CW01376088

WATCHES
EYE ON THE TIME

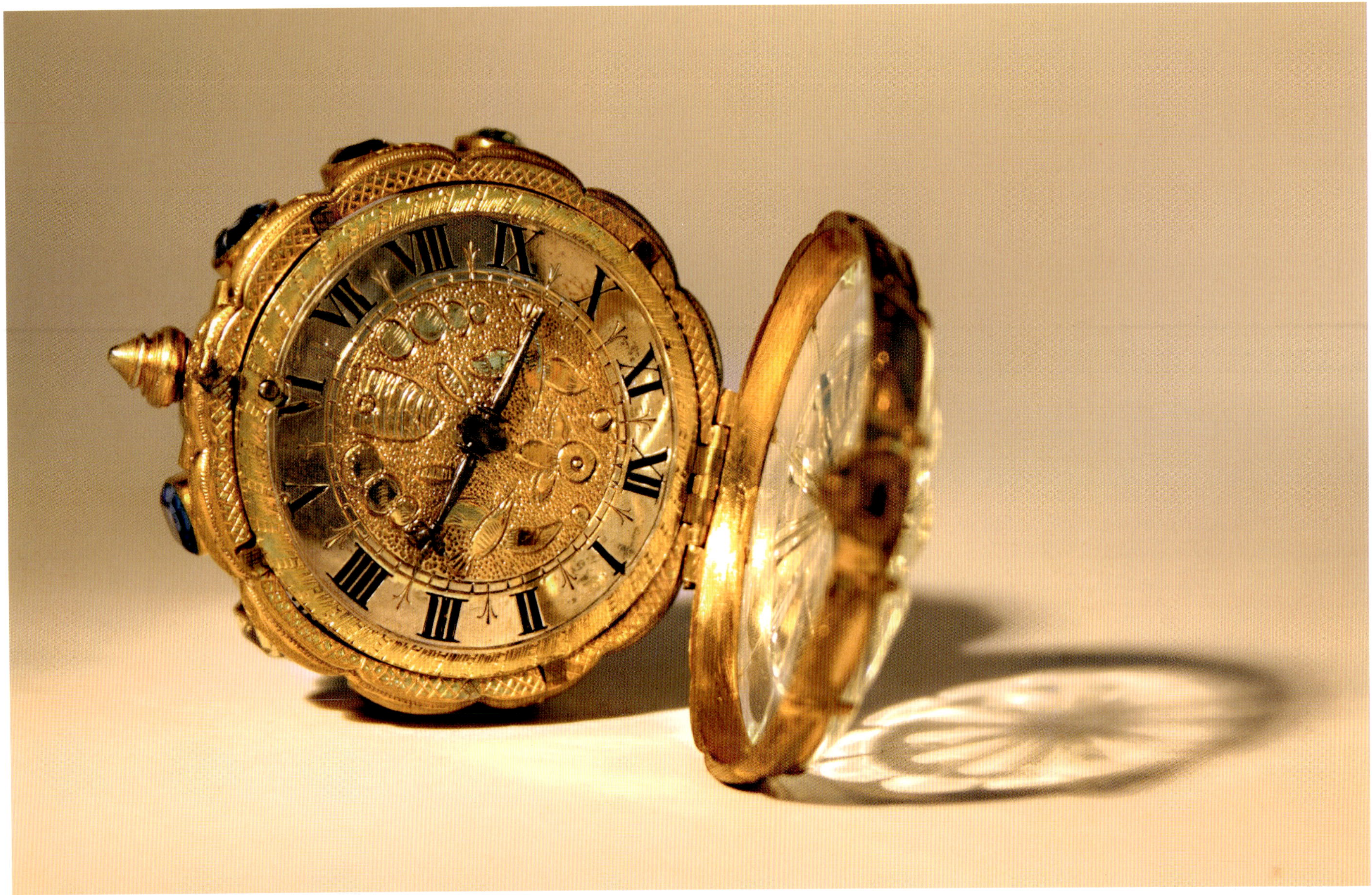

WATCHES
EYE ON THE TIME

Tessa Paul

© Greene Media Ltd

This edition published in 2012 by Park Lane Books
www.parklanebooksltd.vpweb.co.uk

ISBN: 978-1-9069-6907-3

All rights reserved. With the exception of quoting brief passages for the purposes of review, no part of this publication may be reproduced without prior written permission from the Publisher.

The information in this book is true and complete to the best of our knowledge. All recommendations are made without any guarantee on the part of the author or Publisher, who also disclaim any liability incurred in connection with the use of this data or specific details.

We recognize, further, that some words, model names, and designations mentioned herein are the property of the trademark holder. We use them for identification purposes only. This is not an official publication.

Cover photographs use manufacturers material.

Produced for Greene Media Ltd by:
Editorial Developments
Edgmond
Shropshire
England.

Design by: Bacroom Design and Advertising, Birmingham, England

Index: Marie Lorimer Indexing Services

Printed in China

Contents

6	Introduction
12	Marking Time – the story of watchmaking
	22 Breguet
	30 Greenwich Mean Time
44	1900–1920s – Military Advances
	50 World War I
	58 Patek Philippe
	64 Rolex
70	1930s – Dilemmas of Time
	76 Breitling
	84 Vacheron Constantin
	90 Tissot
96	1940s – A Slow Time
	102 Girard-Perregaux
	110 Longines
	116 Omega
120	1950s – Moving Forward
	126 Montblanc
	134 Van Cleef & Arpels
	140 Enameling
146	1960s – In Sea and Space
	152 Seiko
	160 TAG Heuer
	166 Citizen
172	1970s – Design and Opportunity
	178 The Ball Watch Company
	182 Tourbillon
	186 Quartz crystal and liquid
198	1980s – Time for All
	204 Fortis
	212 Oris
	218 Swatch
224	1990s – Outside the Boundaries
	230 Audemars Piguet
	238 Ebel
	244 Jaeger-LeCoultre
250	2000s – The Artistry of Time
	264 Ulysse Nardin
	282 Accurist
	292 Roger W. Smith
300	Novelty watches – In Disguise
	304 Michelle Ong of Carnet
308	A visit to R. W. Smith – Watchmaker
318	Glossary
318	Credits
319	Index

WATCHES

RIGHT: The complex engineering of this watch has been achieved after centuries of invention and experimentation. Patek Philippe presented this chronograph at the prestigious watch fair, Baselworld 2010. The watch epitomizes the best in traditional and contemporary craftsmanship.

WATCHES

Introduction

Centuries of research and science have been devoted to ways of measuring time, but this is the story of the watch and the work of watchmakers, the skilled craftsmen who ensure the survival of quality and engineering, despite the wonders of modern mass production. It is a fascinating story, and interacts with the art of the jeweler, and the fashion world.

Time is surrounded by folk wisdom and cliché, such as 'time is money' or 'time heals all' or 'time is short' and it is for good reason that many phrases relating to time have entered every language. Time is a mysterious element that underlies the natural world and it has demanded the attention of scientists and mathematicians, navigators and merchants. The relentless need to measure time involved the study of shadows, calculations to assess the movement of the moon and the stars, and the construction of mechanical devices.

Inventors found ways of making scientific and public timepieces and clocks; some of these involved towers, water, scales and weights and many were very large. Navigational timepieces demanded careful construction and expense, and their use was largely confined to sailors and explorers. In the 16th century the first small watches were constructed, and these – known as fob or pocket watches – were hung from chains, hidden in the pocket, or carried in small bags.

WATCHES

At last, in 1868 a wristwatch was designed. An intricate timepiece, its construction relied on craftsmen who could build the delicate mechanisms to fit the size of such a small 'clock.' Initially, this engineering made the wristwatch an expensive purchase and it was many years before it gained popularity, but by the end of the 20th century, factories were able to manufacture millions of wonderfully accurate, very light and very cheap wristwatches. Fortunately, this has not deterred master watchmakers who continue to make beautiful, intricate and highly accurate wristwatches.

The progress in this one device for measuring time, the wristwatch, reflects the scientific advances launched by the Industrial Revolution and perfected by the computer technology of the late 20th century.

Sometimes the motivational power behind the advance of the wristwatch was war – soldiers in the trenches of World War I longed for rustproof watches – but also inventions such as aeroplanes, submarines and space ships inspired watchmakers to refine their products.

Qualities beyond timekeeping were added to watches, and these watches, giving more than a measure of hours, minutes and seconds, are known as 'complication' watches. Some were given sound effects, showed the phases of the moon and calendars, or world time. Wristwatches were designed as jewelry. Or they were deliberately robust, designed to be waterproof, set in shatterproof glass, and able to withstand the most extreme physical activity of the wearer.

Introduction

LEFT: Since the Wright brothers used a Vacheron-Constantin watch during the early days of aviation the company has been associated with adventurers. This recent creation has a dial decorated with historical ships and maps, designed as a tribute to explorers.

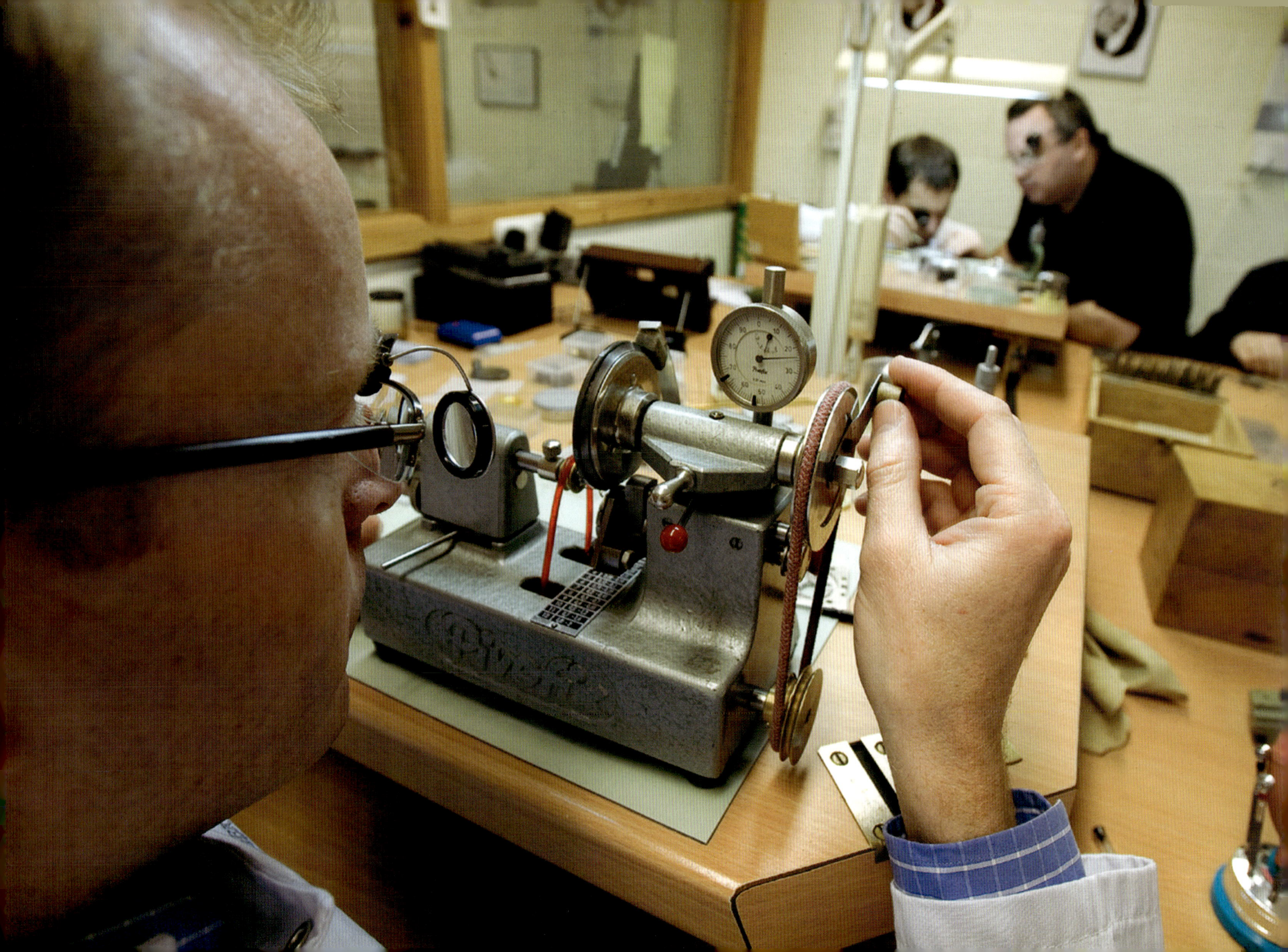

Introduction

By the 1970s, the development of mass-produced quartz watches set a standard of accuracy that could not be surpassed. But mass production has not stopped craftsmen from improving the timepieces they create. They continue to work on complex mechanisms to improve the possibilities of the wristwatch, and their work symbolises the grand and ancient task of measuring time.

They keep the wristwatch alive as a robust, accurate and beautiful timepiece. Carefully designed, made from precious metals and set with gems, modern luxury watches continue a long heritage in scientific craftsmanship.

LEFT: In the workshops of Roger W Smith, artisans follow traditional manufacturing methods to make unique timepieces. Advanced technology has made intricate engineering unnecessary to timekeeping, yet many people appreciate the beauty of engineered construction, and admire the craftsmanship it demands.

WATCHES

Marking Time
– the story of watchmaking

The earliest humans, making their first hesitant steps on two feet began, also, to contemplate the mystery of time. They could not ignore the regularity of sunrise and sunset or, over longer periods, but with similar regularity, the changes in the weather, and in the growth of plants. Over and over again, the moon would swell then shrink, and with monotonous regularity, the sea would flood the beaches then withdraw. All creatures, including humans, were limited by the passing of time. They were born small, grew into adults and died. Time was a measure that underpinned the entire natural world.

But what did it mean? How could time be measured and used?

LEFT: Painted in 1955 by Hugh Chevins, this scene imagines Christiaan Huygens and his contemporary, the watchmaker Salomon Coster in close discussion as, behind them, an artisan works on a timepiece. Huygens, a Dutch physicist, designed the first clock controlled by the movement of a pendulum.

WATCHES

The very first scientists measured the daily journey of the sun by pacing out the shadow cast by a stick in the sand. The Ancient Egyptians and Greeks used sundials and plumblines, and with these simple instruments they could also measure the movement of the moon and planets of the night sky. The medieval Chinese built a mighty tower to mark time. Over the centuries, elaborate weights, wheels, and other mechanical devices were successfully constructed to make clocks but it took some time to invent a small portable timepiece – a watch.

BELOW: One of the earliest timepieces, the sundial, measured time through the movement of the sun. On this small version, the gnomon, the narrow stick 'hand' throws a shadow. If the day is known, the hour can be calculated from the shadow moving as the sun moves.

ABOVE: This is a replica of a Chinese timekeeper from the Song Dynasty. It is a water clock, known as a clepsydra, and the Greeks and Romans used similar apparatus. It measures time through the steady dripping of water from a reservoir through a series of buckets. An overflow of water activates the little figure so that it clashes its cymbals every quarter hour.

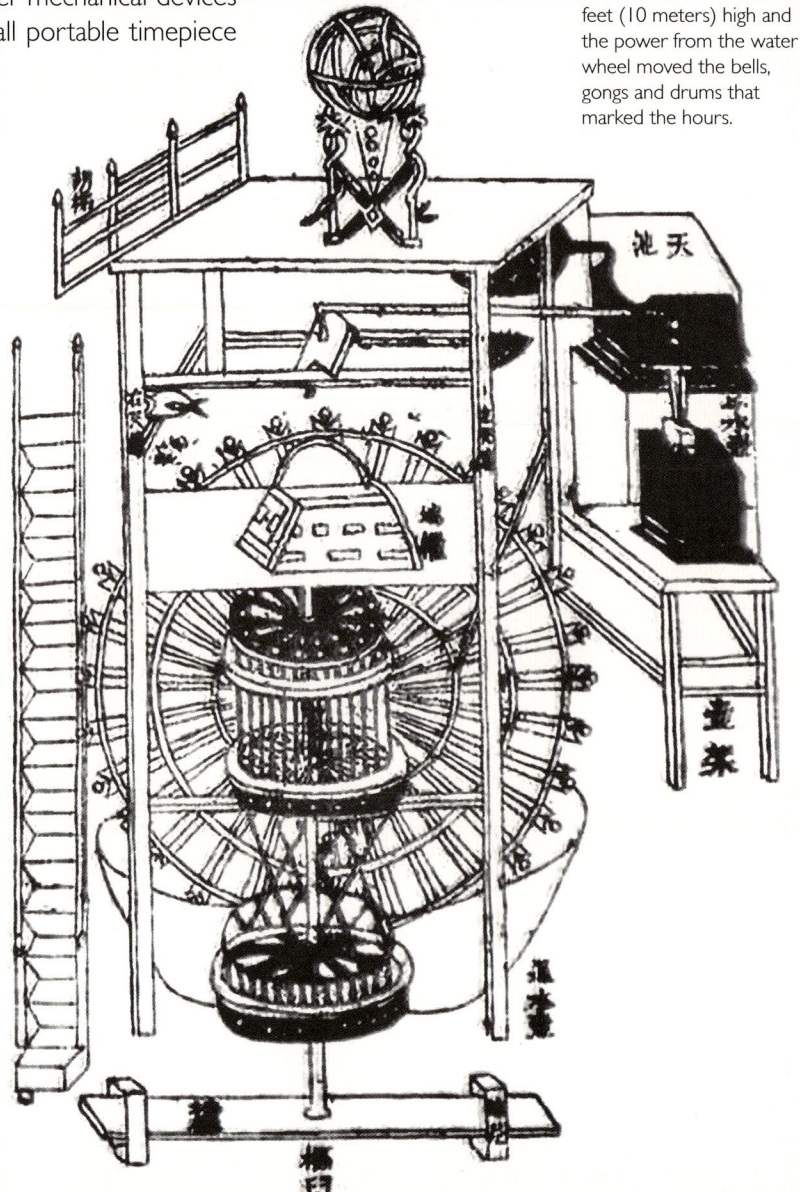

BELOW: A sketch made by the Chinese scientist Su Song shows the inner workings of his clock tower. Built in 1088, it stood 35 feet (10 meters) high and the power from the water wheel moved the bells, gongs and drums that marked the hours.

Marking Time – the story of watchmaking

LEFT: The original clock on the Town Hall in Prague was built about 1486. It is an astronomical clock with automata – the figures fitted in niches above the clock. These emerge to mark the time. The tower also has a calendar dial and a normal time dial.

ABOVE: It is thought that the sandglass first came into use during the Middle Ages. Time was measured by the interval it took for the sand to fall into the lower bulb; then, the glass was turned upside down to repeat the process.

ABOVE: This folding, portable sundial has a string gnomon that can be adjusted for different latitudes, and shows the hours and the position of the sun. It dates from the late Medieval period, and is not only useful but the ivory is beautifully etched.

Its origins are disputed. Some historians think the watch was first made in Italy, but in 1510, a watchmaker, Peter Henlein (also known as Peter Hele) of Nuremburg (1479-1542), announced the development of small 'clocks in iron with many wheels which can be wound up at will, have no pendulum, go for forty hours, and strike and can be carried in the bosom or in the purse.' His work has not survived but a watch made by Casper Werner in 1548 is one of the earliest extant examples of such a timepiece.

WATCHES

These watches were made of iron and were globe shaped; they resembled the spice-filled pomanders many Europeans carried about to ward off bad smells, so the watches were known as 'musk-apple watches.' Initially, they were carried about in boxes but, by the end of the 16th century, they were being hung from a chain or ribbon round the neck or at the waist, and had become 'form watches' – that is, the case came in many shapes – cruciform, egg-shaped, star-shaped, and even skull-shaped (thus reminding the wearer that time passes and we all move towards death).

ABOVE: An early portable watch has a fretwork cover to protect the dial. It dates from about 1600, and although greeted with excitement, its timekeeping was not strictly accurate. This example is known as a 'Nuremburg Egg' denoting both its place of origin and its shape.

LEFT: This intricately worked watch includes an alarm mechanism. It was made in about 1600.

Marking Time – the story of watchmaking

BELOW: This timepiece made by the watchmaker, Johanne Sayller c.1650, has both an hour dial and a calendar.

ABOVE: The movements of a 17th century watch reveal the complex settings of a watch. A team of artisans crafted each little piece before the watchmaker assembled them.

ABOVE: Watches with unusual shapes are known as 'shape' watches. The skull, a 'momento mori', a reminder of death was popular in the 16th century. The doomed Mary Queen of Scots owned just such a watch. Marc Lagisse of Geneva made this example.

17

WATCHES

BELOW: This pocket watch is decorated with enamel and constructed with gold. It was made in France during the reign of Louis XIII. Early watches were available only to the wealthy who were able to pay for a timepiece and naturally, wished to show it off as a thing of beauty not one of mere utility.

Marking Time – the story of watchmaking

Although not very reliable as timekeepers, these early watches were beautifully crafted. The dials were not covered by glass, but hinged, decorative lids gave sturdy protection to the delicate porcelain dials. Thus watchmaking demanded not only craftsmen expert in miniature clockmaking but involved a team of ingenious craftsmen – springmakers, silversmiths, engravers, and jewelers. The watch lids were made of elaborate metal fretwork or worked tortoiseshell and many were decorated with gems, but these watches were produced in small quantities during the 16th century and were very expensive. Ownership denoted great wealth and status.

ABOVE: Pious Christians appreciated the crucifix shape watch. This version has a leather case to protect the timepiece. It comes from the workshop of Charles Bobinet, mid-17th century.

ABOVE: Early watches were scaled down versions of table clocks and were made of iron. F Sermand created this pocket watch in about 1650 and gave it covers of rock crystal.

WATCHES

Elizabeth I of England is reputed to have had many watches, and even had a watch 'armlet'. Made of rubies, diamonds, and gold, it resembled so strongly a bracelet that no one thought to exploit the useful positioning of a watch on the wrist. A painting, once thought to depict Mary, Queen of Scots, kept in the National Portrait Gallery, London, shows a richly dressed noblewoman wearing a watch on a chain round her neck, while another dangles from her belt. The keys required to wind up the watches are attached to the chains.

ABOVE: An obituary recorded that Thomas Tompion (1639-1713) was 'one of the most eminent persons for making clocks and watches... Indeed, he was the most famous and most successful'.

LEFT: Such fat pocket watches were sometimes known as 'onion' watches due to their shape. Gold embellishments pattern a coat of arms on the cover. The watch dates from about 1650, and can be seen in the Patek Philippe Museum, Geneva, Switzerland.

ABOVE: Christiaan Huygens (1629-93) the Dutch physicist was credited with the invention of the pendulum clock, and the balance spring in watches, although the inventor of the latter remains a point of debate. The Englishmen, Thomas Tompion and Robert Hooke also laid claim to the innovation.

Marking Time – the story of watchmaking

LEFT: A watch made by Martin Hyllios of Dresden in 1675. It has only an hour hand, but is crafted of gold and enamel, and hangs from a pretty fob chain.

In 1675, the Dutch physicist, Christiaan Huygens (1629-93) invented the spiral hairspring. Prior to this, clocks were driven by weights. His watches could also carry a minute hand, and this made his timepieces reasonably accurate. But two Englishmen, Thomas Tompion (1639-1713) and Robert Hooke (1635-1703), both master watchmakers, claimed the balance spring as their invention. Whatever the truth, watches were now able to carry a minute hand and thus, of course, measure time more closely. Tompion's craftsmanship and watchmaking skills helped place his country in the forefront of watch making. The development of this industry was helped by the many watchmakers who were among the thousands of Protestant Huguenot refugees from France and Belgium who fled to England in the 17th century.

LEFT: Robert Hooke (1635-1703) had an inventive mind, and is credited with the invention of the Georgian telescope and microscope. He was fascinated by watches but he needed his colleague, Thomas Tompion, to translate his ideas into working realities. This watch is credited to Hooke.

WATCHES

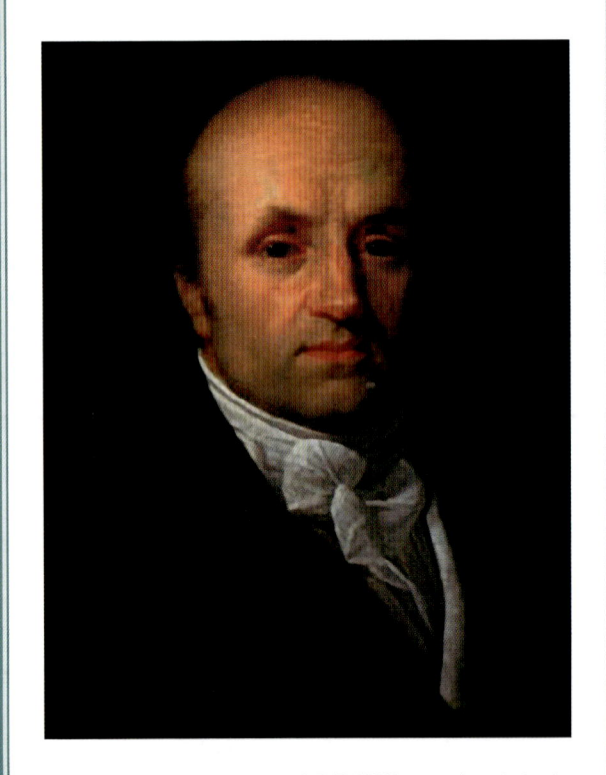

ABOVE: Abraham-Louis Breguet (1747-1823) was acknowledged as a brilliant, inventive watchmaker and every aristocrat in Europe wanted his watches. Marie Antoinette of France ordered several but apparently paid for none.

RIGHT: The simple design of the 'Montre a Tact' belies Breguet's engineering skills. Such was his success that other watchmakers produced fake 'Breguets' hoping for a quick profit. To counteract the counterfeits, he signed his work in finely engraved lettering, placed below the number '12' and difficult to see.

Breguet

This is one of the oldest surviving watchmaking groups in the world. Founded in Paris, 1775, by the wildly inventive Abraham-Louis Breguet (1747-1823), his watches were innovative, and beautiful. Breguet invented the perpetuelle, or self-winding watch, the parachute, or shockproof balance pivots, and the tourbillon. Throughout its history, Breguet has served the great and the good from kings and aristocrats to movie stars and footballers. The Swatch Company under the late Nicolas Hayek bought the company in 1999, and with heavy promotion, sales were increased. These are never high because the craftsmen at Breguet did not change the ideology of their founder. The company continues to innovate and invent, and has kept its place at the top of the Haut Horologie list – those recognized as luxury, high quality watchmakers. Its most recent reward was for the women's watch, 'Crazy Flower' chosen as Best Jewelry Watch in 2010. The headquarters, like many of the other established companies, are in Vallee de Joux, Switzerland.

LEFT: A gold mounted watch from Breguet. It has a ruby cylinder escapement and parachute shock protection. Breguet improved the accuracy of his watches with his invention of the tourbillon. He mounted the escapement on an epicyclic train; this means the center of one circle is carried round the circumference of another circle. The circles are wheels – called 'trains' by watchmakers. He fitted it all into a 'cage'. This rotates completely on its axis over a regular time period, usually one minute. The trains' rotation controls the hands, but before the tourbillon the trains worked inadequately in half rotation.

WATCHES

The watches of the 17th and 18th centuries were works of art. Generally, they were designed to look like jewelry rather than make a frank display as a 'mere' timepiece although the watches were complex and fairly accurate. Watchmakers presented a range of complications, meaning the watches measured not only the hours and minutes but also gave other information, such as the date, astronomical calendar, and some marked the hours with sound.

Abraham-Louis Breguet (1747-1823) emerged as a leading watchmaker. He designed a slim watch, perfect for slipping into a pocket. He created his montre perpetual, a self-winding watch wound by a bouncing weight. He added another quality, a shock absorber so that even if the watch were dropped, it would continue to work. This was known as the parachute. Napoleon carried a Breguet during his campaign in Egypt.

LEFT: This watch is richly patterned with enamel work, but the figures on each side of the dial move their arms to mark the hours. It was made by the French maker, Duchene et Fils in the late 18th century.

RIGHT: This view of the watch's movements reveals the use of ruby pallets. Although English makers kept this innovative use of jewels secret for some time, Louis Breguet ferreted out the information and took it to Paris.

Marking Time – the story of watchmaking

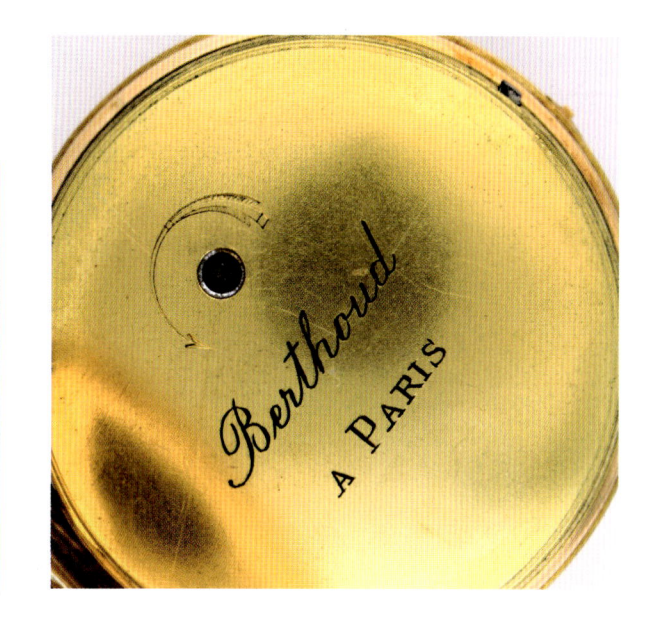

ABOVE: Berthoud designed an equation watch that could go for a month without re-winding. A boastful man, he also claimed the invention of the spring detent escapement chronometer but the Englishman, John Roberts patented this device in 1787.

ABOVE: The maker's signature is marked with some flourish on the back. Berthoud knew this would help sell his timepiece. He was not only famous as a watchmaker but for his suspected role as an industrial spy when he visited England in the 1760s and tried to uncover the secret of lessening friction in the mechanics through the use of rubies.

LEFT: The Swiss watchmaker, Ferdinand Berthoud (1727-1807) worked in France. He was a clever horologist and spent many years perfecting the workings of watches, particularly complication watches. This is a sample of a beautiful equation watch, one that tells hours and minutes, made by him.

25

WATCHES

The popularity of pocket watches stimulated a rash of tradesmen's cards describing a wide variety of watch designs and chains. Gold, enamel, and diamonds adorned the most costly watches, but paste, marquisette, and garnets were used on less expensive versions. Intricate chains and 'safety hooks' were advertised.

Women wore their watches at their waist, hooked to their girdle or dangling from a chain; these hooks and chains were elaborate, ornamental, and fixed into a design that incorporated the watch, forming a unified decoration, known then as an 'equipage' but later called 'chatelaines'. Watches were pinned to the corset or hung round the neck. The watch lids showed landscapes, portraits, religious, or classical scenes. The subjects were engraved on gold or silver, and after a craftsman, Jean Toutin, found a way of painting enamel onto metal, colourful images became popular.

LEFT: This is the work of the Englishman, John Arnold (1736-99) who made marine chronometers as well as precision pocket watches. He was a skilled craftsman and for George III, he constructed a ring watch that sounded the hours and the quarter hours. In the timepiece shown here, the hinged covers of rock crystal allow views of both the face and the movements.

Marking Time – the story of watchmaking

LEFT: The portrait seen on the equipage (far left) is turned over to reveal that it is backed by a watch bearing the maker's signature.

ABOVE: A separate case has been specifically designed to hold this equipage. Although apparently intended as a household item to wear hanging from a belt, in reality this was a precious, expensive timepiece to be displayed as jewelry and worn occasionally. It deserved a special storage box.

FAR LEFT: This rococo gold equipage, or chatelaine, would have been hung at the wearer's waist. It is of elaborate design, but a useful one. On the left hangs the key to wind the watch, and on the right the lady's seal. The portrait is painted in enamel. This pretty timepiece comes from Dusommerard of Rouen, France and is dated 1780.

27

WATCHES

Right: The metal is brass and the enamel painting is in the naïve style, but its careful praise of European leaders cannot be faulted. The Emperor Napoleon is at the apex above the number 12 while Alexander I of Russia and the last Holy Roman Emperor, Francis II, can be seen below him on either side. It was made around 1805.

Above: Nicolas Facio (1664-1753) has been described as 'a mathematician, astronomer, religious enthusiast and political intriguer'. He was the first to propose the use of drilled gemstones as bearings in watches. In London, he met with hostility, but continued to work secretly using this innovation for many years with Peter de Baufre and his brother until the French horologist Breguet uncovered the secret.

Men's pocket watches were attached to a 'fob', a chain or cord that became as showy and decorative as the watch itself. There was a Regency fashion for men to wear an equipage at their waist, from which dangled a watch, a seal and keys but, generally, men continued to carry their fob watches in the depths of their pockets while women displayed their watches on chains and ribbons, and this gender specific way of wearing watches persisted into and throughout the 19th century. There are records of housewives keeping watches in pockets or small pouches hung on their belts but this style never became fashionable.

Marking Time – the story of watchmaking

LEFT: John Harrison (1693-1776) spent years perfecting seagoing timepieces. In this detail from a painting by Thomas King, the famous H.4 is seen in Harrison's hand. On its test trip to Jamaica, the H.4 was inaccurate by a mere one and a quarter minutes, a triumph at that historical period. The watch is fully jeweled with diamond pallets and a center seconds hand. It can be seen in the National Maritime Museum, London, England.

RIGHT: John Harrison was a carpenter with little education, but fascinated by timekeeping. He used crude methods to measure the movement of the stars, and it took him thirty years to perfect his H.4 marine timepiece. Despite the wonder of his invention, the government refused to reward him, other horologists tried to steal details of his invention, and he was an old man before proper recognition was given to his timepiece.

The next major advance in watchmaking came from Nicholas Facio (1664-1753) a Swiss working in London. It was known that the spiral springs running in metal bearings were subject to friction, and this affected the accuracy of all watches. Facio suggested the springs be run through bearings made of drilled gemstones. He used rubies to demonstrate that gems eliminated this friction.

The manner of drilling the gems remained the secret of a few English watchmakers until the late 18th century. The Swiss watchmaker, Breguet learnt the secret and by 1823 he had set up a jewel-making factory and European watchmakers began to jewel everyday watches.

WATCHES

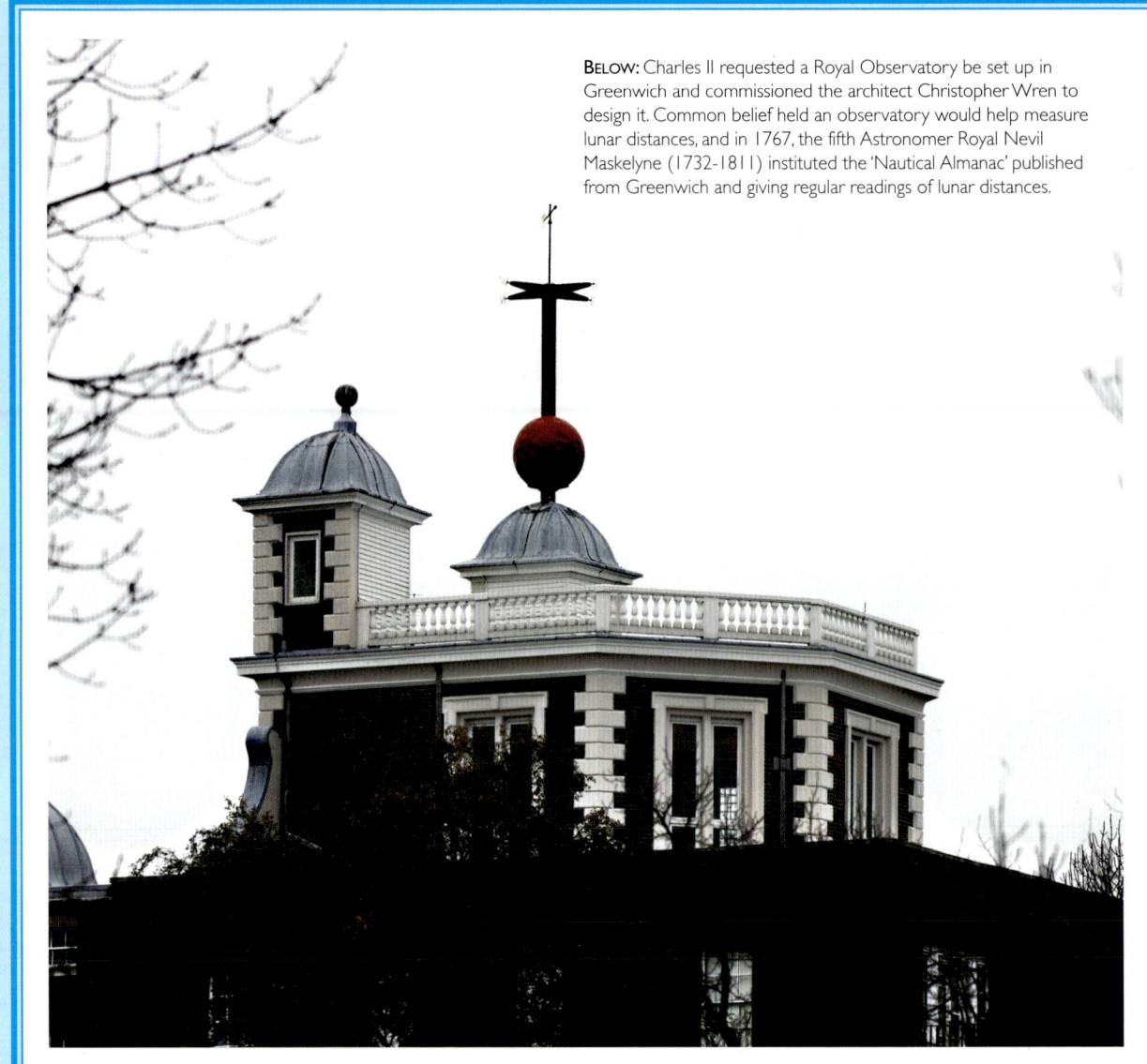

BELOW: Charles II requested a Royal Observatory be set up in Greenwich and commissioned the architect Christopher Wren to design it. Common belief held an observatory would help measure lunar distances, and in 1767, the fifth Astronomer Royal Nevil Maskelyne (1732-1811) instituted the 'Nautical Almanac' published from Greenwich and giving regular readings of lunar distances.

ABOVE: This is the old datum method of marking the Greenwich astronomical meridian, here represented by the stainless steel strip. The Prime Meridian of modern reference systems is 102.5 meters east of the Greenwich astronomical meridian.

Greenwich Mean Time

Greenwich became significant in horology when John Harrison (1693-1776) invented the chronometer, a timepiece that gave an accurate measure of longitude. This was of huge importance to mariners who needed to know how far they were in distance and time from land. Harrison used the Greenwich meridian as his zero measure. Then in the 19th century, sailors made frequent reference to 'The Nautical Almanac' introduced by Nevil Maskelyne (1839-1917). This, too, used the Greenwich meridian. In 1883, the Greenwich Observatory devised a signal by which ship crews could set their chronometers before sailing. John Pond, the Royal Astronomer, set a large ball on a mast on top of the Observatory and, daily, at precisely 01.00 the ball dropped. At an international conference in 1884, the majority of those attending agreed that, due to the familiarity of its use by all mariners of many nations, the Greenwich meridian be accepted as the global time reference – Greenwich Mean Time.

ABOVE: Every night, from the Observatory in Greenwich, a laser beam can be seen as a line of green light shooting through the dark across London. It marks the Prime Meridian on which Greenwich Mean Time is calculated.

ABOVE: This is an early example of an electric slave clock, that is one that has a master clock controlling the pendulum, dial and clock. It sits at the Shepherd Gate entrance to the Observatory.

WATCHES

Despite this advance, fob watches were not yet completely accurate but people accepted time had variable measures. Timekeeping was eccentric, often specific to local measurement, so that, for instance, one district worked on a fifteen-minute time difference from the neighbouring district. But in the early 19th century, railways were becoming a major form of public transport, and these quirky local time differences caused chaos with timetables, and even caused train accidents. A national time standard became essential in the maintenance of train schedules and safety.

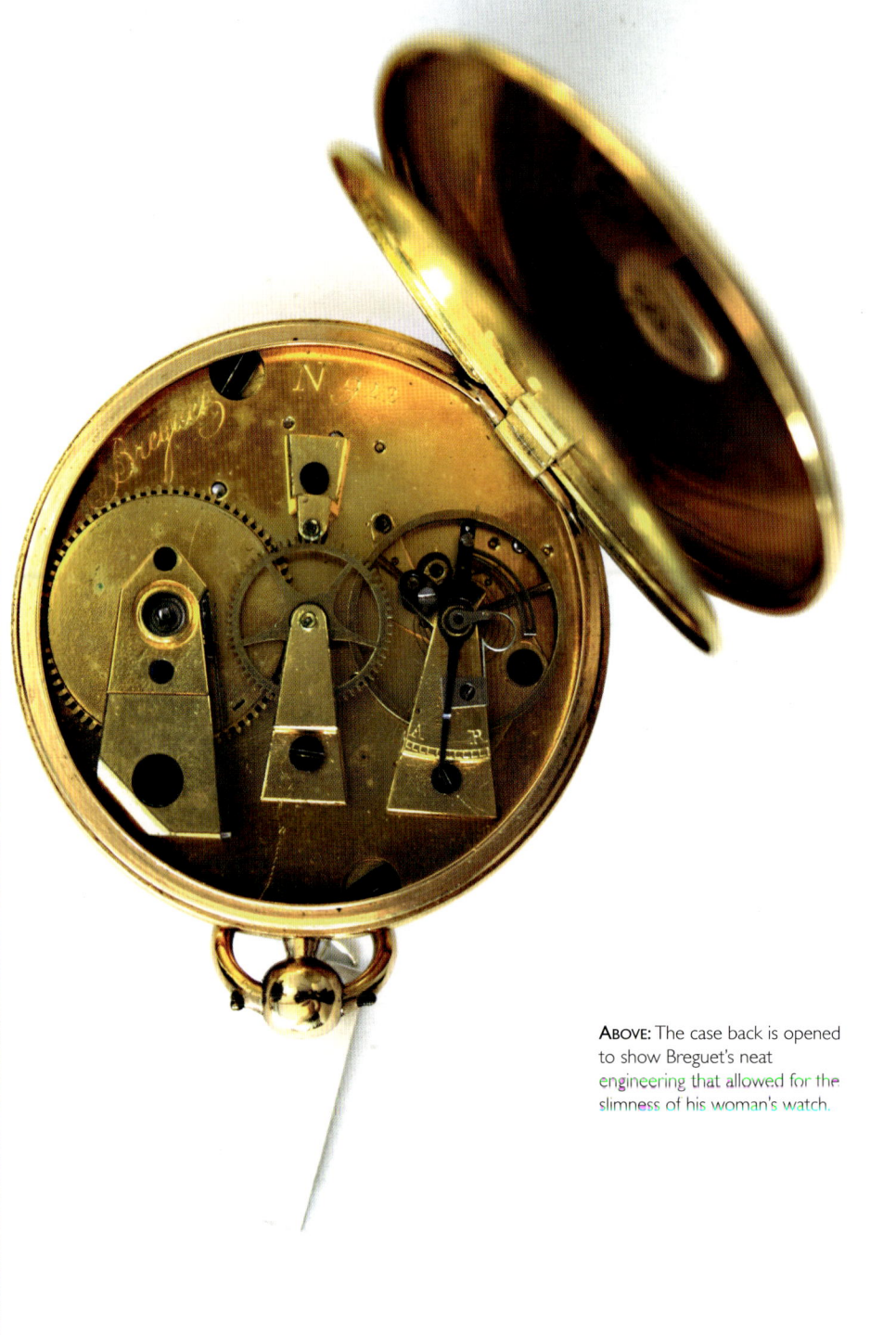

RIGHT: The French horologist, Breguet, made this watch for women. He broke with convention in that he did not disguise his timepiece as a pendant or a brooch, nor did he include it in a chatelaine. He created slim, simple pocket watches easily read and elegant to wear such as the example shown here.

ABOVE: The case back is opened to show Breguet's neat engineering that allowed for the slimness of his woman's watch.

Marking Time – the story of watchmaking

Left: Since their invention watches have served as betrothal gifts, so unusual or decorative versions were preferred for this purpose. This watch, made by Du Bois et Fils in c.1820, may have been aimed at this market. The image on the face is perhaps meaningful: a dog indicating loyalty, doves symbolizing the soul, and a winged boy, perhaps Cupid for love. The dial is calibrated for the hours and is further divided into minutes. The hour figures, and figures for the minutes traverse the aperture to indicate the time. As it moves, a reverse spring is set in motion and when the hand completes its cycle, the spring returns the numbers to the beginning.

33

WATCHES

In 1880, the British Parliament required all railway stations to follow Greenwich Mean Time (GMT), a measure that had long been used by mariners across the globe. But the land-dwelling inhabitants of other countries followed other standards, and the vastness of the United States caused great problems in setting a co-ordinated system of time keeping that the entire nation could observe. Universal time was settled at an international conference in 1884 where the European and American delegates accepted John Harrison's use of the Greenwich meridian when measuring time across the 24 longitude zones: he knew each zone covers 15 degrees and he measured the global time changes using the Greenwich meridian as his zero time base. This became known as Greenwich Mean Time. Harrison established this zero when he invented the marine chronometer in the 18th century.

ABOVE: The workings of the watch reveal a tourbillon and a spring detent escapement, and there are further mechanics to control the thermometer.

RIGHT: This is comes from an anonymous French-speaking maker, possibly Swiss. The small lower dial gives the seconds while the semi-circle on the upper section of the dial is a thermometer, an unusual complication at the turn of the 19th century when the watch was made.

34

Marking Time – the story of watchmaking

The United States were divided into five time zones but all were measured against the Greenwich meridian. The French were the last European nation to accept the British observatory as the universal standard, giving their reluctant acquiesance in 1911.

Of course, these developments inspired watchmakers to make watches that showed 'world time' although as early as 1856, a while before the international time conference, the French watchmaker, Anquetin, made a timepiece with rotating discs back and front. One showed the hours, the other was marked with city names and showed the time at each place. Another advance was made in 1855, when E D Johnson invented the chronograph. This watch could measure time intervals, a boon for sporting events and medical care. Rudimentary stop watches appeared as early as the 1690s and were used by the medical profession to measure heartbeats.

LEFT: The face is enameled and the hands ornamental although the case is not of precious metal. The watch comes from the maker Moilliet of Geneva and was made in c.1800. The small dial placed on the lower half of the face indicates seconds, while on the upper half on the left, the day of the month is revealed, and on the right, the day of the week can be read. The night stars are purely decorative.

35

Left: This is the other side, where the dial shows the days of the week – here in French. A head servant would be trusted with this key, and thus expected to keep an accurate record of regular watch winding, and to ensure that the householder and his family would be tended to on time.

Right: The jewelers, traditionally part of every watchmaking team, became very creative when designing watch keys. These were decorated with gems, engraved, enameled, or made of pierced and cast metal work.

Below: One side of this key is painted to look like a watch but actually the head and its pointy hat moves to show the time when the watch was last wound up.

Marking time – the story of watchmaking

LEFT: American watchmakers of the late 19th century wanted to make watches accessible to a wide market. The so-called 'dollar watch' was their aim. To drop the cost of the parts, watchmakers reverted to the mechanisms found in clocks. These used fewer pieces than the amount used in watches. After some false starts, Ingersoll produced their 'Yankee' dollar watch. In 1896 the company sold a million Yankees. Each watch was packed in a cardboard box and this had instructions pasted inside to help the customer take proper care of their purchase.

RIGHT: Ingersoll bought 12,000 small clocks with two-inch dials (five centimeters) from the Waterbury Clock Company. The movements included a traditional tourbillon. Robert Ingersoll designed a case to fit the clocks' dials, and the Yankee was born. A guarantee of reliability was glued to the case.

RIGHT: The watches carried in a simple, unassuming font the name of the watch, the company's name, and their base in New York, USA.

37

WATCHES

Late 19th century men's watches were severe in design but the fob and key became more and more ornate, some chains growing ridiculously long and multi-looped. There was a busy market in 'railway watches' that copied the design of the big, sturdy pocket watches used by rail workers.

BELOW: Railway workers were obliged to use pocket watches that had passed the US government regulations regarding accurate timekeeping. But the employees were proud of their role and one rail worker attached to his watch chain his 9-carat gold, enameled National Union Of Railwaymen badge.

ABOVE: The American Waltham Watch Company passed the government test for accurate timepieces, and made watches for the Lynton and Barnstable Railway that started operating in 1898.

RIGHT: The company name is engraved inside, while the rail line's initials were put on the outer case.

38

Marking Time – the story of watchmaking

Left: Walker duplicated his name on the inside back, but on the nickel case Great Northern No. 65 is engraved on the rear. It is thought to be the earliest extant Great Northern watch.

Around 1860, American watchmakers began to develop factory methods of watch making; their ambition was to produce inexpensive watches for the masses. Among the most successful was the 'dollar watch' made by Ingersoll. This timepiece was sold under the slogan, 'The watch that made the dollar famous.' Factory pocket watches began to dominate the market, but those marketed for women remained jewel-like and ornamental. They were worn as pendants and brooches in flower designs, or heart shapes, and many continued to be hung on chains at the waist.

Left: This watch was made for a British railway company by John Walker of London. The name Great Northern is on the face to indicate the rail company and in much smaller letters, John Walker's name and address is allowed.

WATCHES

During the first half of the 19th century, on the European side of the Atlantic, English and Swiss watchmakers dominated the market, but the English lost their footing as US factory production gained strength. The English resented the change, seeing it as a threat to their traditional craft and livelihoods. The Swiss, however, were more positive and began to successfully exploit US methods of production. These craftsmen retained skilled, expensive methods of watch making but developed a parallel industry in factory production watch making. Famous Swiss firms such as Breguet, Patek Philippe and Audemars Piguet established themselves during this tumultuous period in the history of watches.

RIGHT: At the turn of the 20th century, dandies in New York wore fobs a yard long, the chain draped from chest down to knee. But conservative gentlemen looked for something like this nicely wrought fob chain, modest, a sensible length, and attached to an elegant watch. A Eppner of Breslau, Germany made this gold timepiece and fob in 1870.

40

Marking Time – the story of watchmaking

As proof of their continuing inventiveness and creativity, craftsmen found ways of staying ahead of factory production. Patek Philippe made a wristwatch in 1868, and Omega produced a version in 1902, closely followed by a Louis Cartier design, a wristwatch made specifically for a pilot. However, this sensible innovation was not popular and the market was sluggish. Cartier and the jeweler, Tiffany, had some success in wristwatches for women but only because the timepieces resembled bracelets.

Right: Longines made masculine watches but also exploited the market in women's watches. This gorgeous rococo style piece was intended as an eye-catching bracelet with a small watch included in the design produced in 1901. This was typical of watches made for women who because of their preference for jewelry wore wristwatches long before men took to the habit.

Left: The owner of a small watch and jewelry shop in Knoxsville, USA attends to a broken timepiece. The tools and implements at his disposal can be seen on the desk, whilst more watches are hung waiting for their owners to collect them. This picture was taken around 1899.

WATCHES

Left: The back of a Roskopf watch shows there is no center wheel. Also, steel pins replaced jewels for the escapement pallets. These innovations considerably reduced manufacturing costs.

Right: When Roskopf was working on his pin-pallet watch in the 1860s there were no patent laws in Switzerland. He patented his invention in some foreign countries, but this did not protect him from other manufacturers making free use of his work.

It took a catastrophe for this innovation to find favor. Officers in World War I realised that, for a soldier sitting in a battlefield, wearing a heavy Sam Browne belt and carrying arms, a timepiece on his wrist was more efficient than a watch in his pocket. The fob watch had dominated the market for over 200 years but it was finally conquered in the trenches of war, and the 20th century opened to a great new era, that of the wristwatch.

Marking time – the story of watchmaking

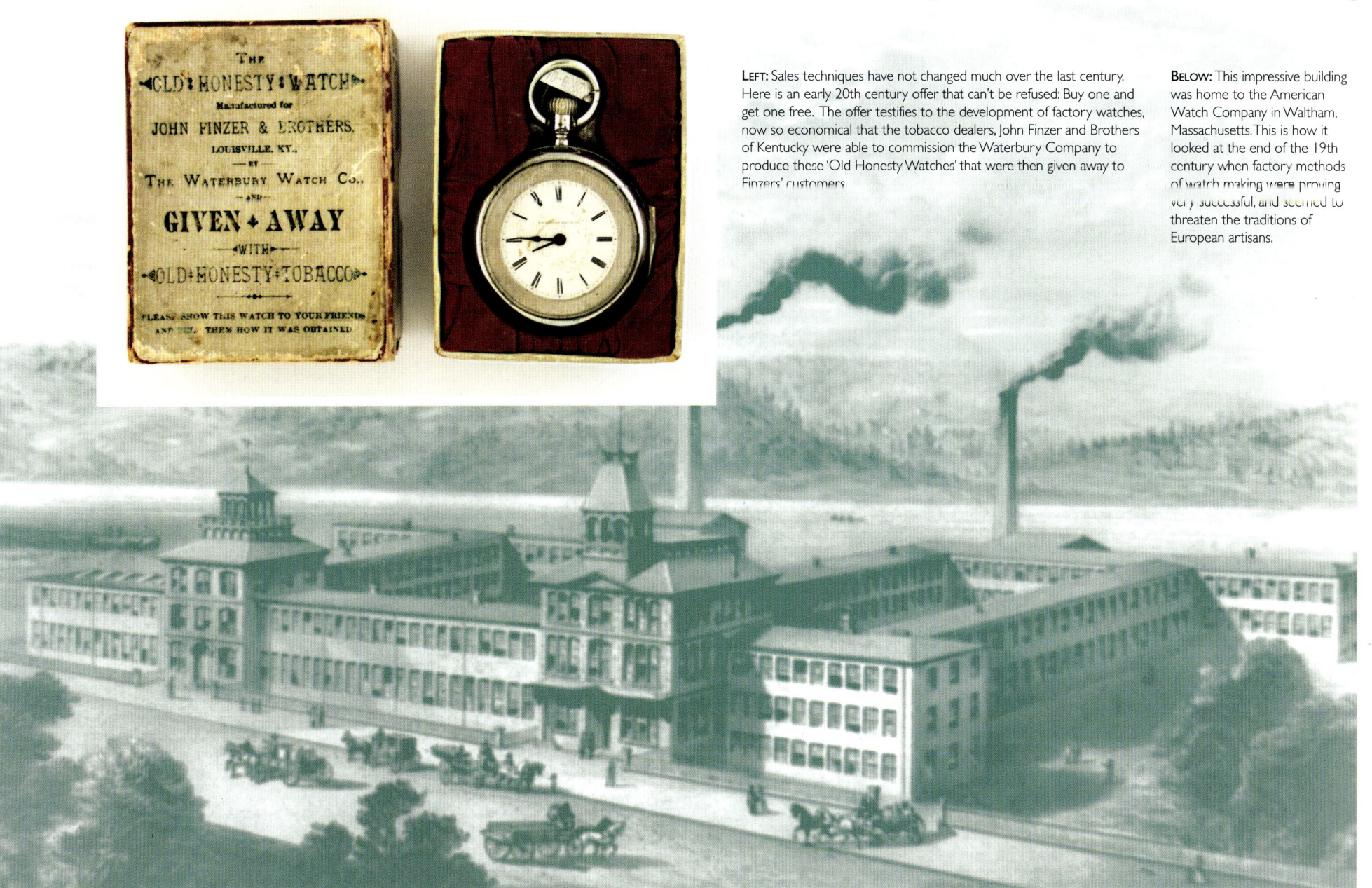

LEFT: Sales techniques have not changed much over the last century. Here is an early 20th century offer that can't be refused: Buy one and get one free. The offer testifies to the development of factory watches, now so economical that the tobacco dealers, John Finzer and Brothers of Kentucky were able to commission the Waterbury Company to produce these 'Old Honesty Watches' that were then given away to Finzers' customers.

BELOW: This impressive building was home to the American Watch Company in Waltham, Massachusetts. This is how it looked at the end of the 19th century when factory methods of watch making were proving very successful, and seemed to threaten the traditions of European artisans.

43

WATCHES

RIGHT: This pocket watch comes from the Illinois Watch Company, USA. It has an unusual double case, and the winding stem is lined up with the number 3. This is placed at the top of the watch so it has to be turned to read the hours in the usual sequence.

1900-1920s
Military Advances

ABOVE: This pocket watch could be hung on a chatelaine. The case is decorative metal, while the face is enamel, prettily but lightly decorated. The watch dates from about 1870.

Historically, men and women wore watches in different ways, and these gender preferences persisted into the 20th century. Initially, many early wristwatches were designed and sold to men for specific activities and professions – even as late as the 1950s, watchmakers were advertising their wristwatches as designed to suit 'every special need' whether the male buyer was a mechanic, salesman, serviceman, or sportsman. And historically, the long search for accurate timekeeping was strongly motivated by the demands of male mariners who needed to know how far they were in terms of time from their nearest coastline.

WATCHES

The technological advances of the 19th century created new kinds of work, generally undertaken by men. The trend started with the railway watch, sturdy pocket watches designed for rail workers.

RIGHT: The watch featured here, was made by the Japanese company Seikosha, in 1929 and was designed specifically for use by railroad employees. Kintaro Hattori established Kintaro Hattori & Co. Ltd., back in 1881 and the Seikosha clock supply factory was established 1892. In 1937 watch production was split off as Daini Seikosha Co., Ltd.,(literally translated as second Seikosha) and became the independent predecessor of today's Seiko Instruments Inc.

RIGHT: Rail workers across the world were careful about timekeeping. Governments demanded strict accuracy, and the international acceptance of GMT ensured a standard method of measuring time. Here, two railroad workers, the conductor and the engineer check their time matches before the journey starts from a station in Illinois. Railroad watches were expensive to purchase, but workers were compelled to own them.

1900-1920s – Military Advances

BELOW: The watch was commissioned from the Lancashire Watch Company of Preston, England. They have used Roman numerals on the hours dial but not on the small seconds dial. Despite this, the numbers are clear and easy to read.

ABOVE: Another sturdy rail watch, this one was made for the Great Western Railway, Great Britain. It is good quality nickel and bears the initials GWR and a numbered movement 328340. It used 4 pairs of extra jewels adding to its status and expense.

47

WATCHES

LEFT: Naturally, watchmakers took a little while to catch-up with the unexpected breed of aviators that appeared at the turn of the 20th century. The airmen were obliged to improvise with their timepieces – strap them to their thighs, or wind them round fittings in the airplane. Time pieces can be seen here on the interior section of the Wright brothers' machine.

Then, in 1904, to time their flights as the first aviators, the Wright brothers fixed a Vacheron Constantin pocket watch to a strap. A watch in the pocket was useless for the Wrights' need to observe the timing of their flight as they operated the air machine, and early aviators often strapped a watch to their thigh. Cartier improved on their innovation by creating a specially designed wristwatch for a daredevil aviator, Alberto Santos Dumont and by 1911 this was being marketed as the 'Santos'.

BELOW: Man's ancient dream of flight was, at last, realized by two American brothers, Orville and Wilbur Wright in 1903. On that airborne journey, Orville was the pilot while Wilbur trotted at the wingtip.

1900-1920s – Military Advances

LEFT: The early aviators were adventurers. Alberto Santos-Dumont cut a romantic figure as he packed his Demoisille monoplane in his roadster and dashed down to the practice ground for a flight.

LEFT: Dumont inspired his friend Louis Cartier to design a watch for aviators. Cartier made a rectangular watch with precisely placed numbers on the dial for his aviator friend, and named the watch after the dashing pilot. In 2004, Cartier brought out a retro range of the 'Santos' watch.

ABOVE: Constantin Girard and Marie Perregaux married and formed a watch making company. They were interested in timepieces for the military and the navy. In 1889, a design using a tourbillon with three gold bridges won them gold medals at the Paris Universal Exhibition. It was a pocket watch and can be seen here. The company was also credited with making watches covered with a grill to protect the glass, making 2000 models for the German navy in the 19th century.

49

WATCHES

LEFT: The watchmakers were keen to supply the soldiers of World War I although they could not have anticipated that wristwatches were to become so popular with the men.

World War I

The soldiers who fought in World War I trooped off to the battlefront carrying their pocket watches. Most carried the inexpensive Ingersoll, or a similar model from other companies such as Rotherham and Son. Officers carried their Breguet, Patek Philippe, or Vacheron Constantin. Both classes soon realized a watch kept in the pocket was not useful, and started to improvise by fixing the watch onto a strap, either by fitting it into a purse on a strap or making their own lugs to fit a strap.

ABOVE: This example was given radium luminous figures and pointers, and a separate grid to be fitted over the glass for protection.

World War 1

Surviving samples show the winding button placed above 12 o'clock – the design of a pocket watch. Watchmakers lagged behind in the production of wristwatches because they had never had large sales before the war. A commentator remarked that a watch on the wrist might be efficient, but one never stopped a bullet entering a man's heart, as the pocket watch was known to have done.

Left: The Waltham Company of the USA designed this wristwatch with a circular grid of petal-shaped cutouts. This grid allowed a clear view of the boldly numbered dial. This model was called the 'Trench' and appeared in 1914.

WATCHES

BELOW: When shopping at the first Vacheron Constantin boutique, the clients, who were generally wealthy and well-known, were drawn aside to specially designed private rooms for consultation on timepieces suitable to their taste and station.

Even earlier than this, Girard-Perregaux was commissioned to create wristwatches for the German Imperial Navy in the 1880s, and Panerai was asked to develop a waterproof watch for the Italian naval authorities. Soldiers, as well as aviators and sailors, found they needed a timepiece that could be consulted while the wearer was working with his hands. Pocket watches were not good enough.

In the Boer War (1899-1902) British officers, impatient with the hassle of digging into their pockets for a watch, improvised ways of affixing their fob watches to straps and some watchmakers, quick to spot a new market, began to advertise a 'reliable timekeeper for Gentlemen going on Active Service'. In 1906, strap makers started to design and sell watch straps, usually of leather but, also, they revised flexible, expandable bracelet chain links to make straps. Often, fob watches were modified with loops to fix to these straps and such watches are known as 'transition' watches.

1900-1920s – Military Advances

RIGHT: This narrow bangle with chased metal work and precious gems had a watch fitted into a side plane, and not into the usual top panel. The Maharajah of Patiala owned it, confirming his love of decoration above any useful timekeeping facility.

ABOVE: In 19th century European men's clothes became conservative and drab, but in India the fabulously wealthy princes and provincial rulers reveled in flamboyance and the beauty of jewels. Here the Maharajah of Patiala is festooned with pearls and clusters of precious gems and was a regular visitor to the Vacheron Constantin boutique.

53

WATCHES

THE GOLDSMITHS & SILVERSMITHS COMPANY, LTD.

THE COMPANY'S "SERVICE" WATCH.

The most reliable timekeeper in the World for Gentlemen going on Active Service or for rough wear.

£2 10 0   £2 10 0

No. 128.
In Oxidised Steel Case.
£2 10 0

Gentleman's Keyless Lever Watch, Jewelled in all holes, guaranteed a perfect timekeeper, specially adapted for Military use, on account of its shallow and smooth Case, from which it can only be removed by raising Winding catch, and unscrewing from the front, thus rendering it both Dust and Air-tight.

No. 129.
In Solid Silver Case.
£3 10 0

No. 130.
In 18-carat Gold Case.
£12 0 0

UNSOLICITED TESTIMONIAL.

June 7th, 1900.

Please put enclosed Watch in a plain Silver Case. The metal has, as you see, rusted considerably, but I am not surprised, as I wore it continually in South Africa on my wrist for 3½ months. It kept most excellent time, and never failed me.—Faithfully yours,

Capt. North Staffs. Regt.

These Watches are manufactured abroad specially to the order of the Goldsmiths and Silversmiths Company, Ltd., who examine them in London and guarantee them.

. The Prices in this Catalogue are for Cash, without Discount. Orders should be accompanied by a Remittance or London Reference. Goods not approved may be exchanged, or the amount paid will be returned.

But the popular market was not persuaded by the supposed advantages of the wristwatch. Then, the soldiers of World War I, who were not 'Gentlemen' but ordinary men conscripted in their thousands into the army found the wristwatch suited the conditions found on the front. Many of the troops fitted their pocket watches into primitive cupped leather straps.

LEFT: The Service Watch advertised itself as entirely suitable for 'Gentlemen on Active Service' or going to 'rough wear'. Such wording was soon outmoded as millions of young men became involved in 'rough wear' and the fob watch, too, proved inefficient and old-fashioned in the trenches of World War I.

1900-1920s – Military Advances

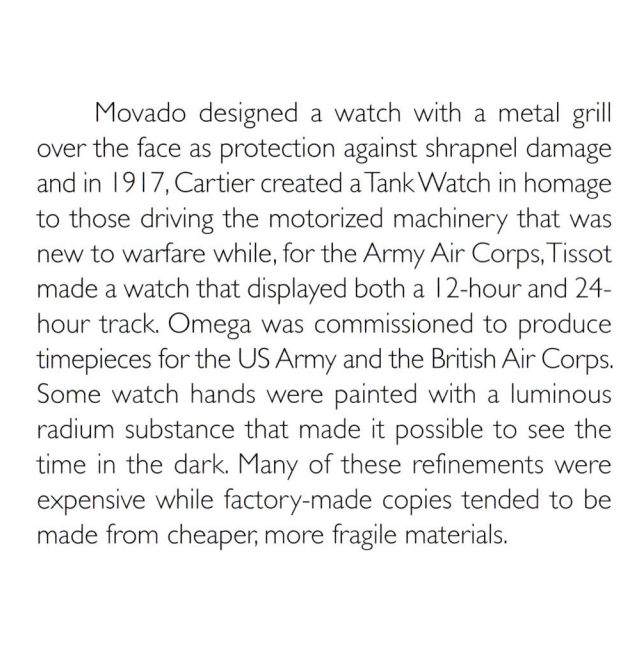

Movado designed a watch with a metal grill over the face as protection against shrapnel damage and in 1917, Cartier created a Tank Watch in homage to those driving the motorized machinery that was new to warfare while, for the Army Air Corps, Tissot made a watch that displayed both a 12-hour and 24-hour track. Omega was commissioned to produce timepieces for the US Army and the British Air Corps. Some watch hands were painted with a luminous radium substance that made it possible to see the time in the dark. Many of these refinements were expensive while factory-made copies tended to be made from cheaper, more fragile materials.

LEFT: This watch from Seiko shows signs of tarnish, but the dial is clear, the numbers presented with great clarity. It dates from 1913, is called the 'Laurel', and is the first timepiece ever produced in Japan. It is one of the first Japanese timepieces presented in the west, and marks the beginning of Seiko, now one of the largest watchmakers in the world.

WATCHES

Until this war, most men were reluctant to wear wristwatches even though manufacturers tried to persuade male customers by calling the product a 'strap watch' to differentiate them from women's wristwatches. Man perceived these timepieces as effeminate because women wore them as pretty, expensively decorated bracelets that happened to include a timepiece in the design. Louis Cartier, while busy making accurate complication watches to suit men's work, confirmed the idea that women preferred form to function and, he revived the traditions of handcrafted watchmaking.

Right: This wristwatch makes it clear why men of the early 20th century were slow to abandon their fob watches. Most wristwatches were conceived as jewelry for women. In 1919, Audemars Piguet gave a tiny watch a dazzling frame of diamonds and fitted it on a grosgrain strap with a jeweled catch.

1900-1920s – Military Advances

At his Paris offices, he assembled teams of craftsmen to design watches as fashion accessories, beautiful, elegant items of jewelry. These bracelets, fashioned from precious metals and stones, often had a hinged cover obscuring the watch face. The hinged cover would be disguised under a great emerald, or the diamond pattern of the strap was repeated seamlessly on the lid. But both Cartier and Tiffany also incorporated the dial as part of the bracelet design.

Left: Longines designed this pendant in 1923. The design, with its curled rhythmic lines recalls the style of Art Nouveau. The surface is in enamel work, but the numbers one to 12 are worked in jewels and placed outside the dial, whilst the 24-hour watch numbers are faintly marked on the inner side. It is a lovely decorative timepiece.

57

WATCHES

Patek Philippe

The Patek Philippe company has a proud history of craftsmanship, and their artisans continue to make every part of each Patek Philippe watch. In 1839, Anton Patek and Franciszek Czapek, both Polish, opened in Geneva as Patek, Czapek & Cle, watchmakers. By 1851 Czapek had left, and was replaced by a Frenchman Adrien Philippe, so the company became Patek Philippe & Cle.

Right: As an independent family owned company, Patek Philippe enjoys total creative freedom to design, produce and assemble what experts agree to be the finest timepieces in the world. Today, Patek Philippe includes the main workshops and headquarters at Plan-les-Ouates, the case and bracelet workshops at Perly and the Patek Philippe Museum at Plainpalais, all in Geneva.

Left: One of their latest creations, the Nautilus chronograph in rose gold on a leather strap. Consummately crafted in Patek Philippe's workshops, the perfectly hand-finished movement with the 21K gold winding rotor is visible through the sapphire-crystal display back.

Patek Philippe

There were some other changes but the biggest came in 1932 when Charles and Jean Stern of Geneva purchased the group, calling it Patek Philippe. It maintains very high standards, every mechanical piece tested before being incorporated into the watch. Each timepiece must pass rigorous testing before qualifying for the Patek Philippe Seal. Because of this process, Patek Philippe's watches are highly valued and respected. The company has been in the same family for four generations. The President is Thierry Stern, while the Honorary President is Philippe Stern.

ABOVE: This is a Patek Philippe pocket watch made for the Bailey, Banks & Biddle company of Philadelphia, USA, around the 1910 period.

ABOVE: Bailey, Banks & Biddle, one of the oldest US jewelry brands, can trace its roots back to 1832. Here the rear of the watch clearly shows the beautiful and intricate work that went into making it, with the tourbillon visible at the bottom left and the fine adjustment lever directly above it.

WATCHES

A very rich class emerged in post-World War I society, and the Americans were particularly wealthy. The wives and daughters of American industrialists trawled Europe for their shopping thrills, and Cartier and other jewellers, such as Tiffany and Bulova, exploited the situation. Women from lower economic brackets shared the attitude of their rich sisters, and demanded factories make cheaper but equally elaborate wristwatches disguised as bracelets. A German company, Theil, made a 'proper' wristwatch for women, that is to say, a watch that was not disguised as a bracelet. They called it Darling, and brought it out in 1912.

RIGHT & INSET: This gold bracelet has an elaborate strap of gold, pearls and enamel work, and shows the jeweler's art at its best. The central rectangle is hinged and, when opened, reveals a watch. This jewel watch comes from Henry Capt of Geneva, and is dated 1850, marking it as an early example of a wristwatch.

1900-1920s – Military Advances

Above: The hinged lid is opened to reveal a space that is carefully organized to fit the watch. A close look at the base of the lid shows a slot to take the watch's crown and ring. And, of course, the watch could be worn separately, hooked onto a chatelaine or hung on a chain round the neck.

Left: This watch fits into the decorative bracelet that is featured on the facing page. The metal face shows signs of ornamental engraving and the Roman numerals are not clearly presented, indicating that reading the time was not of primary concern to the wearer.

61

WATCHES

RIGHT: Nurses inspired a watch design that was efficient for their work. Worn as a brooch, the watch was hung 'upside down' with the number 12 in the lower arc. A busy nurse needed simply to glance down to read the time. This is an early version; ideally, a nurse's watch has a seconds hand to help measure patients' pulse rates.

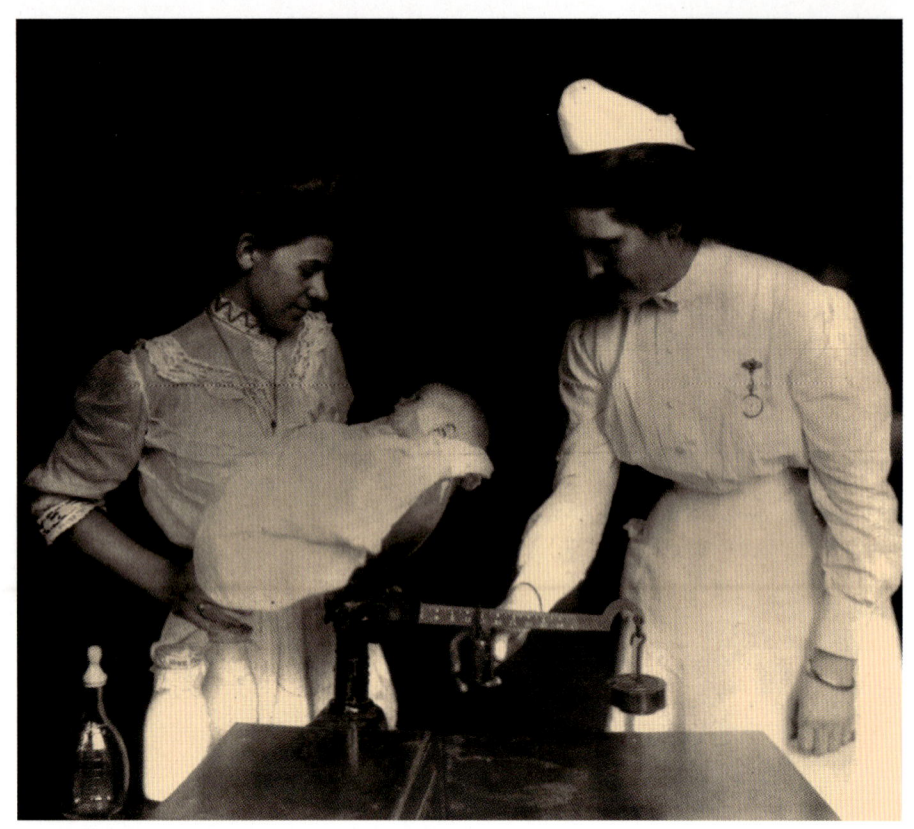

ABOVE: A nurse weighs a baby at the Cincinnati pure milk station in 1908. Her crisp uniform proclaims her authority and her brooch watch is very much part of her medical arsenal.

And the one watch designed specifically for professional women came as a brooch. These were made for nurses, and were pinned to their tunics, chest height. The watch was hung upside down, so that the nurse, glancing down at the pinned watch could see the correct time while measuring the pulse rate of her patient. This brooch watch was standard equipment from the late 19th century and into the mid-20th century.

1900-1920s – Military Advances

Case makers such as Francis Baumgartner and Borgel worked hard to overcome problems of dust and grit creeping into the mechanism of watches. Everyone in the industry longed to find a reliable method of properly rust- and waterproofing these timepieces and they were determined to destroy the widespread public belief that such a small timepiece could not keep time with any accuracy.

ABOVE: In the early 20th century, men were reluctant to wear wristwatches fearing the slur of daintiness. A watchmaker known as Borgel gave them a compromise design. He created a watch that could be fitted into a broad, masculine leather strap, or removed and worn as a pocket watch.

63

WATCHES

Far left: These glistening glass headquarters were completed in time for the celebration of the Rolex centennial two years ago. The building is in the industrial area Plan-les-Ouates, Geneva.

Left: The founder of Rolex, Hans Wilsdorf was an innovative watchmaker and a clever businessman. Among his most famous designs was the hermetically sealed Rolex Oyster, water resistant with a screw-in crown.

Rolex

In 1905, Hans Wildorf and his family opened a company in London. From here, they ordered parts from Switzerland and made watches. Soon they moved to La Chaux de Fonds, in Switzerland, and in 1904, Kew Observatory granted Wilsdorf a chronometer certification, a high accolade. In 1919, the company moved to Geneva where it operated under the name 'Rolex' (the origin of the name remains a mystery) and, in 1926 Wilsdorf created his earliest masterpiece wristwatch, the 'Prince'. Rolex is now a household name,

Rolex

LEFT: This image reveals the delicate skill required to set gems in the movements of a watch. This craft is practiced by Rolex craftsmen in the site at Chene-Bourg.

RIGHT: The Rolex Prince, first introduced in 1926, has remained popular over the years. The rectangular form, the clarity of the numerals, and its long time span before rewinding is required, are appreciated by aficionados. This is a modern, reworked design of the old favorite.

famous for carefully crafted, inventive engineering and superb complication watches. The company is listed among the world's 100 most valuable global brands while the vast number of counterfeit Rolexes available on the black market confirms their popularity. It comes as a surprise that this global company remains in private hands under the Hans Wilsdorf Foundation and a percentage of profits is dedicated to charity. Currently the Chief Executive Officer is Bruno Meier.

WATCHES

This decade saw major advances in watches that helped establish wristwatches beyond the preferences of servicemen. Watches with chronograph and central date indicators were available, and in 1923 John Harwood patented a self-winding watch thus eliminating the need for keys or a winding button on the watch.

ABOVE: The historic workhouses of the Tissot watch company reveal a light and airy atmosphere. Tissot, however, is responsible for a highly technical advance in timekeeping. Its 1999 'T-Touch' disposed of many functions; a mere touch of the finger conjures a digital display of time, or altimeter, or chronograph and so forth.

ABOVE: John Harwood perfected the self-winding or automatic wristwatch in 1923. Here he can be seen inspecting one of his timepieces.

1900-1920s – Military Advances

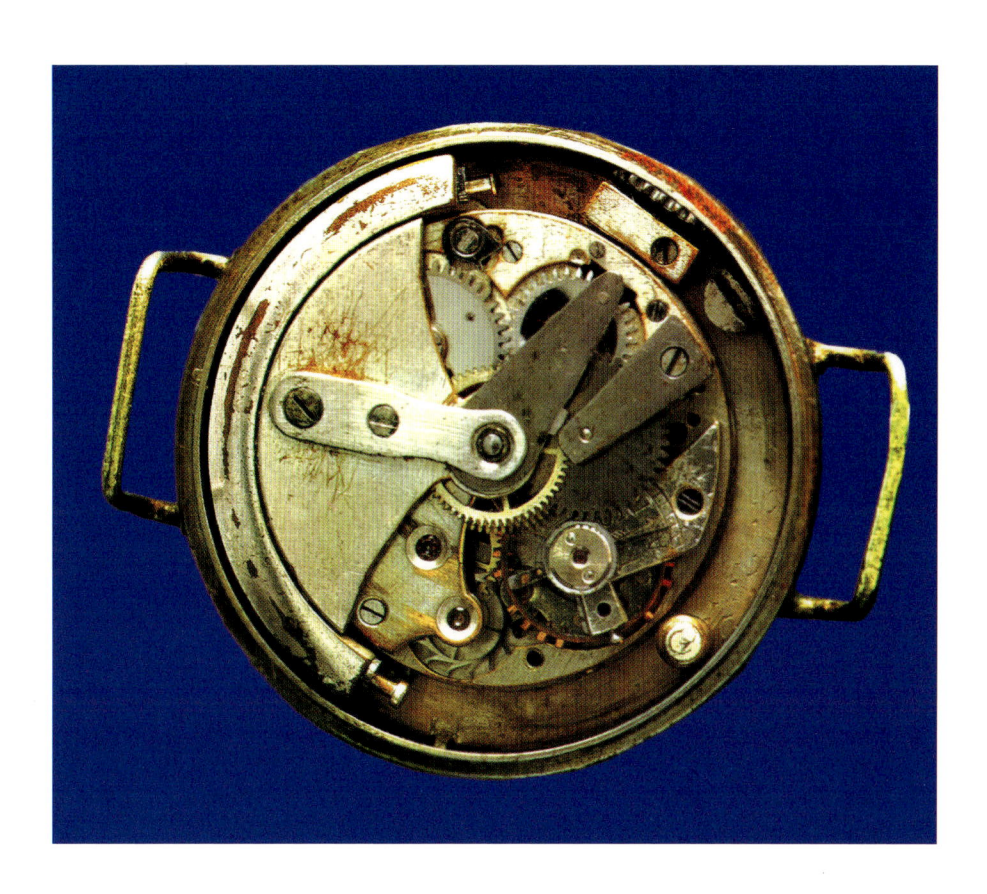

ABOVE: This Harwood watch shows the oscillating winding weight with spring-loaded buffers at the ends. It took some time for the world of horology to recognize Harwood for his invention.

RIGHT: Brietling designed this clear, simple design with dials for day of the month and seconds. It is a chronometer, or stopwatch and is dated 1923.

WATCHES

Hans Wildorf of Rolex introduced his Rolex Prince, and this established firmly the ascendancy of the wristwatch. The shape was unconventional; it was a rectangle that allowed the use of a large mainspring barrel and a larger balance. This design gave space to a big seconds dial, easily read. The Prince was constructed with great efficiency. Wildorf ensured it had been checked in every which way – upside down, left, right, and sideways and in all temperatures. It could run for 58 hours and only needed to be wound every two days.

Of course, the Rolex creation prompted many imitators, and not least among the watchmakers who worked out of factories. The retail market was quick to manufacture and promote wristwatches that were not jewelry accessories but simple, efficient timepieces. Advertisements appeared for rugged little watches made for busy women.

Right: This is an early model of the Rolex Prince. The spare design made the watch easy to read, but its timekeeping qualities and robust construction brought this range lasting popularity.

1900-1920s – Military Advances

ABOVE: Mercedes Gleitze was the first woman to swim the English Channel. The British newspaper, The News of the World, awarded her with a check for her achievement. She can be seen accepting this gift from the paper's representative, Mr Emslie.

ABOVE RIGHT: The Rolex Oyster wristwatch was the first truly waterproof timepiece. When Mercedes Gleitze swam the English Channel, she wore a Rolex Oyster on a chain round her neck.

And, ironically, it was a woman not a man who became the first 'celebrity' to promote a particular watch. When Mercedes Gleitze swam the English Channel in 1927, she wore the Rolex 'Oyster' watch, proving it not only gave an accurate reading of time but that it was indeed waterproof. And her feat gave watchmakers pause for thought: women as athletes? Could this prove a new and strong market?

69

WATCHES

1930s
Dilemmas of Time

The connection between time and sport began in the late 19th century. Montblanc revived its Nicolas Riveussec stopwatch, and gamblers in the US horseracing world took to using their own stopwatches to measure the time it took for the champion to romp past the winning post.

LEFT: In the 1920s, the stopwatch was used with great excitement, but perhaps without great accuracy, by crowds at the horse races, and in betting shops. The punters felt they could beat the bookies with this chance to personally measure the horses' racing times.

WATCHES

The first stopwatch dates back as far as the late 17th century, when it was used by doctors and the military leaders, who found them helpful when conducting campaigns. In 1822, a small, boxed timepiece appeared that, at the press of a button, squirted ink onto the dial, thus recording the moment the button was pressed. It was called a chronograph, but forty years later, Heuer was making pocket watches that were very similar to modern stopwatches and, by 1916, their invention was accurate to a hundredth of a second. They called it the Micrograph.

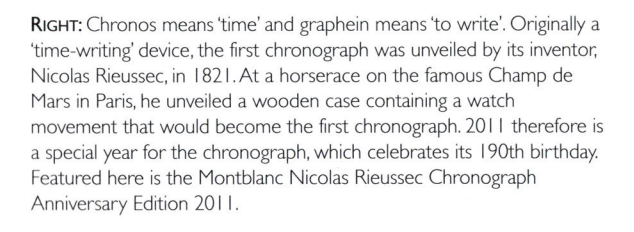

RIGHT: Chronos means 'time' and graphein means 'to write'. Originally a 'time-writing' device, the first chronograph was unveiled by its inventor, Nicolas Rieussec, in 1821. At a horserace on the famous Champ de Mars in Paris, he unveiled a wooden case containing a watch movement that would become the first chronograph. 2011 therefore is a special year for the chronograph, which celebrates its 190th birthday. Featured here is the Montblanc Nicolas Rieussec Chronograph Anniversary Edition 2011.

1930s – Dilemmas of Time

Auguste Piccard not only explored the deep ocean but also the skies. He designed an aluminum gondola specially adapted so that passengers did not need to wear a pressure suit. In 1930, he and his colleague, Paul Kipfer took off from Augsberg, Germany and reached a record altitude of 51,775 feet (15,785 m). A chronometer proved an important part of the flight equipment.

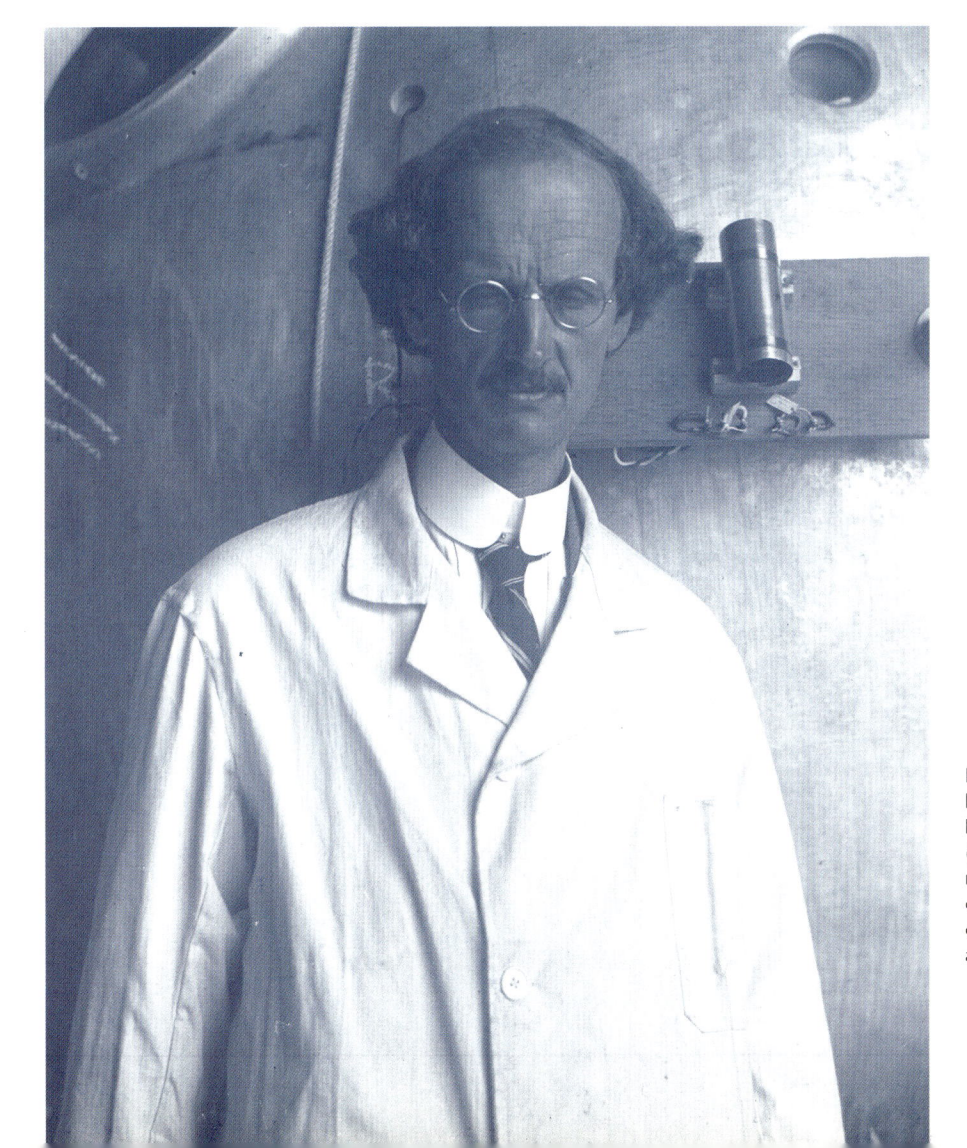

Left: In recognition of his achievements, the German city of Biel presented Piccard with this TAG Heuer chronograph.

Left: Auguste Piccard made his heroic balloon journey reaching a height of over 51,000 feet (15,000 meters). He was able to make significant measurements of cosmic rays and collected other scientific data on the upper atmosphere.

WATCHES

Motor racing became a sport soon after the invention of the automobile but, initially these races were a test of endurance, drivers proving they could complete difficult courses. However, by the 1930s, these races began to concentrate on speed, and stopwatches proved their worth. Longines and Tissot made stopwatches used at the Brazil grand prix, Omega took stopwatches to the 1932 Olympics and in 1933 TAG Heuer were producing stop watches for car dashboards. But this method of measuring speed had its disadvantages – seconds could be lost while a thumb sought the button to stop the hands. Moving pictures – film – and digital clocks thereafter superseded this slightly inaccurate method of timing athletes, cars, and horses.

RIGHT: Omega was selected for the 1932 Olympic Games, and their poster was a confident presentation of its watches. It was, of course, a great commercial coup to be credited as the official timekeeper of the Olympic Games, but it was also a confirmation of the high reputation of the watchmaker.

1930s – Dilemmas of Time

LEFT: Proper stopwatches with independent dials, the hands of which can be started, stopped and reset while not affecting timekeeping appeared in the early 19th century. This Omega is a splendid example. Stopwatches were phased out of Olympic use in 1964 when they were replaced by electronic timing devices. This is one of the actual timekeeping watches at the games.

BELOW: This is an overview of the opening ceremony of the Olympic Games at the Los Angeles Stadium in 1932.

WATCHES

Breitling

Leon Breitling opened as a watchmaker in Saint-Imier, Switzerland in 1884. He was a dedicated watchmaker, but when he became fascinated by the new wonder of flying, he determined his watches would "measure time, rather than tell time". As a result, Breitling is famed for its chronometers, and its watches are much appreciated by civil aviators. The watches have large faces, and analog time; they also have a flyback function, split seconds, phases of the moon, the date, and other complications. The mechanical models are self-winding, have 38 jewels, with straps and cases of steel, titanium, or gold. The quartz models have rubber straps. Every watch is certified with an Attestation de Chronomatique by the Swiss horology authority. Among the famous Breitling models are the 'Navitimer' and the 'Cosmonaut'. The company, based now in Grenchen, Switzerland has been in the family for five generations, and the CEO in 2010 is Theodore Schneider.

ABOVE: Leon Breitling, founder, concentrated on chronographs and loved the development of flight and airplanes. He would be proud and pleased to know that over a hundred years after its establishment, his watch company is host to aviation displays and is sponsor to aviation associations.

ABOVE: Breiling instrument watches are among the world's finest. This variation of its Navitimer Chrono-Matic tells the hours, minutes, subsidiary seconds, and shows chronograph, calendar and moon phase. It has also an integrated slide rule.

Breitling

RIGHT: For a long time, Breitling imported movements for its watches but in 2006, the company presented its Caliber B01, a highly advanced technical chronograph made by in-house craftsmen. Artisans' and designers' workstations are housed in bright cheerful conditions in the modern Breiling headquarters.

LEFT: The fine buildings of the Breitling watch company in 1892 were testament to the rapid rise of Leon Breitling as a businessman and a craftsman.

WATCHES

LEFT: The informality and excitement of early motor racing is captured in this scene. Such events were terribly important to watchmakers who were keen to promote the accuracy of the timepieces they made. Longines was an early enthusiast for this sport, and was eager to be associated with automobiles and fast drivers.

BELOW: Timepieces, no doubt stopwatches, are lined up so that Frau Steinweg can keep track of times during a race in which the great driver, Rudolf Steinweg, participated. Frau Steinweg was photographed keeping her records in Berlin, 1933.

1930s – Dilemmas of Time

Above: In 1933, TAG Heuer made a robust timepiece for automobiles. It could be screwed to the dashboard, and was called the 'Atavia-Dashboard'.

WATCHES

In 1933, Anne and Charles Lindbergh set off on a voyage of some 47,000 km around the North Atlantic. The navigational instruments that they took with them on their journey included a directional gyroscopic compass, an artificial horizon and an ice indicator, as well as two aperiodic compasses and a Longines chronograph developed specially by the watch brand for this flight over Greenland and the far north. The Longines Lindbergh's Atlantic Voyage Watch was re-issued in honour of the long voyage undertaken by the Lindbergh's.

At the beginning of this decade another connection between watches and sport was made. It is a curious, romantic story. Cesar de Trey, once a denture manufacturer who had become a watchmaker, was a spectator at a polo match in India. The players complained to him that the glass protecting their watch dials was constantly breaking. De Trey submitted a design for 'a watch that can be slid in its support and completely turned over' and thus, the glass was protected while the rider was playing a vigorous game of polo.

RIGHT: Charles Lindbergh has signed the sketch he prepared for the kind of timepiece he wanted for his exploration of the North Atlantic. He devised a system to improve aerial and nautical navigational methods, and Longines incorporated his ideas. The timepiece had a wristwatch chronograph movement with a 30-minute counter. It measured time to the fifth of a second, and the chronograph mechanism also had a tachymeter that could measure speeds of up to 500 kph.

80

1930s – Dilemmas of Time

BELOW: Longines re-issued the exceptional timepiece made for Lindbergh, naming the new model the 'Longines Lindbergh's Atlantic Voyage Watch'.

ABOVE: The watch company were rightfully proud of the wristwatch chronograph they made for Lindbergh, and this advertisement reveals that Longines were ready to consult with their clients and meet their special needs.

81

WATCHES

The resulting 'Reverso' watch was made by Jaeger-LeCoultre and proved hugely popular, not only with polo players but also among women. It seems that, at this time, it was not 'ladylike' to consult the time in public but with a Reverso a gal did not need to leave her timepiece at home because she could hide the dial as she sipped her cocktail. Technology had now advanced to make possible a mechanism that could fit into odd shapes that were also thinner than previous watches. The Gruen Curvex appeared in 1932, and it was curved to follow the shape of the wrist.

LEFT: The patent for the design of the Reverso was filed in Paris in 1931, and it remains the most famous watch made by Jaeger-LeCoultre. The sketches show the ingenious system that allowed the face to be turned over within its case. Reverso comes in many designs. This black face with gold marks to indicate numerals is simple and elegant.

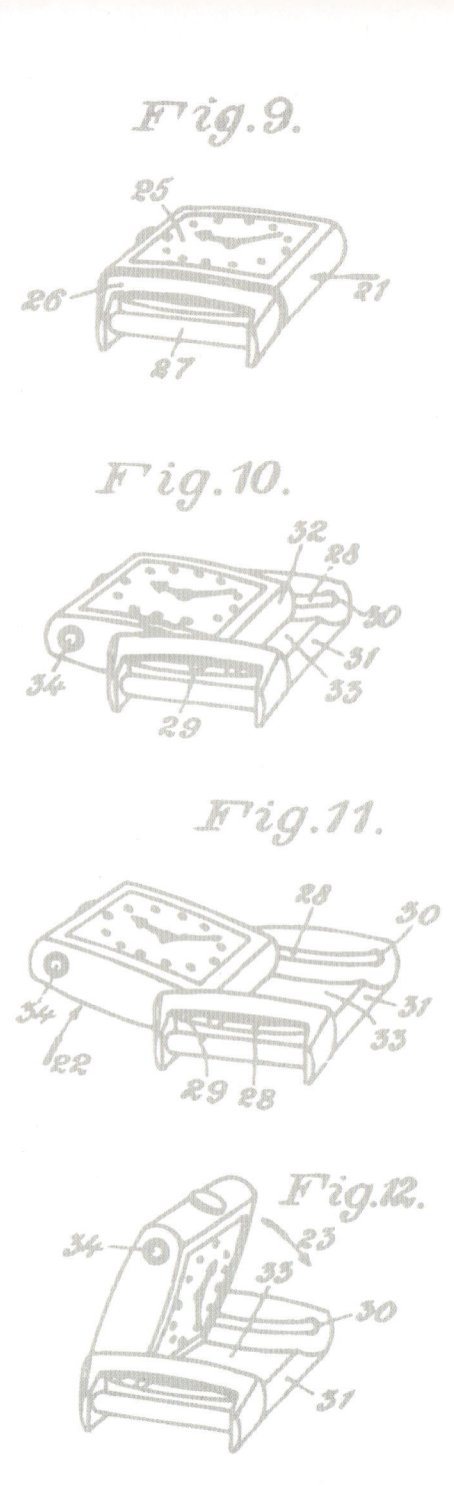

1930s – Dilemmas of Time

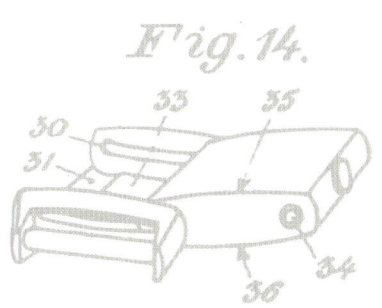

Left: This advertisement shows, in sophisticated style, how the Reverso can be a wristwatch, or with a simple action, become a decorative item worn on the wrist. The design was loved by sportsmen who wished to protect the dial of their watch, and by women who liked to hide their watch, pretending they had no dull concern with time.

Right: The Reverso has been issued in many models, such as this version with a subsidiary dial for seconds. All versions retain the basic rectangular shape, and every Reverso needs wide lugs to support the box into which the watch is slid and turned.

WATCHES

Vacheron Constantin

Vacheron Constantin is recognized as the oldest watchmaker in the world, and one of the most luxurious. In 1755, Jean-Marc Vacheron opened in Geneva. Francois Constantin joined in 1819. Over the years, Vacheron Constantin invented, among other things, the first complications in a timepiece, engine-turned dials, and a pantographic device to engrave the tiny parts of a watch. This creativity continues to mark the company in the 21st century, with the world's thinnest watch, the 'Patrimony' and one of the most exquisite, the 'Kallista'. This took 6,000 hours to construct, then 20 months of work by jewelers. Watches for women appeared in 2003 and in 2007, Vacheron Constantin presented their 'Les Masques', a series of 12 watches, each carrying an image of an African mask on its dial. Vacheron Constantin sells only in 15 dedicated outlets, and in 1996 became part of the Richemont Group. In 2010 Juan Carlos Torres is the CEO and has been since 2005.

Left: To honor the brand's long history with China, Vacherin Constantin created a limited series of three 'Dragons' watches, each series carrying nine numbered pieces. These watches were only sold at the following locations: 1881 Heritage in Hong Kong, Vacheron Constantin Mansions in Geneva and Shanghai, and the Vacheron Constantin boutique in Moscow.

Above: Vacheron Constantin has its headquarters in this distinctive modernist building in Geneva.

Vacheron Constantin

ABOVE & LEFT: This piece exemplifies Vacheron Constantin's luxe standards. The Caliber 2450 shows hours, minutes and sweep seconds, and is a mechanical watch with automatic winding. The movements have a brass plate with perlage, and 27 jewels; the Seal of Geneva confirms the high quality of this watch.

WATCHES

These were practical applications of timepieces, but the progress in the intricacy of watch engineering and design excited intellectual and artistic interest. Picasso could not resist such contemporary developments in the old, fascinating science of measuring time. In his 1931 painting, 'Girl Reading', he included a reference to the rectangular Rolex watch. Another painter, Gerald Murphy, created a wonderful geometric pattern in his painting of the mechanics of a Vacheron-Constantin minute repeater.

But perhaps the most famous 1930s artistic reference to time came from Salvador Dali. In his painting 'The Persistence of Memory', watches melt and dissolve in a wide landscape, and the work is Dali's metaphor for the mystery of time. The curious design of the Cartier Libre wristwatch was thought by some to have derived from the Dali painting, while others saw the shape as a watch that followed the form of a woman's torso.

RIGHT: Watchmakers were aware of changing attitudes among post-war women who began to demand 'proper' timepieces, not jewel watches. The manufacturers made wristwatches that were elegant but practical, promising the same accuracy and complications that had long been available for men.

1930s – Dilemmas of Time

Of course, this was not the first era artists had commented on time. In the 16th century, Holbein made a mysterious study The Ambassadors and, within the scene, he depicts a calendar, a sundial, astrological devices and other timekeeping devices contemporary to his time. Numerous Renaissance paintings were gloomy meditations on the passing of time, the artist juxtaposing a watch with a skull to emphasise the point.

ABOVE: Omega found an answer to the famous Reverso watch, with this bracelet watch designed so that the dial could be hidden. It was called 'Armure' and was aimed at the ever-increasing market of sportswomen.

LEFT: Gruen, a US company, catered for a popular market, and found ways of convincing their customers that wristwatches were both beautiful and useful. The curved line of the watch promised a snug fit and sophisticated style, suitable to wear with the most gorgeous outfit.

WATCHES

Watchmakers in the 30s made strong use of artists and craftsmen, not only to design jewelled timepieces for women, but in making cases for watches so that the timepiece was protected from the strenuous activities of golf and tennis players. In 1927, an hermetic or sealed watch was patented, and in the early 30s, Ebel was marketing the design. The two halves of the case were pulled apart to reveal the watch. The Ebel watch opened when two small buttons on the case were pressed. A stud screw in the case was engineered to wind the watch. Women were given the choice of beautiful Art Deco cases while men were offered the Rolex chased silver 'masculine' case.

ABOVE: Watches had a novelty value in the early 20th century and manufacturers presented them in all sorts of fun ways. Here, a watch is fitted snugly to the side of a cigarette case. It was made by Van Cleef and Arpels, a company with a history in the making of jewel watches.

LEFT: The Swiss company Ebel made the first hermetic or sealed watch in 1926, but other manufacturers soon followed. It was of a design and construction that could be carried in a pocket, bag or purse while keeping the watch secure. The case opens with two sliding halves, and a winding device works whenever the watch is opened. The case allowed for some gorgeous decoration in enamels or gemstones.

RIGHT: Another offering from Van Cleef and Arpels, the timepiece set on a powder compact is lavishly framed with gems. The hand shows only the hours, an unusual element in 1937.

1930s – Dilemmas of Time

This began a craze for watches not worn on the wrist but fitted into cigarette lighters, purses and powder compacts. Movado created their popular Ermeto watchcases that they called purse watches; many manufacturers produced handbags sporting watches on their exteriors, and powder compacts were adorned with a watch on their lids. But these were novelties and did not detract from the growing popularity of wristwatches for men and women, and factories in Germany, Switzerland and the USA continued to make affordable wristwatches for the mass market.

LEFT: A watch, encased in a glittering diamond-shaped frame, adds a little pizzazz to a nondescript evening bag. This was a stylish touch in 1935.

WATCHES

Tissot

Founded in 1853 by Charles-Félicien Tissot and his son, Charles-Emile, in Le Locle, Switzerland, the business and the profits were helped when Charles-Emile made successful sales trips to Russia. The company was not afraid of the unconventional. Some of the designs used wood, mother-of-pearl, and Alpine granite to decorate the faces. Their jewelry watches have been successful – clients include Grace Kelly. Tissot introduced its first mass produced pocket watches in the 19th century, and ever innovative, recently created the 'T-Touch'. This uses touch-sensitive sapphire glass, and shows compass, barometer, altimeter, thermometer, and the time. Angelina Jolie wore one in *Lara Croft Tomb Raider*. In 1930, Tissot and Omega became partners of a convention linking the two houses under the corporate name of Société Suisse pour l'Industrie Horlogère (Swiss Company for the Watch Industry). But since 1983, Tissot has been part of the Swatch empire. In 2010 George Nicolas Hayek Jnr became the Chairman of the Board, and the President is François Thiébaud.

ABOVE: With the success of the Tissot Company, a factory was built in 1907. The building would grow with the notoriety of the brand.

LEFT: Charles-Félicien and his Son Charles-Emile, founded their company in the mid-19th century, in the house where they lived with their family; an official wall plaque honors where the famous Tissot brand was born.

FAR LEFT: : Charles-Emile Tissot presents a sober, respectable face that belies his daring as watchmaker and a businessman.

Tissot

ABOVE: Tissot combines digital and analog display with neat, minimalist design. The striped glass gives the watch an appearance that suits the city clothes of professional men and women.

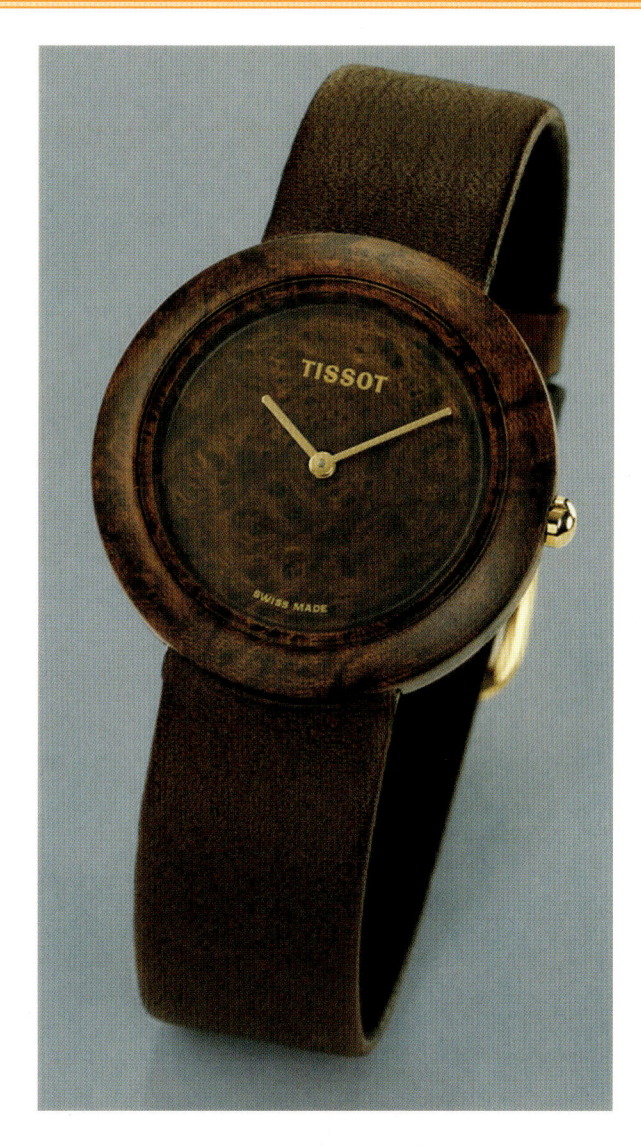

LEFT: The wooden watch presented by Tissot in 1988 is proud of its material. There is no attempt to hide the wood; indeed, not even numerals are permitted to mark the surface. It has a reassuring, eco-friendly air about it.

WATCHES

LEFT: The factory manufacturer, Mido, stormed the market with their 'Evolution' range. In this watch, the numeral for the hour clicked to show itself in one aperture, while below it the minutes appeared in another aperture. The seconds, however, show on a dial.

Ingersoll, ever democratic in their determination to make watches affordable for all, presented their famous 'Mickey Mouse' watch. The dial showed Disney's much-loved cartoon character, with Mickey's arms serving to show the time. Images of Mickey were reproduced on the child size strap, and the whole was advertised as unbreakable. Christmas advertisements from the 30s show a wide variety of wristwatches for men and women. Dials come with round faces, square, oblong and curved.

LEFT: In the 1930s, the terms analog and digital were not familiar to the general public. The 'Evolution' seemed digital, but it was not operated by electricity or quartz. It was an imaginative design, seeking sales among those who wanted a less than conventional timepiece.

1930s – Dilemmas of Time

Yet watches were not a frivolous buy. Even factory products were costly enough to qualify as gifts for special occasions such as birthdays, anniversaries, or an academic achievement. To emphasise the special quality of watches, makers boasted of 'original and artistic designs' for their women's watches, or of 'master craftsmanship' when selling to male customers. Bulova also announced that their creations 'made no compromise with accuracy.'

ABOVE: Some watchmakers couldn't resist the temptation to be artistic with their timepieces. This watch is of unusual shape, and the numerals are interesting rather than clear and simple. Elia added a gold bracelet-style strap on this woman's watch.

RIGHT: This man's watch has a fine snakeskin strap, but its most distinctive feature is the display of the passing seconds in a small aperture placed where the numeral 9 would normally appear. It was created by Waltham in the 1930s.

WATCHES

Unlike the wealthy era of the 20s, this period suffered from the great financial Depression of 1929, and as the decade progressed, Europe confronted a growing militarism. Spain erupted into a civil war, and the aggressive men who led Germany and Italy nursed grand ideas of conquering all Europe. Another world war seemed inevitable. These developments affected, of course, the watch making industry. Customers had less money to spend, and materials and supplies became more difficult to find. Switzerland seemed the one country that could withstand the threatening political and economic upheavals.

RIGHT: For many decades, Swiss watchmaking held the respect of the world. Bulova had a classical figure frolicking through a variety of women's watches, because she carried implications of tradition, quality and good looks. Tissot made a proud display that included the Swiss flag. The purchase of a watch was 'the gift of a lifetime' and a Swiss timepiece was of such quality it was a gift for a lifetime.

1930s – Dilemmas of Time

ABOVE: Breitling establishes their dedication to the aviation industry while also confirming the advanced technology of their chronometer. The Montbrillant range has proved to have enduring popularity.

95

WATCHES

RIGHT: The Tissot company building sits confidently in Le Locle, a town in the Jura area. Here, the company sustains the traditions of the Swiss watchmaking industry, manufacturing luxury, crafted timepieces while employing a skilled labor force.

1940s
A Slow Time

The watchmaking industry was among the calamities of World War II. Materials were diverted for the use of the military and, besides, craftsmen and factory workers joined the fighting forces. In England, and most of Europe the industry came to a standstill – except in Switzerland.

WATCHES

This landlocked, mountain-ridged land was a neutral zone during the war. This did not mean the country played no role at all. Switzerland is a country with few natural resources and no seaport, so, to counteract these disadvantages, it had built up industries of high value, high quality products, such as specialised machinery, luxury textiles, and watches, and they sold these things to both sides fighting the war.

Below: The villages of the Jura region of Switzerland have long been involved in watchmaking, and during the religious wars of the Reformation, many French craftsmen found refuge and work in the area.

1940s – A Slow Time

ABOVE: World War II restricted production but did not halt the Swiss watchmaking industry. Tissot maintained a busy output as this view of workers in 1940 reveals.

WATCHES

By 1936, the Swiss had passed the USA in the production of watches. A reciprocal trade agreement eased the market for Swiss imports into the USA while it killed the production of American jewel-lever watches. Roskopf, the Swiss watchmaker of inexpensive products, were so successful they opened branches in the USA, and war conditions helped the Swiss industry.

RIGHT: Georges-Frederic Roskopf (1839-89) was a German watchmaker who worked in La Chaux-de-Fonds, Switzerland. Some historians believe that he has never been given proper credit for his ingenious pocket watches 'affordable by all purses,' although he won a bronze medal for his timepiece at the 1868 Universal Exhibition, Paris.

1940s – A Slow Time

ABOVE: The Roskopf watch was known also as the pin-pallet or pin-lever watch, and many manufacturers copied this construction. The watch earned a poor reputation thanks to shabby copies, but authorized Roskopf watches were so accurate that they were supplied to Belgium railway workers. The Reconvilier Watch Company made this model in the 40s.

The founder of this company, Georges-Frederic Roskopf (1813-89) was determined to make affordable watches. He came up with an ingenious design, managing to eliminate the center wheel that drove the seconds hand, and he replaced the escapement cylinder with a kind of pin-pallet. Later changes included a simplified keyless winding system. These innovations lowered production costs, and his company maintained his aspirations for low cost timepieces, increasing manufacture even during the hardship years of the 40s.

WATCHES

Girard-Perregaux

This company joins luxury brands Gucci, Bedat, and Boucheron under the umbrella of the Sowind Swiss Group. Girard-Perregaux has modern premises in Geneva. The company was started in 1791 by Jean-Francois Bautte but was bought by the watchmaker, Constant Girard and his wife, Marie Perregaux in 1852. The couple continued Bautte's policy of keeping his artisans under one roof although it was customary at that time to out-source work to craftsmen. The company maintains their policy. In 1880, Girard-Perregaux was first to make a series of wristwatches when Kaiser Wilhelm commissioned them for his navy, and in 1967 the watchmakers won the Astronomical Observatory de Neuchatel prize for their 'Observatory Chronometer.' They are respected for complications watches, the most iconic being the 'Tourbillon' range. One model adjusts time between lunar and mean time. In the women's range, the 'Vintage 1945' and 'Cat's Eye' are admired. The Chief Executive Officer is Luigi Macaluso.

RIGHT: This is the Caliber GPFAY08. It has manual winding, a tourbillon cage and a slot machine with three cylinders activated by a hand lever that includes a sound signal. This kind of original approach to its timepieces has long been company ethos. To make a game extension as part of a watch, Girard-Perregaux embarked upon a completely new design and months of development were needed to conceive the GPFAY08 Jackpot Tourbillon.

Girard-Perregaux

ABOVE: This design of a tourbillon under three gold bridges, and automatic winding was patented in 1867. Girard-Perregaux cherishes the quality of this movement, and still uses this construction as can be found in its modern watch 'Caliber 9600'.

ABOVE: Constant Girard-Perregaux was particularly acclaimed for his research into escapement systems, notably the tourbillon escapement. In 1889, his famous tourbillon with three gold bridges won a gold medal at the Paris Universal Exhibition. With his wife, he bought an established workshop in his hometown of La Chaux-de-Fonds and so the famous company was born.

WATCHES

LEFT & BELOW: Allied prisoners-of-war had their watches confiscated by the German forces, so captured soldiers had to find ingenious ways of concealing their precious Rolex 'Speed King' from the enemy.

Despite Roskopf's success, Swiss watchmaking was hardly vigorous during World War II, but, of course, watches played a role in warfare. Famously, the Allied prisoners-of-war planning the Great Escape from Colditz Castle relied on their Rolex 'Oyster Chronograph' watches to time the movements of their guards. Many soldiers wore the smaller, and less expensive, Rolex 'Speed King'.

BELOW: A scene from the film 'Coldtiz' made in 1954 about the doomed attempts of Allied soldiers to flee imprisonment. It was claimed that a Rolex watch was used to time the prison guards' comings and goings around the prison.

1940s – A Slow Time

Right: This watch was commissioned by the British navy in 1942. Longines were asked to make a watch for deepsea divers, hence the robust design, with a crown held firmly on a chain. The arms are luminous.

WATCHES

For aviators, Breitling made the 'Navitimer' that showed a circular slide rule on its dial, and the Aircraft Owners and Pilots Association adopted this watch. The Russian state factory, Sekonda, manufactured Poljot watches of great accuracy for the Soviet armed forces. An American company, the Hamilton Watch Company, managed to mass-produce marine chronometers that were widely used by the Allies during World War II.

RIGHT: The Breitling Chronomat was an early chronograph with a circular slide rule. It was presented in 1942, and was admired for its technical advance. But as automatic watches from competing countries began to take the market, the Swiss industry sensed the need for change. In collaboration with the movement maker Dubois Depraz, the watchmakers Heuer and Breitling began work on an automatic chronograph movement.

1940s – A Slow Time

When motor racing was resumed after peace was declared, Heuer launched chronographs that proved popular with racers, who favored especially the 'Carrera' and 'Daytona' models, named after famous racetracks. (Some terms are easily confused. A chronograph measures short intervals on demand, that is, a stopwatch. A chronometer is a high precision watch with an extremely regular time rate.) All these watches were bought also by men who were neither aviators nor racing drivers but who appreciated the appearance and the various complications offered by these timepieces.

Left: TAG Heuer presented their 'Carrera' timepiece for motor racers in the 1940s, but the range has endured for over 50 years, and TAG Heuer continue to present updated variations. This is the modern 'Grand Carrera Calibre 17 RS'. It has a rotating disc display, and has chronograph and date functions as well as telling the time. It is made of stainless steel.

WATCHES

At the start of the war, another well-liked model was created for the medical world. This was the Hamilton 'Seckron Doctor's Duo-Dial' watch: its rectangular dial was divided in half, with one section showing hours and minutes while the other showed, in a large and clear fashion, seconds. It had a beautiful minimalist design and stylized numerals, and was sought by customers outside the world of hospitals.

RIGHT: Watch designs grew more and more interesting and some, like this example, acknowledged customers' fascination with the mechanics of watchmaking. Described as a skelletonized movement, this timepiece made in 1946 by Audemars Piguet displays its movements uncovered. The numerals are placed outside the dial, allowing no interruption in the skeleton display.

1940s – A Slow Time

Of course, neither war nor recession hinders the very rich who, even in the 1940s, longed for luxury and wealthy women continued to regard watches as jewelry. Vacheron Constantin made a silver dial with gold numerals, markers, and gold hands, adding a gold case and gold snake bracelet strap. Movado produced an ornate design of platinum set with diamonds. Cartier, Tiffany, and other jewelers managed to cater for this small luxury market.

LEFT: The Portuguese singer Carmen Miranda (1913-1955) was a flamboyant and much adored entertainer who inspired musicians, artists, designers and watchmakers. The latter were eager to have her endorsement for their timepieces. Here Carmen Miranda is photographed in a scene from an unknown film.

ABOVE: So famous was Carmen Miranda, that Tissot gave this jewel watch her name. It seems to be a pretty bracelet but the central medallion is hinged and, when opened, reveals a watch.

WATCHES

Longines

This company has been closely associated with sport and athletes since the early 20th century. Lindbergh wore the Longines 'Lindbergh Hour Angle Watch' when he made the first flight across the Atlantic, and the aviatrix, Amelia Earhart relied on Longines when she was flying. In 1988, the company formed a partnership with the luxury and racing car manufacturer, Ferrari, but they are associated also with the Olympics, gymnasts, equestrians, and skiers. August Agassiz founded the business in 1832 in St-Imiers, Switzerland and, as his business expanded, he moved to the neighborhood of Les Longines. The brand name 'Longines' was registered in 1880. The company aims for modern innovations combined with a strong sense of contemporary design – the 'Flagship Heritage' shows a clean, minimalist look, whereas the 'Chronograph' range includes heavy, impressive sports watches; both men and women favor the brand. The company became part of the Swatch group in the 1980s.

RIGHT: Despite its attachment to sporting events, Longines has long been associated with watches for women. This spectacular clasp was called 'Cleopatra' and it was designed in 1978, an era when showy accessories were much admired.

LEFT: This decorative pocket watch is one of the early timepieces made by August Agassiz, founder of Longines. It was probably worn as a pendant. The movements show a cylinder escapement that requires a key to wind it.

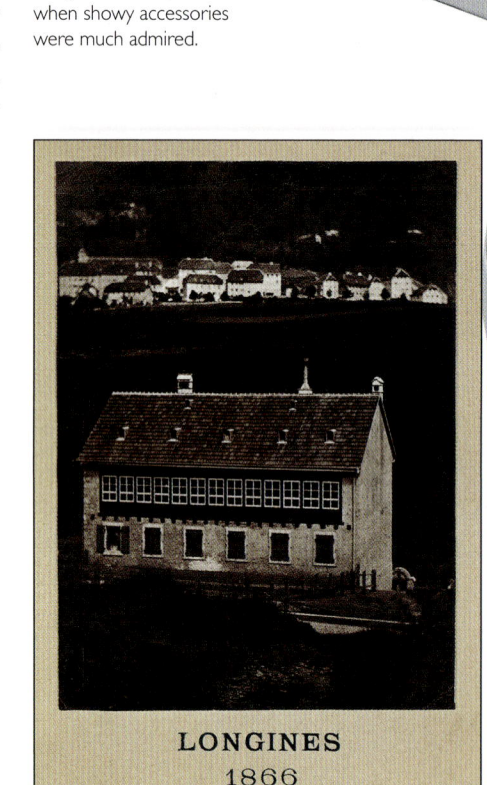

LEFT: This was the home of the Longines company in 1866. It was located in a suburb of St-Imiers, a watchmaking center in Switzerland.

Longines

LEFT: Longines watches are characterized by traditional values and classic design combined with progressive technology. These qualities are demonstrated in this sophisticated timepiece from the 'DolceVita' collection.

BELOW: The simplicity of this pocket watch with its seconds dial won Longines awards at the Paris Exposition in 1867.

111

WATCHES

But even less wealthy women, who found ways of overcoming war rationing and other restrictions to buy shoes and purses, found the means to own a pretty watch. For this market, Jacques Kreisler and other factory manufacturers marketed decorative bangle-style watches. Advertisements from the time show firm bangle 'straps' closed with a clasp and the dial set into the ornate bangles, made of twisted or engraved non-precious metal.

But the market for watches as jewelry was small during wartime for another reason. Many women found themselves thrown into jobs vacated by the men who had gone to war. A postal worker, a factory hand, or a bus driver needed a sensible watch, appropriate to their work. Their changed lives demanded sensible watches rather than jewel-like objects.

RIGHT: Commercial manufacturers understood that many women prefer a jewel watch, and Jacques Kreisler marketed wristwatches as 'sculptured curve watch bands'. These resembled interesting bangles and sold well.

1940s – A Slow Time

LEFT: Women were urged to abandon their usual homemaking role and take on 'men's work' during World War II. The model in this campaign poster sports a neat, gold wristwatch.

Roskopf catered for their needs, but that other great purveyor of commercial watches, Ingersol, had been diverted to the war effort, producing fuses and timing devices for bombs. Omega and Rolex presented women's watches that had small, circular dials marked with clear precise numerals and all held on leather straps, and even the grand jewelers, Tiffany, ventured out with a simple but dainty dial and a narrow strap of reptile skin.

ABOVE: Watchmakers began to create simple, uncluttered watches for women such as the 1948 'Seamaster' range from Omega. These ranges did not imitate the heavy design of men's sports watches but neither did they pretend to be jewelry.

WATCHES

And, for the first time, the art world acknowledged that the watch itself could be regarded as a work of art. The Museum of Modern Art, New York displayed the 'Museum' watch designed by Nathan George Horwitt in 1947 for Movado. The dial had single gold dot to symbolise the moon while the hands suggested the movement of the Earth.

LEFT: In 1946, Rolex marketed the 'First Datejust'. It showed hours, minutes and seconds but also gave the date. The design was sturdy, emphasizing an air of reliability and accuracy.

LEFT: Ten years after the original Eterna watch made its epic journey with Thor Heyerdahl, the company decided to introduce an anniversary version, called of course the Kontiki after the name of the expedition.

RIGHT: In 2010 the Kontiki collection of watches by Eterna, are still part of their line and not so different from the original.

1940s – A Slow Time

But output in the 1940s was small at every level of the watch industry, and unsettled post-war conditions ensured that emphasis remained on practical timepieces. In 1945, Rolex produced the first wristwatch with a date function, naming it the 'Oyster Perpetual Datejust'. Incidentally, the word 'perpetual' used on these historic watches refers to the automatic winding by rotor and not to a perpetual calendar, and it was Rolex that improved the rotor mechanism introduced by Breguet. Panerai worked on the 'Mare Nostrum' chronograph for sportsmen, while Eterna looked for ways to improve waterproof watches. Their efforts were given extra impetus when Thor Heyerdahl sailed his balsawood raft, the Kon-Tiki, across the oceans in the late 1940s.

LEFT: The Norwegian Thor Heyerdahl (1914-2002) set out to prove that the ocean trip from Peru to Polynesia was possible in a balsa raft. His daring expedition inspired watchmakers to create timepieces that could serve such an arduous journey.

WATCHES

Omega

The Co-Axial escapement, introduced in 2007, has given Omega a top place in the ranks of innovators. Based on George Daniel's invention the Co-Axial involves, among other changes, a decrease in movement frequency caused by decoupling the drive impulses from the balance. Omega intends to fit Co-Axial in all their watches. Now, over 150 years since its humble founding, this luxury brand is a household name. Opened in La Choux-de-Fonds in 1848 by Louis Brandt, the company relocated to Gurzelen in 1882 and has been there ever since. Paul-Emile Brandt, a part inheritor of the firm, took over in 1903. World War I and the 1930s Depression affected the company badly. It had a revival in the 1960s when an Omega watch went to the moon and President of the United States of America, John F Kennedy, also wore an Omega. But the counterfeit market affected sales and, after various financial difficulties, the company joined Swatch in 1998.

ABOVE: In the 18th century, Abraham-Louis Breguet contrived to make a repeating watch in a fine, slim form. He eliminated the bell with a rod that gonged. Omega used the model for a repeater in 1892. They have produced variations on these movements ever since, such as this version.

Omega

ABOVE: Watchmakers were keen on sport, and the needs that sportsmen required of their timepieces inspired interesting designs. Aviation attracted many watchmakers, and this 1909 ballooning event in Zurich found sponsors in Omega.

ABOVE: Omega recognized the changing needs of their women customers, many of whom appreciated the movements and preferred the appearance of a sports watch to a jewel watch. This is the Omega 'Ladymatic'.

ABOVE: Louis Brandt opened Omega in 1848, and chose the Greek letter as a company name and as its logo. He felt it symbolic of a belief in invention, and beautiful design. These are qualities that continue to motivate Omega, helping it to overcome difficulties and introduce interesting innovations.

117

WATCHES

In the late 1930s, a Swiss watchmaker, Louis Cottier invented a 'world time' watch. This had a system of superimposed discs that simultaneously gave local time in different cities. In the years following this advance, Cottier reworked his invention for Patek Philippe, and the craftsmanship was so refined Cottier made the smallest watch in the world to feature such a complication.

The jewelers included in watchmaking teams began to concentrate on the lug of the wristwatch. The lugs are the rings holding the watch to the strap. Gruen created fancy, flexible lugs to sell to car drivers, while on another of their designs, the lug was carried in a line around the case then angled to open for the strap. These watches were curved to sit easily anywhere on the wrist. Bulova's 'Drivers' Lug Tank' watch showed a smooth unbroken line from the case to the lug. Leather straps were used on these models and all the watches carried an extra, small dial for timing seconds.

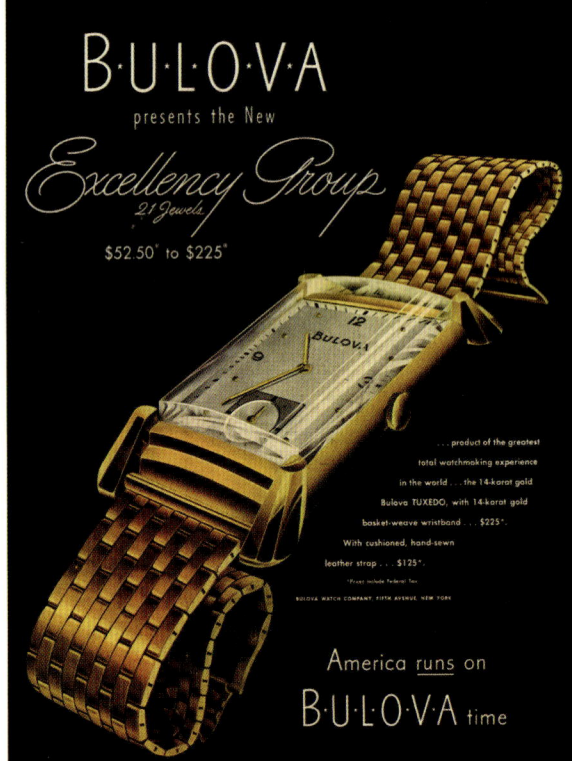

RIGHT: It was an era when watches were gifts given at special occasions and intended to last a lifetime. This Bulova watch has 21 jewels and the advertisement is promoting the sleek design of its Excellency range, with claims that America runs on Bulova time.

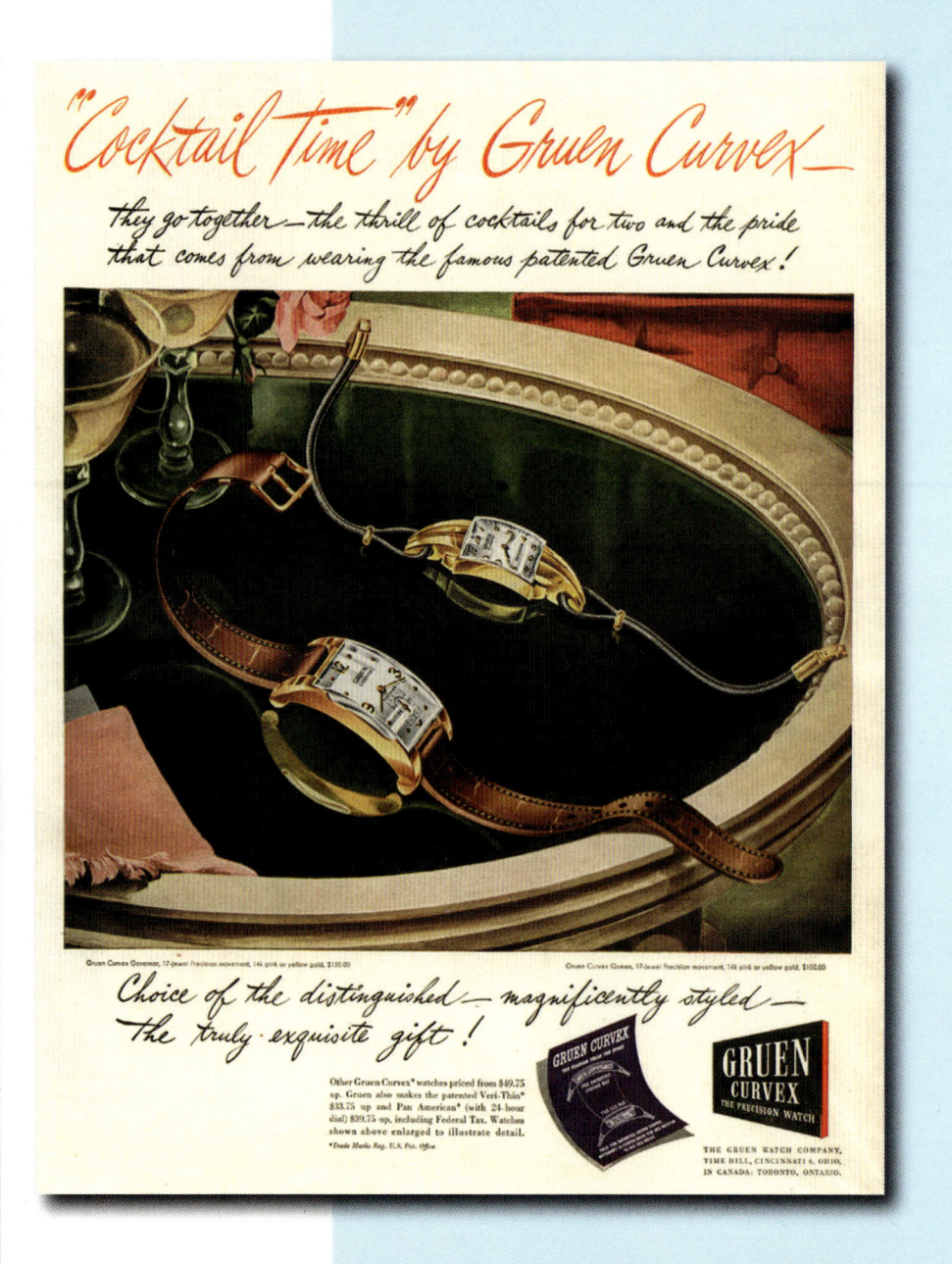

1940s – A Slow Time

LEFT: Gruen watches for men and women relied on a modern, curved design, and the lugs on the woman's watch are extended and decorative. Both models were intended to bring an elegant, sophisticated note to the cocktail hour.

LEFT: The Longines Caliber 30CH is regarded as having one of the finest wristwatch chronograph movements. The silver-gray dial and crisp black printing give the timepiece a chic value despite the relatively large size of its 38mm diameter.

Swiss watches used friction-free jewels in the construction of their watches, and specifications described how many jewels were included in the works. Some used diamonds, some rubies, and yet others were of synthetic origin. Obviously, this affected the price and people learnt to appreciate that the type of jewel, and the number included reflected the value of the watch. And, of course, a high number indicated the wearer's status. As the next decade approached, Switzerland was poised to dominate the watchmaking industry.

RIGHT: The complex and beautifully arranged movements of the Caliber 30CH explain why true aficionados prefer the mechanical watch over any other. The craftsmanship and intelligence of the workings intrigue the eye and the mind.

119

WATCHES

1950s
Moving Forward

In 1953, a prestigious commission for a woman's watch was granted to Jaeger-LeCoultre. They were asked to create a watch for Queen Elizabeth II of England, to wear during her coronation in Westminster Abbey, London. The watchmaker devised a tiny watch with the world's smallest mechanical movement, and set it in a bracelet of two linked rows of diamonds. The whole made an exquisite piece of jewelry and, of course, the Queen's choice helped revive the market for beautiful, elegant women's watches.

LEFT: Jaeger-LeCoultre could not have hoped for a grander exposure than the coronation of Elizabeth II in 1953. It was a day of tradition and splendor. The watch they made for the monarch was unobtrusive but this did not detract from the status it brought the watchmaker.

WATCHES

RIGHT: Limited editions were made of the Jaeger-LeCoultre watch worn by the Queen at her coronation ceremony. Her Majesty was obliged to wear state jewelry and a crown, so the dainty Jaeger-LeCoultre timepiece complemented but did not detract from the splendor of the precious gems adorning her that day.

1950s – Moving Forward

During this decade, the world learnt to love Swiss watches. Roskopf were exporting 28 million watches every year, while the nation's other watchmakers led the market in quality and luxury watches. The inexpensive Roskopf watches, that used a pin-pallet instead of jewels, were popular while Jaeger-LeCoultre created the 'Futurematic', a watch that withstood violent sporting activity, extremes of temperature, and lost only 30 seconds a week. It was also distinguished by its winding mechanism. This was not the usual button on the side of the watch, but a cunning little sliding mechanism placed on the back.

Above: The 'Futurematic' was developed by Jaeger-LeCoultre in 1952. It is a 17-jeweled watch with a lever escapement and had an oscillating winding weight that was an advance on John Harwood's automatic winding watch of 1929.

WATCHES

Vacheron Constantin were rightly proud of their thin women's watch, and in 1954, renowned actress Zsa Zsa Gabor chose a Vacheron Constantin timepiece as a special gift for actor Marlon Brando to commemorate the release of 'On the Waterfront', for which Brando won an Oscar. Its case back was engraved 'To Marlon Love Zsa Zsa June 24, 1954.' The timepiece sold at The Important Collectors' Wristwatches, Pocket Watches & Clocks auction held by Antiquorum in New York for six times its estimated value. The 18K yellow gold wristwatch went for a final price of US$18,000 to an unknown buyer.

RIGHT: American actors Marlon Brando and Eva Marie Saint, embrace in a still from director Elia Kazan's film, 'On The Waterfront' (1954).

1950s – Moving Forward

RIGHT: Held in high regard by watch collectors and enthusiasts alike, Vacheron Constantin's strengths lie in its superlative technical mastery of highly complicated movement manufacturing, its award-winning aesthetic sensibility, and its extremely high level of finishing. Featured here is the Vacheron Constantin timepiece that renowned actress Zsa Zsa Gabor chose as a special gift for actor Marlon Brando, to commemorate the release of the 1954 film "On the Waterfront", for which Brando won an Oscar.

ABOVE: As can be seen, its case back was specially engraved "To Marlon Love Zsa Zsa June 24, 1954".

WATCHES

Montblanc

This company had established a strong reputation as the makers of writing tools before it started manufacturing watches in 1990. The first range was brought out in 1997 and customers looked for design elements that resembled those of Montblanc pens. The company had absorbed a small watchmaker Minerva, and one of the first watches from Montblanc, the 'Villeret 1885' paid homage to the Minerva artisans and designers, and the date in the name refers to the year Minerva was established. In 2008 Montblanc produced two excellent chronographs. They are automatic and manual, having numerous complications including measurements of three time zones. In the 'Caliber MB 16.30' has parts of the dial and upper plate removed to show the movements. Montblanc makes its watches and is a luxury brand, designed for men and women. Its success in the market has surprised some by its speed. It is part of the Richemont group.

LEFT: Wilhelm Dziambor one of the founders of Montblanc, a company initially famous for fine pens, but when it turned to watch making produced equally excellent timepieces.

RIGHT: Claus Johannes Voss, partner in the Montblanc business, helped establish standards of excellence and fine craftsmanship.

Montblanc

Above: Montblanc maintains a team of artisans who manufacture its watches working from this historic building in Le Locle, Switzerland.

Above: This is one of the great watches to come from the relatively new Montblanc watch company. The 'Rieussec Chronograph' has rotating scaled discs instead of hands functioning as thirty-minute and sixty-second counters. The range has been produced as limited editions in both hand-wound and automatic models.

WATCHES

But Omega too were advertised a very thin watch by photographing it sideways, thus admitting that its daintiness, not its timekeeping quality, was the most distinguishing feature. Despite the publicity given to the Queen's bracelet watch, this was an era when celebrities did not have high consumer appeal so advertisements showed beautiful young women in evening gowns displaying cleverly designed Reverso watches. Some turned to show a 'daywear' dial with an 'evening occasion' design on the reverse. And the fashion for watches that didn't look like watches was revived among high society women who, harking back to grand old days, decided it was impolite to be seen checking the time.

The Mikuna bangle of multicolored, densely packed rhinestones had a spring opener that opened the intricate web of stones to reveal a watch dial. Others hid the watch under a lid of gold and pearls that swiveled to reveal the dial, while the Russians made amber bracelets in which the central amber was hinged to lift and show the watch beneath. Cartier, Piaget, Chopard, Vacheron Constantin, and other fine jeweler-watchmakers offered straps of woven gold or platinum chains, with the dial patterned to blend, or they set precious gems set round the face of the watch.

RIGHT: Competition among post-war manufacturers was fierce. Omega designed this 'Constellation de Luxe' a dignified masculine watch with complications and claimed it was 'the finest watch that man can make.'

1950s – Moving Forward

Right: So-called 'cocktail watches' were popular. Often, the designs were small and feminine and relied on curved, decorative lugs such as those on this watch produced by an unknown maker.

WATCHES

The factory manufacturers came up with fun designs for the popular market, and Ingersoll designed dials illustrated with cowboy images, football teams, and in 1952, launched its 'Dan Dare' model. The watch had this cartoon hero painted on the face. After the war, the company opened a factory in South Wales from where they delivered millions of watches. The Russian state-owned company, Sekonda, also achieved a high production rate.

These factory-made watches were accurate and hardy, but the public trusted quality Swiss watchmakers, and their timepieces continued to be regarded as 'special' gifts, tokens of love, respect, or awards of distinction. Few children wore wristwatches, and few women wore precious bejewelled watches, but a reputable Swiss watch, nicely made and well designed, would be accepted with joy and due appreciation.

RIGHT: Watches were perceived as special presents because they were expensive purchases and intended to last many years. For this reason, Hamilton marketed their products as tokens of love.

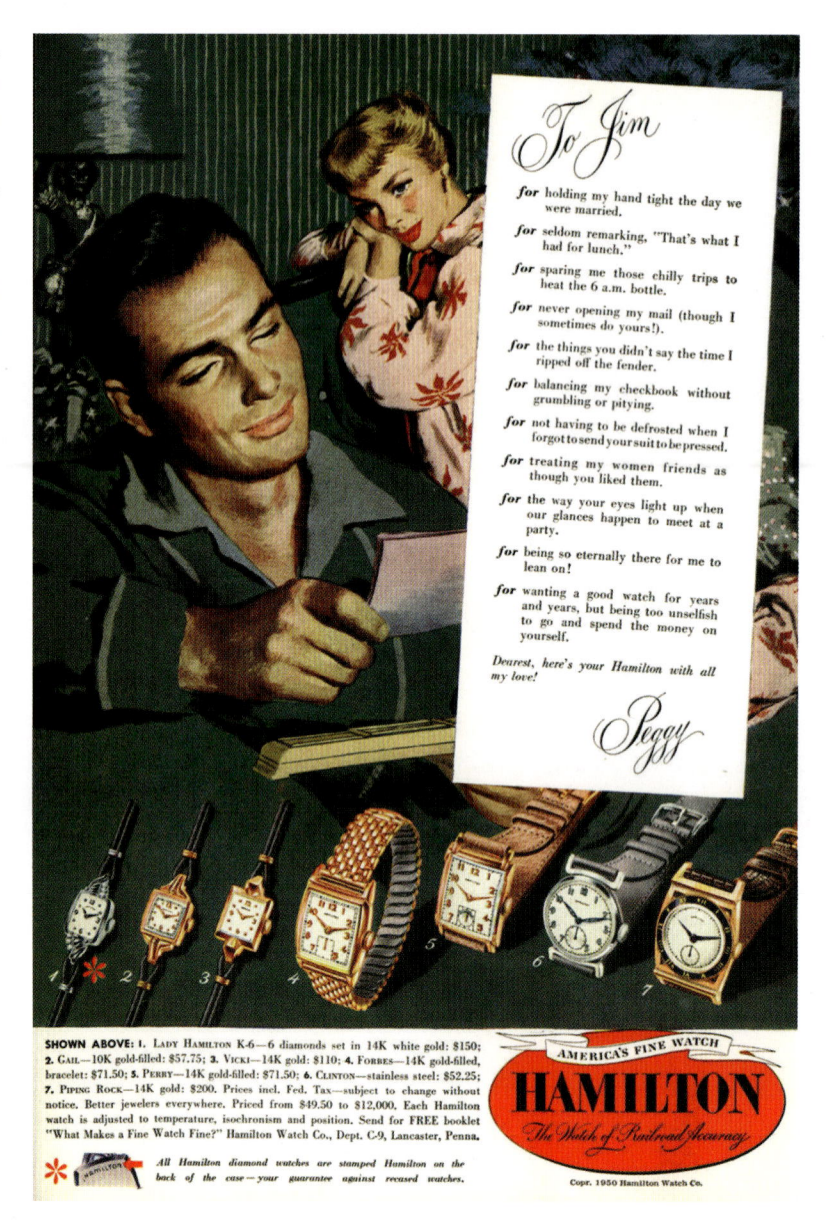

1950s – Moving Forward

Left: Despite the growth of excellent American and Japanese companies, Swiss watches continued to command respect. Longines maintained dignity in design, and its 'Flagship' watch of 1957 showed a minimalist appearance of a modernity that appealed to fashionable customers.

Right: In the 1950s, Rolex were making timepieces that were to cement its position as one of the best known names in the world of watches. This fine example is the 'Day-Date' of 1956. It shows hours, minutes, sweep seconds, day and date. The glass is sapphire crystal with a magnifying lens over the date. It has a Breguet balance spring and 31 jewels.

131

WATCHES

The regard given to Swiss watches was emphasised by the grand people who bought them to confirm their own status. American president, Lyndon B Johnson, was an avid admirer of Rolex watches and was known to give important colleagues a Rolex to show his appreciation for their work; the cowboy film star, Gene Autry, was proud of his Patek watch that had his name engraved on the strap, and the Bey of Tunis swanked about with his Rolex 'Oyster'.

LEFT: Lyndon Johnson gifted precious watches to his colleagues. Often, he chose Rolex but he gave his friend Senator Smathers a gold Patek Philippe. On the dial was engraved, "Do unto others as you would have them do unto you."

1950s – Moving Forward

LEFT: The fabulous customized wristwatch made in 1948 for the 'yodeling cowboy' Gene Autry. It is a Patek Philippe 18 carat gold chronograph with moon phases, and it sold for $254,000 at a New York auction in the summer of 2010.

WATCHES

Van Cleef & Arpels

1896 saw the marriage of Estelle Arpels and Alfred Van Cleef. Alfred and his brother-in-law Charles founded Van Cleef & Arpels in 1906. This same year they moved into the prestigious Parisian boutique at 22 Place Vendôme.

Julien Arpels joined the company in 1908 and Louis entered the family business in 1913. The design collaboration between René Sim Lacaze and Renée Puissant, daughter of Alfred Van Cleef and Estelle Arpels commenced in 1926, thus starting two highly creative decades for Van Cleef & Arpels.

In 1939 Claude Arpels crossed the Atlantic and opened the Van Cleef & Arpels boutique in Rockefeller Centre in New York – one of the first European luxury firms to make this move. Soon afterwards it relocated to its definitive address at 774 Fifth Avenue.

'Cadenas' a gold chain with a padlock in which a watch was hidden, was much admired in 1936. The 1940s saw the introduction of the 'Snowflake' collection, which made its debut alongside the Cristaux de Neige clip in 1948. Julia Roberts recently wore a 'Snowflake' bracelet at the Oscars.

One of the latest pieces, the 'Pont des Amoureux' has modified mechanics to work not only the time but to move the golden figures of two lovers across the dial. Enameling is used to create a Parisian scene behind them.

Van Cleef & Arpels retail through selected outlets; its client list includes Queen Elizabeth II, Madonna, and Sheryl Crow. The family was part of the company until 1999 when it was incorporated into the Richemont group.

LEFT: In 1906, the company conducted their jewelry and watch business from this building in Paris, but by 1909 branches were opened in Nice, Monte Carlo, and other wealthy, fashionable holiday resorts.

ABOVE: Who could guess that this lovely brooch, fashioned from exquisite gems, is also a watch? The central core of rubies can be lifted to reveal the timepiece. Van Cleef and Arpels created this piece in 1941 and it is a fine demonstration of their skills as jewelers and watchmakers.

Van Cleef & Arpels

RIGHT: This company is constantly seeking interesting ways of combining jewelry with watch making. It helped revive enameling, a skill that had been neglected for fifty years, and making use of this craft, a new range 'Poetic Complications' was conceived. One of the most intriguing models is the 'Pont des Amoureux'.

LEFT: Estelle Arpels and Alfred Van Cleef pose for the camera on their wedding day in 1896.

135

WATCHES

The great Swiss watchmakers continued to refine the purpose and practicality of their watches. In 1953 Rolex launched their Turn-O-Graph, classed as an adventure watch. The following year They made the first completely waterproof wristwatch, the 'Oyster Perpetual Submariner', which was followed the next year by the 'GMT Master', a wristwatch that displayed two time zones at once – all Pan Am pilots were issued with this timepiece. The Cuban guerrilla fighter, Che Guevara, favored the 'GMT Master'. No doubt its complications proved useful as he sneaked through different time zones in the jungles of South America. 1954 also saw TAG Heuer introduce their 'Ring Master' stopwatch, which had interchangeable rings of scale for timing various sports.

BELOW LEFT: The Rolex 'Explorer' was a self-winding, waterproof with a 25-jewel chronometer movement, and in the 1950s the watch was used by the Royal Society of London on scientific explorations. The advertisement uses the imagery of a majestic, strange landscape to emphasize the notion of an advanced, new timepiece.

BELOW: Another timepiece from Rolex was the 1953 Turn-O-Graph 'Adventure' watch. It was stainless steel, with 31 jewels and showed hours, minutes, sweep seconds, and date.

136

1950s – Moving Forward

LEFT: The timing of sports events, and the courage of athletes have always been elements attractive to watchmakers. TAG Heuer gave the sports world the 'Ring Master', a pocket watch that did not measure time in a conventional manner, but was able to measure the timing of athletic events. It was a very superior stopwatch allowing more than one reading at a time.

ABOVE: The 'Speedmaster' produced in 1957 was the first in a range that Omega has maintained and developed over the years. It has subsidiary dials for chronograph, seconds, and date, and a screw-in crown and buttons.

WATCHES

Rolex again proved a favorite among watch wearers. One of the two men who first conquered Mount Everest, Tenzing Norgay, wore a Rolex 'Oyster' when he climbed this mountain with Edmund Hillary in 1953, although Hillary is reputed to have worn a Smiths 'Deluxe'. Despite this, Rolex designed 'Explorer' and 'Explorer II' for high altitudes.

LEFT: Mount Everest, the Himalayan Mountains that defeated many climbers was conquered by two men in 1953. Edmund Hilary, a New Zealander and his Sherpa fellow climber, Tenzig Norgay were feted across the world. The English newspaper 'The Times' devoted a color magazine to the adventure. Rolex were pleased to announce that Norgay wore a Rolex 'Oyster'.

RIGHT: Edmund Hilary wore a Rolex Oyster Perpetual during his expedition of the Antarctic 1955. But to celebrate the 20th anniversary of his ascent of Everest, he bought a Rolex Explorer like the one shown here and recently, his watch was valued at £12,000.

138

1950s – Moving Forward

The Swiss were proud of their skill and craftsmanship in making reliable, accurate mechanical watches but others were looking for ways to improve the costs and mechanics of watchmaking. In 1953, the British Horological Institute invited a well-known French watchmaker, Fred Lip, to give a lecture on his new electronic wristwatch. He wore such a watch to impress his large audience but, despite the excitement his innovation caused, he found difficulties in putting the watch into production.

Another French firm, ATO, came forward in 1956 with the same innovation but, again, it was not in production. After working in great secrecy, the American group, the Hamilton Watch Company, announced they had solved all manufacturing problems and on February 3 1957, they showed and marketed their electric wristwatch. To emphasise the grand launch, the watches were sold in gold cases.

Hamilton — the world's first electric watch!

It's no secret that electricity is the best way to run a wrist watch. Greater accuracy. Fewer parts. Less care. But it was real news early this year when Hamilton was *first* to produce the electric watch. Your Hamilton jeweler will tell you more about this, the biggest watch news in 477 years. *(Left to right)* Spectra, $150; Ventura I, $200; Van Horn, $175. Hamilton Watch Company, Lancaster, Pennsylvania.
Patents pending

HAMILTON
the watch fine jewelers recommend more often than any other

LEFT: The Hamilton Watch Company was the first to find a way of fitting batteries into an electric watch. This advertisement with its 'space age' swirls proclaims the company's modernity and inventiveness.

WATCHES

Enameling

For centuries, enameled faces and cases decorated watches. This ornamental look became unfashionable in the 20th century, but there has been a revival in the 21st century.

Enameling embraces many skills. An artist may paint a picture or use the grisaille technique, painting Limoges white over a dark background, thus creating gradations of color. Cloisonné entails shaping gold filaments to 'draw' the image, then painting enamel into each shape. In champleve the surface is engraved. The enamel is poured in and the depth of the etching mark makes the enamel translucent or opaque. Whatever method, the effect is one of brilliantly colored design.

Teams of artisans used to be involved. Some hand-ground the enamel to powder then mixed it with oil or water. Others prepared the watch face surface. An etcher would be employed; someone else beat and shaped filaments. Nowadays one craftsman may do all preparation and artwork.

Above: This charming and very valuable 'toy' is a little enameled violin that opens to reveal a watch. The enamel work gives it a rich, glittering color and the cloisonné method allows for a detailed patterning of the surface.

Left: Enameled eggs were made famous by the 19th century Russian jewelers, Faberge and this one is an homage to the old and revered firm, made by the watchmakers, Ulysse Nardin. The cloisonné technique has been used. The French term means 'to partition'.

Enameling

ABOVE: Enamel is a colorless, soft glass of silica, red lead, and soda. Elements such as copper and iron are added to bring color. Here is a step in the cloisonné technique. The enamel is being applied with a quill into a shape formed by a lead outline. When the entire design is filled with enamel, the piece is baked to harden the glass.

ABOVE: This is the work of a highly trained and skilled enamellist, and it has been attributed to a 17th century French artist, Robert Vauquer. He has painted his scenes with enamel. The case is decorated with classical scenes and floral patterns, and is quite beautiful. It belongs to the Patek Philippe Museum in Geneva. The watch was made by David Champion of Paris.

141

WATCHES

The electric watch replaced the mainspring barrel with a power cell. A very fine wire was attached to the balance wheel. This wire conducted an electromagnetic impulse, closing a minuscule switch and moving the balance that drove the hands. Watchmakers in Switzerland, France and Germany were quick to follow Hamilton, and adapted the electric mechanism.

There was another change in the craft of watchmaking, but it happened slowly and, at the time, was not widely regretted. Since the 17th century, enameling had been part of the beauty of watches and clocks. Early cases for pocket watches were decorated with landscapes, portraits, and floral studies. The dials of wristwatches, especially those for women, carried enameling. During the 1930s, noblemen asked to have their coat-of-arms enameled on the caseback, and the fabulously rich Maharajah of Kapurtala had a portrait of his wife decorating a Reverso watch.

RIGHT: This Timex electric watch shows that new and synthetic fabrics had replaced faces of enamel and porcelain. This is chrome plated.

RIGHT: The back of an early Timex electric watch shows how different it is from that of a mechanical watch. A circular case holds the batteries that give electric energy to the hands. The base is stainless steel, a new product.

142

1950s – Moving Forward

LEFT: The intricate and the tiny scale of the engineering required in making a mechanical watch demands close attention. The artisan has a choice of oils, each of a different viscosity; he needs to understand which oil suits what part as he constructs the movements.

143

WATCHES

Enameling is a complicated art, embracing a variety of disciplines, such as cloisonné, plique-a-jour, champlevé and grisaille. All these skills are time consuming and labor intensive, and were valued for the highly decorative note they brought to a functional timepiece. But the post-war world of the 1950s preferred a modernist style of simplicity and minimalism and, besides, materials had changed.

In the 1920s, porcelain faces were replaced with metal and now, in the 1950s, plastic and other synthetic fabrics were preferred. Patek produced an enamel dial in this decade but generally this kind of decoration simply fell out of favor. The craftsmen, those who ground the enamel, and others who prepared the surface for the artists, the artists themselves, were no longer part of the traditional watchmaking team, and after 400 years, the craft was all but lost. Craftsmen were reduced to repairing historic enamel work.

RIGHT: In 1630, an artisan Jean Toutin found a way of painting enamel without having to pour it into the metal chambers forming the image. This allowed painters a tremendous freedom – their brush strokes were no longer inhibited by gold metal outlines. Here the artist shows off his talent with a landscape and a portrait.

ABOVE: The Hoaud family of Geneva soon established themselves as leaders in the technique of painting with enamel and the Bayer Museum in Zurich has some fine examples. The new technique attracted many artists, and this pendant watch was perhaps commissioned as a present for a new mother; it doesn't have the characteristics usual to images of the Virgin Mary but cherishes the image of mother and child.

1950s – Moving Forward

This did not mean that all decoration was lost in the world of watches, but precious stones and metals were favored because these could be arranged in a sleek, contemporary style. Women's watches best showed these advantages. Straps were constructed from interesting links of gold; the cases were curved, and ornament was discreet. LeCoultre designed a black face and gold body with a strap that repeated this color combination, while Longines set a white gold watch in a leather strap that was cut and slashed to form an interesting pattern.

There was one aspect of watch wearing that had not changed: men continued to look for a watch that appeared as a functional, but complicated statement while women preferred a timepiece that was a thing of beauty and elegance.

LEFT: In 1953, Tissot presented its world timepiece, the 'Navigator'. A clever design shows city names set in a circle of numerals for 24-hour time then, on the bevel, are numerals for local time in the usual 12-hour cycle. In one movement, the hands point to a city, and the 24-hour time relevant to that city, and also local time. In one glance, the wearer can establish a distant foreign time zone and the local time.

145

WATCHES

RIGHT: Rock and roll singer and actor Elvis Presley, looking very pensive, on the set of *Blue Hawaii* at Paramount Pictures in Los Angeles, California in April 1961. The watch he used while on the set of this film was a Hamilton Ventura.

1960s
In Sea and Space

A marketing element crept into the world of watches when sales departments realized that famous people helped boost sales. Audiences noticed Elvis Presley wore a Hamilton 'Ventura' when he starred in the movie *Blue Hawaii* in 1961.

WATCHES

When Sean Connery played James Bond sporting a Rolex 'Submariner' in 'Goldfinger', everyone longed to own the watch. And then, in 1964, the Bond movie heroine, Pussy Galore played by Honor Blackman, wore a Rolex 'GMT Master', and salesmen's suspicions were confirmed because the watch earned universal recognition after movie audiences nicknamed her watch 'Pussy Galore'. Advertisers began to think about the value of twinning fame with a product.

BELOW: In 1957, Hamilton introduced the world's first electric watch, the Hamilton Electric 500. It was available in a variety of non-traditional asymmetrical case styles including the Ventura. The Ventura was reissued recently and was prominently featured in the *'Men in Black'* movies.

1960s – In Sea and Space

LEFT: A scene from the third film in the James Bond franchise, '*Goldfinger*'. Pictured are James Bond, played by British actor Sean Connery, and Pussy Galore played by Honor Blackman, in a passionate embrace. Although you can't see Bond's watch, the Rolex being worn by Pussy Galore is quite visible.

WATCHES

Publicity shots of movie actors and pop stars began to include the subject's wristwatch as an acceptable fashion accessory. In contemporary photos, Ringo Starr of the Beatles has his sleeve pulled back to reveal his 'accessory', and the British singer, Lulu, showed her girlish cheek by choosing a Mickey Mouse watch. Even Vogue magazine permitted rare glimpses of models wearing a delicate wristwatch.

RIGHT: Ringo Starr, drummer for the 1960s pop group The Beatles, poses during the filming of '*A Hard Day's Night*'. Ringo was well known for wearing rings, bracelets and watches, as can be seen in this photo.

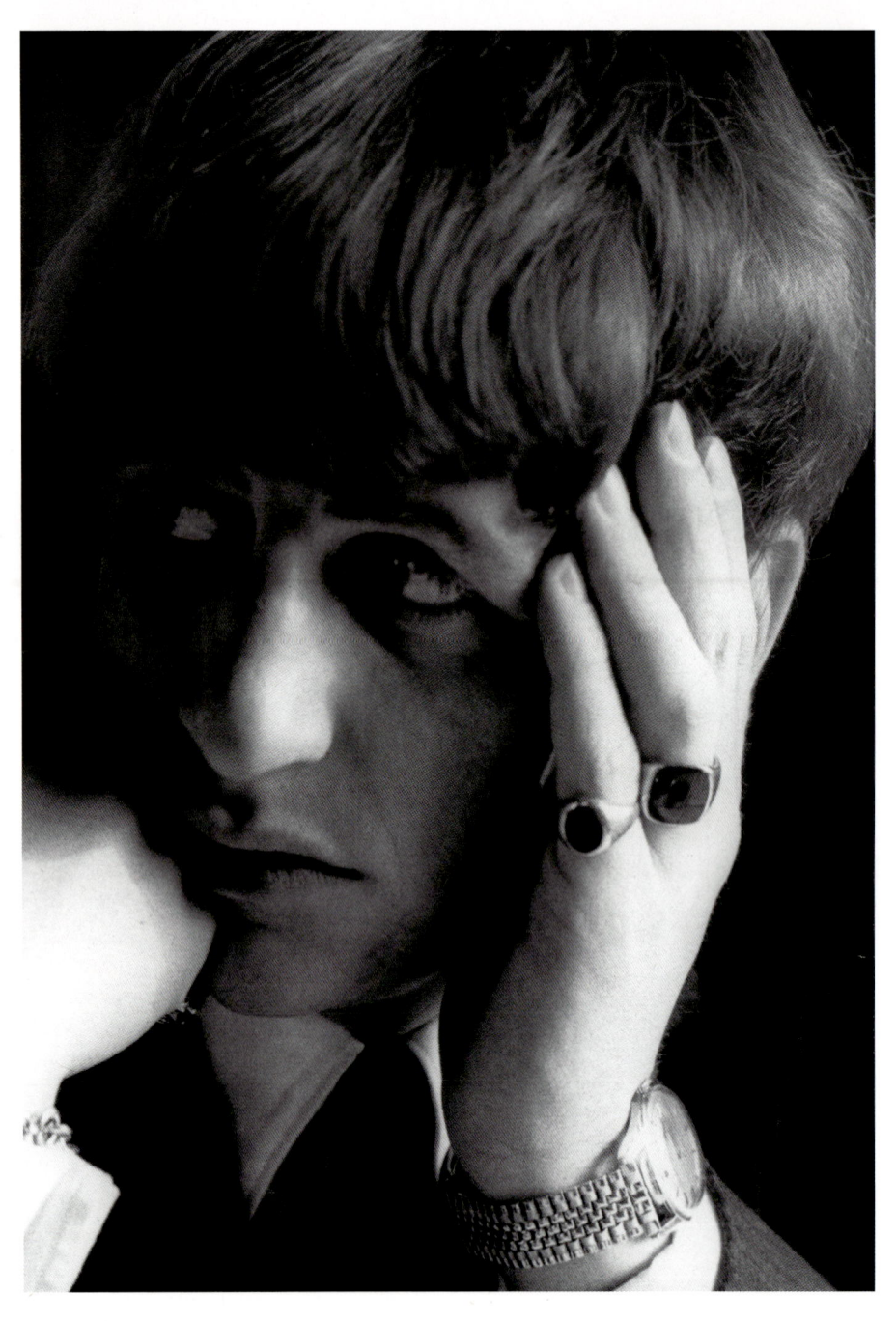

LEFT: This is the iconic Rolex GMT Master, which was originally developed in 1954 at the request of Pan Am Airways, to assist its pilots with the problem of crossing multiple time zones when on transcontinental flights (GMT stands for Greenwich Mean Time).

1960s – In Sea and Space

LEFT: A Mickey Mouse watch goes under the hammer at the Antique and Modern Watch Jewelry Show at a hotel in Hong Kong. These watches now sell for large sums of money and the originals are a real collector's delight.

151

WATCHES

Seiko

Kintaro Hattori opened his jewelry and watch shop in Tokyo, 1881 and the company has always been dedicated to research, setting a base of five functions for its watches: they must be shock resistant, water resistant, give time, day and date, and be automatic. In 1969, the company was the first to market the quartz watch. Production is in-house – even oils are mixed by employees. The 'Ananta' is made of katana metals used in traditional Japanese hand-forged swords. 'Spring Drive' uses Seiko's Tri-Synchro Regulator to energize the spring that turns the trains and a generator, while the 'Kinetic' derives energy from the wearer's movements. Some ranges are available only in Asia but most are marketed across the world. The brand caters for both the luxury and popular markets but won a glamorous reputation when Matt Damon wore a Seiko in *The Bourne Identity*. In 2007, it became Seiko Holdings Corporation. In 2010 the CEO is Shinji Hattori.

RIGHT: The Seiko Spring Drive Spacewalk is designed and built, as the name suggests, for space. It is the first watch ever designed specifically for use in outer space and in 2010 a commemorative edition became available through selected Seiko retail outlets across the world.

Seiko

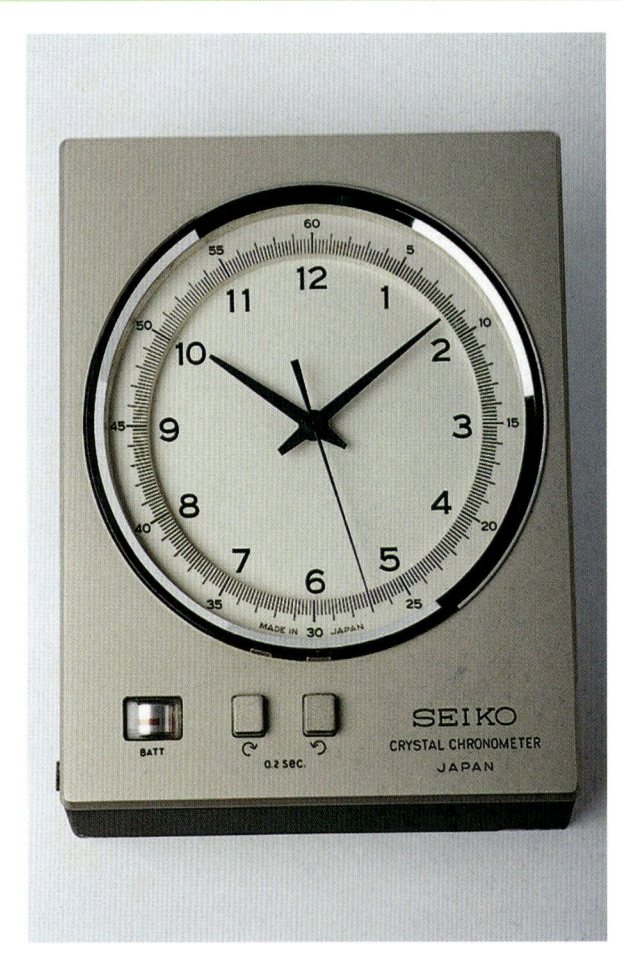

ABOVE: Seiko first served as the official time keeper at the Tokyo Olympics in 1964. They built no less than 1,278 timing and scoring devices from scratch; this is the world's first portable chronograph.

LEFT: 1990 saw Seiko come up with another world first, this is the world's first computerized diver's watch 'Scubamaster'.

WATCHES

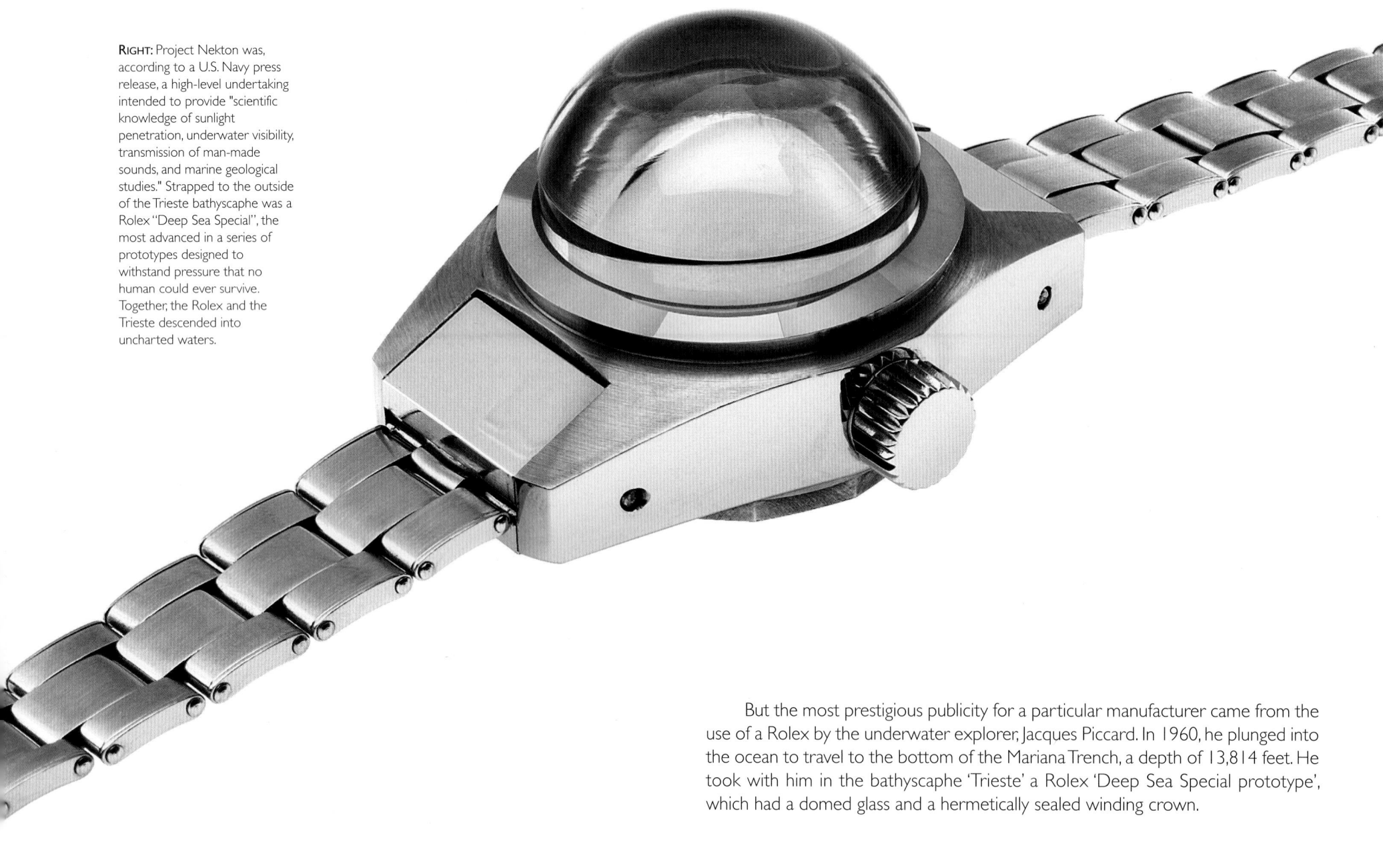

RIGHT: Project Nekton was, according to a U.S. Navy press release, a high-level undertaking intended to provide "scientific knowledge of sunlight penetration, underwater visibility, transmission of man-made sounds, and marine geological studies." Strapped to the outside of the Trieste bathyscaphe was a Rolex "Deep Sea Special", the most advanced in a series of prototypes designed to withstand pressure that no human could ever survive. Together, the Rolex and the Trieste descended into uncharted waters.

But the most prestigious publicity for a particular manufacturer came from the use of a Rolex by the underwater explorer, Jacques Piccard. In 1960, he plunged into the ocean to travel to the bottom of the Mariana Trench, a depth of 13,814 feet. He took with him in the bathyscaphe 'Trieste' a Rolex 'Deep Sea Special prototype', which had a domed glass and a hermetically sealed winding crown.

1960s – In Sea and Space

Piccard's watch was taken to the greatest known depth on Earth and worked perfectly, withstanding pressures of seven tons per square inch. Piccard's remarkable feat brought not only public admiration for him but also for the watchmaker, cemented when Piccard sent a telegram of congratulations, thanking Rolex for the precision of its timepiece.

LEFT: On the evening of January 23, 1960 as the setting sun turned the surface of the Pacific Ocean deep orange, Swiss oceanographer and engineer Jacques Piccard and United States Navy Lieutenant Don Walsh packed up chocolate, nuts and their courage before lowering themselves through the narrow tube and into the cabin of the bathyscaphe, Trieste.

WATCHES

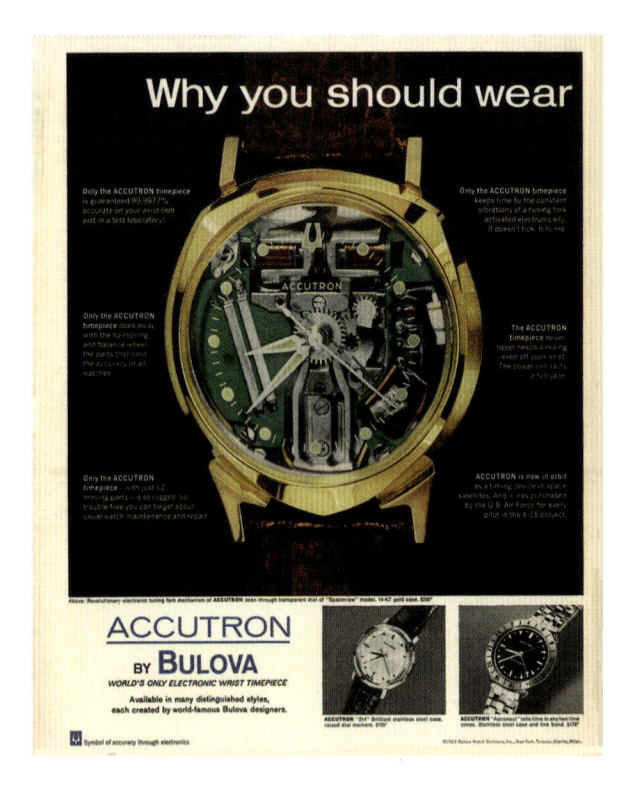

LEFT: On October 10th 1960, the new president of the Bulova Watch Co., Omar N. Bradley, known for his participation in the Normandy Offensive in World War II, announced the Bulova Accutron caliber 214, the first electronic watch in the world.

RIGHT: The Rolex Oyster Perpetual Sea-Dweller Submariner 2000 (it was capable of diving to 2000 ft/610 m) that became available in 1967 was developed from the Submariner, for the Comex S.A. industrial deep-sea diving company. It had increasing crystal thickness and was produced in several variations.

Sales techniques were changing but also, the decade opened to a major development in timekeeping, one that was to shake the complacency of Swiss watchmakers. The change started slowly with the ideas of a Swiss, Max Hetzel, who devised a tuning fork as an oscillator, powered by an oscillating electronic circuit. His native land showed little interest in his innovation, so he turned to the USA. His timing was good; the Americans were working on their space program, and astronauts needed timepieces that functioned accurately under unusual conditions. Bulova saw the potential of Hetzel's invention and improved his basic idea, adapting it for use in a wristwatch. They made the 'Accutron', an electronic watch that guaranteed timekeeping reliable to a minute a month during the life of the watch.

American and Japanese manufacturers were quick to exploit this innovation and they began to dominate the market. The Hamilton Watch Company devised glamorous advertisements, claiming a gift of one of its 'electrically run' watches would 'show the magnitude of your love'. Among the images they displayed was a gold 'Ventura' modified as a woman's wristwatch. Bulova tried to wean men from the macho complications watch by marketing their male products as 'lean, clean, uncluttered'.

1960s – In Sea and Space

ABOVE: The Bulova Accutron was designed by a Swiss engineer, Max Hetzel, and manufactured in the USA. It remained in production until 1976, by which time five million watches had been sold.

LEFT: The Accutron had a revolutionary feature; the time keeping was controlled by a tuning fork. The tuning fork vibrated 360 times per second and the vibrations were maintained at constant amplitude by means of a transistor. The number of parts in the watch had been dramatically reduced to a mere 27, of which only 12 were moving parts. By comparison, a self-winding watch at that time contained about 136 parts, 26 of them moving.

157

WATCHES

Major watchmakers were creating 'proper' watches for women, with prominent faces and leather straps. Some even carried complications, and this reflected the changing world of women. The feminist movement was gaining strength, and more and more women were running careers as well as families. They wanted watches that reflected their serious professional intent, and their determination to storm the masculine world.

ABOVE: Jaeger-LeCoultre's Memovox is one of the classic vintage men's watches. The original, aimed at the international businessman, was the first automatic wristwatch with a mechanical alarm function built in. The model was produced until the late 1960s but has recently been revived.

1960s – In Sea and Space

Left: A beautiful gold ladies Omega watch with matching gold strap and manual wind.

WATCHES

TAG Heuer

TAG Heuer is part of the LVMH group (Louis Vitton, Hennessy) having grown from a little watch business opened by Eduard Heuer in 1860 in St-Imier, Switzerland. He patented an 'oscillating pinion' – still part of mechanical watches today. Heuer specialized in chronographs, making the first dashboard chronograph in 1911, and the first chronograph watch in 1914. The company continues to be associated with motor racing and chronographs, but it is also recognized for its luxury sports watches also. Its ranges – Formula One, Aquarecor, Link, Carrera, Grand Carrera and Monaco – are much sought after, and the brand has won the International Forum Design award more than once. The company is closely associated with sport and athletes. Lewis Hamilton, F1 Grand Prix champion and Maria Sharapova, Ladies Wimbledon tennis winner, wear TAG Heuer, as does the great golfer Tiger Woods, who sports the TAG Heuer Golf Watch. In 2010 the CEO is Jean-Christophe Babin.

LEFT: In 1860, at the age of twenty, Edouard Heuer set up his watchmaking shop in St Imier in the beautiful Jura area of Switzerland.

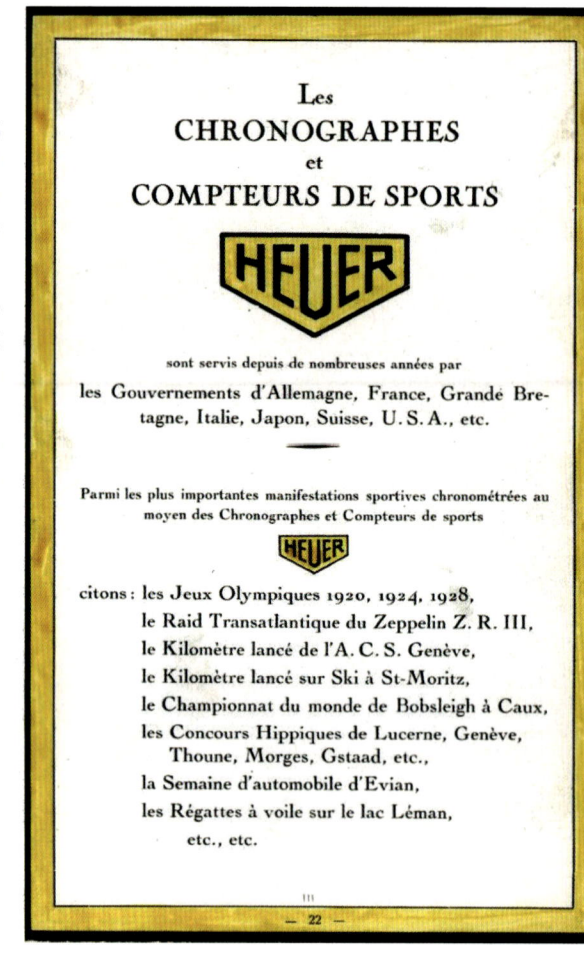

LEFT: In 1920, TAG Heuer put their stop watches to the test in the heat of the moment - their chronometers were used as timekeepers of the speed skiing at St Moritz and the world Bobsleigh championships at Caux, as well as the regattas on Lake Leman and the automobile week in Evian.

RIGHT: In 2010 TAG Heuer presented their Grand Carrera Pendulum. It uses the first-ever mechanical movement without a hairspring. With this concept the traditional hairspring is replaced by an 'invisible' or virtual spring derived from magnets. This watch is a noble addition to the Grand Carrera collection.

160

TAG Heuer

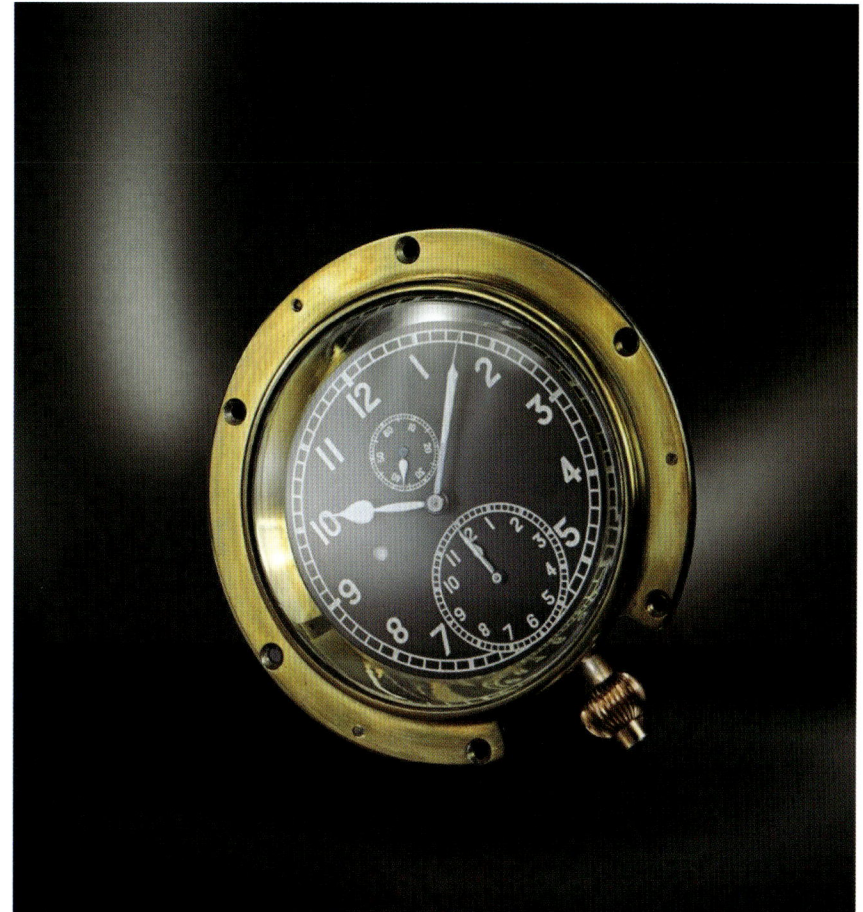

ABOVE: Time of trip – the first dashboard chronograph patented by TAG Heuer in 1911. It was designed to be placed on the dashboard of an automobile or aircraft. The Zeppelin ZR III used one of these chronographs when it flew 8,106 km (66.25 miles) over North America.

161

WATCHES

Factory manufacturers, of course, followed this trend but, even so, the majority of women continued to prefer their watches, however modern and open in appearance, to be dainty and decorative: watches as jewelry or fashionable accessories had not lost their appeal. Cartier was not worried by fads from the feminist movement. Neither were other manufacturers.

Pierre Cardin sold a neatly boxed set comprising a watch and a selection of decorative rings and straps. The fashionable woman could change the look of her watch by simply fixing it into a choice from the rings and straps. Oris were blatant in offering watches as jewelry by marketing a selection of old-time pendant watches in prettily designed cases – including a few with cases enameled in rich colors, one designed to look like a ladybird.

LEFT: Oris were never slow in coming forward when it came to satisfying the ladies and like the 1960s, this attractive Oris watch from the Miles Rectangular range comes with a Silver Quarter Arabic dial, Steel watch case and a White Leather bracelet.

1960s – In Sea and Space

Although the Swiss authorities were alarmed by the development of electronic watches, they were slow in their response and found themselves ousted as watchmakers, reduced to suppliers of parts to their American and Japanese competitors.

Late in the decade, they tried to catch-up, but they had underestimated the Japanese who were determined to develop a post-war industrial economy. For this reason, the nation was not averse to new ideas and theories that would modernize their watchmaking industry. Neither were they hindered by centuries of tradition, nor the wails of craftsmen who feared the loss of their traditional employment, problems that hindered the Swiss.

LEFT: 1960 saw the launch of a watch that would develop into a classic and which would endure for years to come. The Grand Seiko was put on the market.

WATCHES

ABOVE: John Glenn was the first American to Orbit Earth, and he wore a Tag Heuer Stop Watch which had been modified with elastic bands so that it would fit over the spacesuit. This Heuer stopwatch served as a "backup clock" for the timing instruments aboard Friendship 7 and was started manually by Glenn 20 seconds into the flight.

There were further exciting developments that involved watchmaking. The Americans and the Russians were taking the first giant steps in space exploration. Watchmakers were keen to be part of this great adventure. Indeed, Bulova had developed Hetzel's electric mechanism in the hope that they would win a contract from NASA. But it was Omega that won the commission for a watch 'Flight-Qualified by NASA for all Manned Space Missions'. Virgil Grissom wore an Omega 'Speedmaster Professional' chronograph during the space flight of Gemini 3 in 1965; Buzz Aldrin wore one when he landed on the moon in 1969. The watch was nicknamed 'Moonwalker'.

RIGHT: This is a picture of the first footprint on the Moon, which will be there for a million years. There is no wind on the moon to blow it away.

1960s – In Sea and Space

ABOVE: Overall view of astronaut John Glenn Jr., as he enters into the spacecraft Friendship 7 prior to MA-6 launch operations at Launch Complex 14, Kennedy Space Center, Florida. Astronaut Glenn is entering his spacecraft to begin the first American manned Earth orbital mission. His watch is strapped to his right arm and can be clearly seen.

165

WATCHES

Citizen

In 1918, a Japanese jeweler, Yamalki, founded the Shokasha Watch Research Institute in Tokyo, using Swiss machinery and called his range of timepieces 'Citizen'. In 1930 he re-named his company 'Citizen'. The company was the first to market liquid crystal display on quartz watches, but is known for watches made for deep sea diving and other water sports. The 1985 'Promaster Aqualand' included an integrated electronic depth gauge. Also, Citizen has been in the forefront of ecologically sound research, introducing their Citizen Eco-Drive range in 1995. These watches use photocells to transform energy that is saved by a small accumulator, and so never need change a battery. Citizen developed atomic timekeeping with a timepiece that synchronizes with atomic clocks in Japan, North America, and Europe. It tracks two time zones, always displaying 'home' time to the benefit of the watch-wearing traveler. The brand designs elegant, mechanical sports watches for the popular market. The President in 2010 is Makoto Umehara.

RIGHT: The Citizen history goes back to 1924, when their forerunner, the Shokosha Watch Research Watch Institute, produced its first pocket watch. The then Mayor of Tokyo, Mr Shimpei Goto, named the watch "CITIZEN" with the hope that the watch, a luxury item at the time, would become widely available to ordinary citizens throughout the world.

RIGHT: In 1976, Citizen released the world's first analog quartz watch using sunlight as a power source. It was named the Citizen Quartz Crystron Solar Cell watch.

Citizen

RIGHT: The Citizen Men's Red Arrows watch is based on high performance and professionalism. With radio controlled accuracy, this watch is packed with features which include atomic timekeeping, chronograph, tachymeter, alarm and backlight, world time in 43 cities and a perpetual calendar.

WATCHES

Rolex watches, too, played a role in space travel. The astronaut, Ron Evans, relied on his own Rolex 'Oyster Perpetual GMT-Master' during his Apollo 17 Mission in 1968. But the wonders of the Rolex product were truly proved when this watch was taken on the Lunar Module Challenger mission, where the Oyster was left on the moon and ran for almost 75 hours without losing time or breaking down.

These exciting historic events overshadowed some of the difficulties and changes in the watchmaking world. Ingersol had changed ownership so becoming the Timex Company; the Russian company, Sekonda, moved its operation to the United Kingdom, while the Japanese company, Seiko, continued to intensify their research and, as they hoped, they were to revolutionize the craft of watchmaking.

RIGHT: The first Speedmaster making a trip in space was back in the early 1960s, during the Mercury programme. Shown here is a speedmaster professional Mark IV of 1973, which was probably used with Apollo-Soyuz and then later on the space shuttle.

1960s – In Sea and Space

BREITLING FÜR DIE WELTLUFTFAHRT FÜR DIE WELTRAUMFAHRT BREITLING

NAVITIMER

Der berühmte Chronograph mit Navigations-Computer. 17 Rubine, drehbarer Glasring, Leuchtzifferblatt, Zählwerk bis 30 Minuten und 12 Stunden, stoßsicher 17 Rubine, robustes Gehäuse

Mod. 806 S Edelstahl DM 385.- *
Mod. 806 P Goldplaqué DM 395.- *
Mod. 806 G Gold 18 Kt. DM 798.- *

Gebrauchsanweisung auf Anforderung

SPEZIALCHRONOGRAPH FÜR FLIEGER

Der Breitling-Navitimer ist ein ganz einzigartiger Chronograph. Er allein bietet den Piloten, Funkern usw. nebst allen Annehmlichkeiten eines Armbandchronographen die vollständige Logarithmentafel eines Rechenschiebers für die Luftfahrt. Der Breitling-Navitimer hat sich als zuverlässiger Begleiter für alle Piloten erwiesen. Er gibt die genaue Zeit, zählt die Sekunden und läßt sich mit seinen beiden Drückern beliebig anhalten und wieder in Gang setzen. Die Einteilung auf dem beweglichen Glasreif steht der fixen Skala auf dem Zifferblatt gegenüber. Merkzeichen erleichtern die Umrechnung von Land- und Seemeilen in Kilometer und umgekehrt. Eine weitere Skala innerhalb der fixen gestattet das rasche Bestimmen von Stundengeschwindigkeiten oder des zurückgelegten Weges bei bekannter Geschwindigkeit und gegebener Zeit. Der Navitimer zeigt Halte- und Fehlzeiten an, erleichtert die Aufstellung von Navigationsplänen, die Bestimmung des Zeitpunktes für den nächsten Funkanruf, berechnet den Brennstoffverbrauch und dient der Standort- und Richtungsbestimmung, gibt den Zeitpunkt der Ankunft. Der Navitimer ist ein unentbehrliches Navigationsinstrument. Der Breitling-Navitimer ist einzigartig, ein treuer Begleiter für alle Piloten.

COSMONAUT-NAVITIMER

Mod. 809 Edelstahl DM 425.- *
Spezialausführung des Navitimers mit 24-Stunden-Zifferblatt

Diese Uhr hat den amerikanischen Raumflug mit Lt. Commander Scott Carpenter im Mai 1962 erfolgreich bestanden.

* Unverbindlicher Richtpreis

LEFT: In 1959 Lt. Commander Scott Carpenter was selected as one of seven astronauts for the NASA Mercury program. Carpenter was a US Navy test pilot who had flown in combat in the Korean War and who wore a Breitling Navitimer (12-hour version) during that period. After selection he contacted Breitling and suggested they make a 24-hour version of the Navitimer pilot's watch. He eventually received his own 24-hour Breitling on the 21st May, 1962 just three days before his historic flight.

169

WATCHES

ABOVE: First presented by Rolex in 1963, the Rolex Daytona watch was designed for professional race car drivers. With the use of its tachometric scale on the bezel, the Rolex Daytona allows drivers to measure lap time and calculate average speeds with great accuracy.

RIGHT: The Longines Ultra-Chron automatic high-beat-rate wristwatch, was introduced in 1967 to mark the 100-year anniversary of the company, which was founded in 1867. Longines went on to produce several variations of the Ultra-Chron, including different case shapes, between 1967 and 1975.

1960s – In Sea and Space

Despite the struggle to dominate the commercial market, Swiss watchmakers continued to produce high quality, luxury watches. Vacheron Constantin made a defiant statement for the skilled engineering wonder that is the mechanical watch. In 1969, they made a skeletonized and engraved gold wristwatch. The workings, with all the springs, wheels, and so on were displayed on the dial, and it had an engraved 17-jewel movement. It was opulent, expensive, and crafted. But the changes in the industry could not be ignored, and the next decade opened to a major upheaval.

Left: In the late 1960s, Girard-Perregaux was one of the very few manufactures to have its own internal R&D team. This research department enabled the Brand to develop several revolutionary movements. In 1966, it presented the first high frequency movement, with a 36,000 vibrations/hour balance: the Gyromatic HF.

WATCHES

RIGHT: Iconic film star of the 1960s and 1970s, Steve McQueen, fastens the buttons on his racing jacket; the TAG-Heuer logo clearly marked on his chest. On his wrist is the now legendary TAG Heuer Monaco watch that he chose specifically to wear for the film. This is a still from the movie 'Le Mans', in which McQueen portrays a racing driver during the infamous Le Mans 24 hour race in France.

1970s
Design and Opportunity

One development of the 1960s did not alter as much as grow slowly during the 1970s, and this was the advertisers' use of 'the famous' to enhance the status of particular watches. Heuer was delighted when the champion Formula One driver, Clay Regazzoni, wore their 'Montreal' chronometer and they even dedicated a watch to Jackie Ickx, Formula One and saloon car racing champion. But what pleased them even more was when the rugged, popular movie star, Steve McQueen, brandished their 'Monaco' in the film, 'Le Mans' in which he appeared as a racing driver. Consequently, these watches became household names.

WATCHES

ABOVE: In 1969, TAG Heuer broke with tradition by creating the first square-cased, water-resistant watch in the history of watchmaking. Powered by the famous Chronomatic Calibre 11, the Monaco is also the world's first automatic chronograph.

ABOVE: In 2010 the Monaco lives on. Five years after its announcement as a concept watch, the Monaco V4 – the first belt-driven watch - is being manufactured as a limited edition anniversary watch, to celebrate the 150 years of watchmaking by the TAG Heuer Company.

1970s – Design and Opportunity

And a foretaste of future developments showed in the purchase of the Gucci fashion license by the watchmaker, Steve Wunderman. A clever businessman, Wunderman sniffed a commercial link between fashion and the wristwatch as a style accessory. But the real revolution was found in the world of horology. Centuries of watchmaking tradition were overturned with the invention of the crystal quartz watch. The notion of a timepiece as an heirloom, a beautifully crafted work of engineering was abandoned – or so it seemed. The first steps toward this radical change came from the Swiss organization, Centre Electronique Horloger who announced they were working on a quartz driven watch, but admitted it was not yet fully developed. The Japanese company, Seiko, was smarter, and quicker. It put the first quartz watch on the market.

RIGHT: In 1972, as a tribute to racing driver Jacky Ickx, TAG Heuer launched the chronograph 'Easy Rider Jacky Ickx'. The chrome-plated case was constructed in so-called monohull fashion and may only be opened from the dial side, with the pinpallet movement Caliber EB8420 hidden underneath the dial.

175

WATCHES

The Seiko '35 SQ Astron' appeared in 1969. It had no moving parts, except for the hands. A few years later, the Hamilton Watch Company, now calling itself THW, made their 'Pulsar'. At the press of a button, this showed digital time in bright lit-up figures on a dark screen. Allegedly, the design of this wristwatch was based on a clock shown in the hugely successful science fiction movie, '*2001: A Space Odyssey*'. In the early stages, the quartz watch was not cheap to produce. The manufacture of microcircuits and microprocessors was costly, and initially, large US computer companies supplied them.

RIGHT: Featured here is the Seiko Astron wristwatch, formally known as the Seiko Quartz-Astron 35SQ, the world's first quartz wristwatch. Within one week of it going on sale, 100 gold watches had been sold, at a retail price of 450,000 yen (US$1,250) each. At the time, this was equivalent to the price of a medium-sized Japanese automobile.

RIGHT: After ten years of research and development at Suwa Seikosha, a manufacturing company of the Seiko Group, a team of engineers headed by Tsuneya Nakamura produced the first quartz wristwatch to be sold to the public. The Seiko Quartz-Astron 35SQ was introduced in Tokyo on December 25, 1969.

LEFT: The crucial elements of the Astron included a quartz crystal oscillator, a hybrid integrated circuit, and a miniature stepping motor to turn the hands. It was accurate to within five seconds per month.

1970s – Design and Opportunity

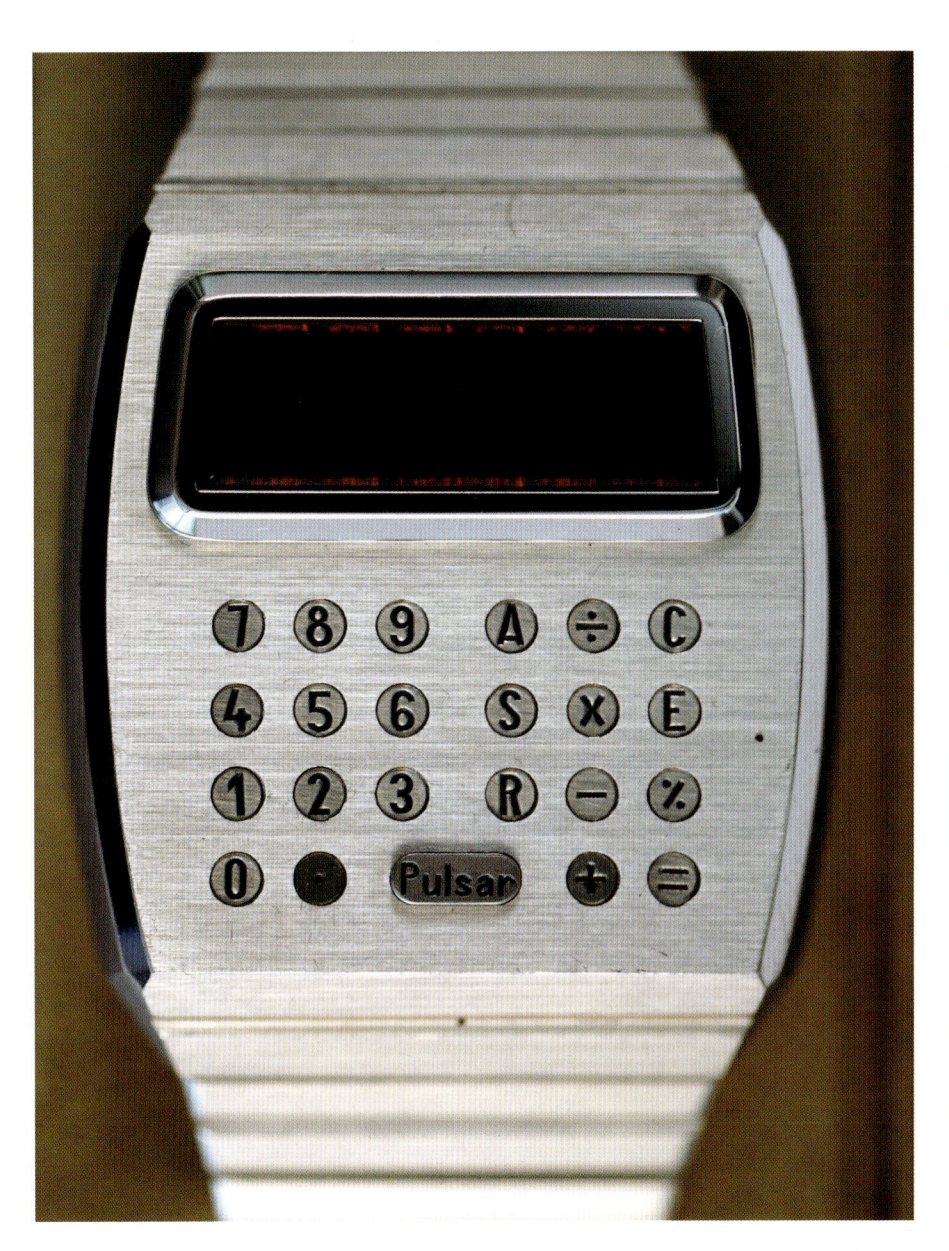

The Swiss made contracts with these conglomerates, but still, their watchmaking industry went into recession while the American and Japanese made huge sales with their quartz watches. There were various disadvantages to be overcome in this new invention, but by the end of the decade, most had been sorted, especially with the introduction of liquid crystal that made the figures easier to see when lit. The factory watchmakers and some of the grander houses were quick to cater for the women's market. Gucci boxed a set of interchangeable bezels, each a different color, into which the watch could be fitted, then attached to a slender gold strap. A penchant for gold cocktail watches dominated the market.

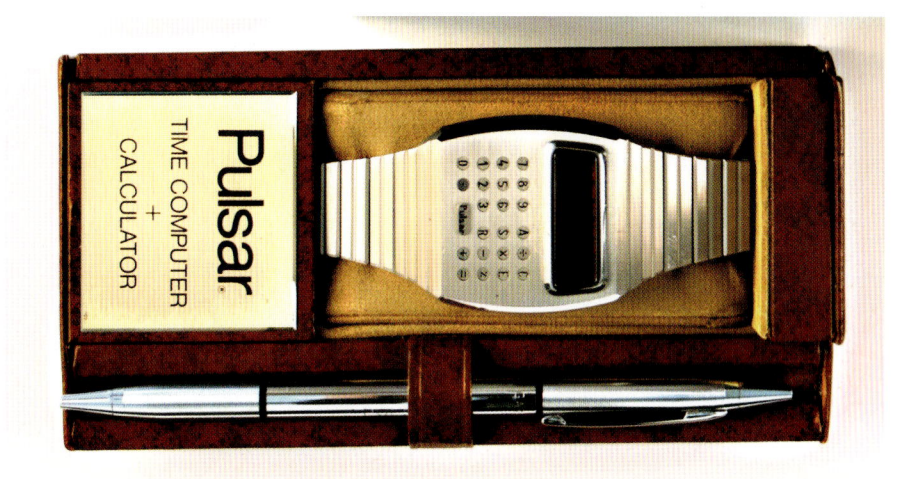

Left: With electronic parts now so small, it seemed easy to incorporate several different applications to a watch. In 1975, Pulsar introduced the first electronic calculator watch, which came in gold or silver. Due to the excessive amount of power used when the display is live, it turns itself off when not being used. To re-activate the time display, the button marked 'Pulsar' can be pressed.

Above: This is the special case in which the watch came, along with a Pulsar pen/stylus, which has a retractable ball point pen at one end and a retractable stylus at the other, for operating the tiny calculator buttons.

WATCHES

The Ball Watch Company

Webster C Ball had a long apprenticeship in watchmaking and business before, in 1879, founding the Webb C Ball Company in Cleveland, Ohio USA. He responded to the need for time precision demanded by the newly invented railroads, and not only developed a worthy timepiece but became Chief Inspector for Lake Shore Lines, governing timekeeping over thousands of miles of railroads. The names of Ball's ranges honor this early connection – 'Trainmaster', 'Fireman', and 'Engineer' – and their watches are robust, concentrating on clarity and reliability. The company continues to support the new and adventurous, forming the Ball Explorer's Club in 2004 to collaborate with explorers and athletes. The 2008 world record holder in free diving, Gillaume Nery, helped design the 'Engineer Master II Diver GMT'. The family owned the company until the 1990s when they sold the rights to the name. The new owners, based in Switzerland, maintain the traditions of the American company.

LEFT: When standard time was adopted in America in 1883, Webb C Ball was the first jeweler to use time signals, bringing accurate time to the railroad in Cleveland. Ball was later made Chief Inspector for all the Lake Shore Lines, which was just the beginning of the vast Ball network.

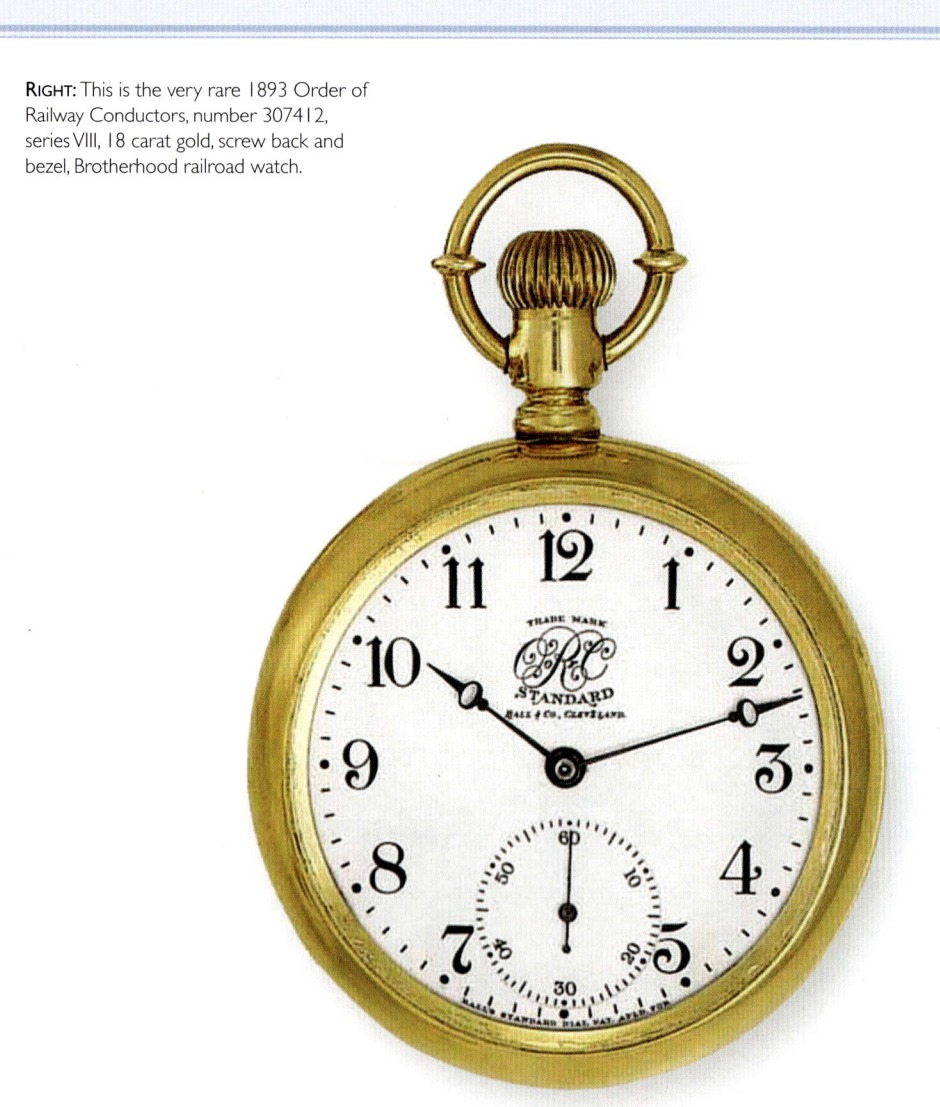

RIGHT: This is the very rare 1893 Order of Railway Conductors, number 307412, series VIII, 18 carat gold, screw back and bezel, Brotherhood railroad watch.

The Ball Watch Company

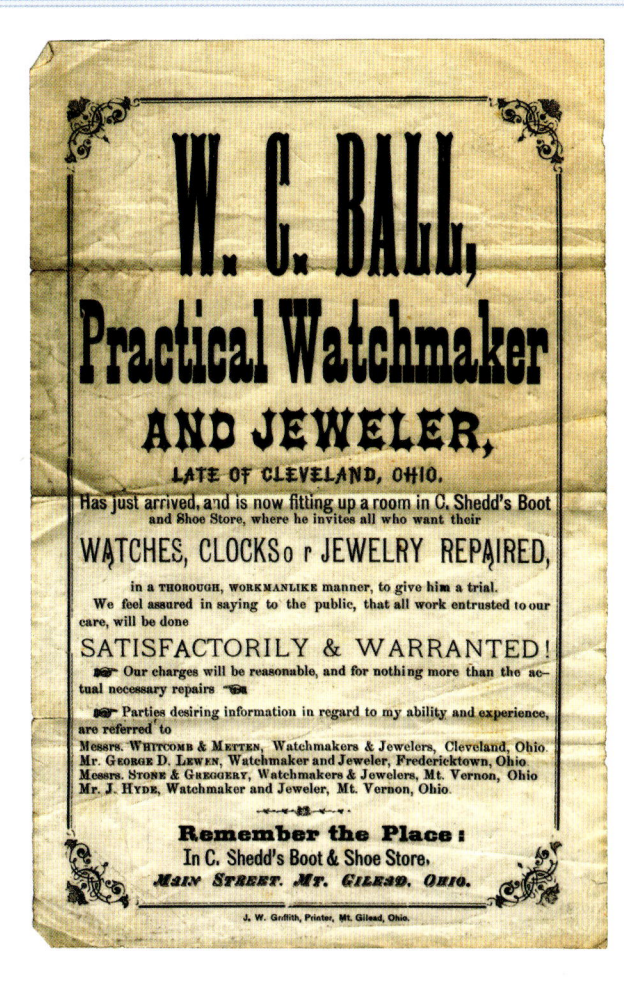

LEFT: One of the 2010 models produced by the Ball Watch Company is the Engineer Master II, which can be seen here showing off its night-time capabilities.

BELOW: Webb C. Ball's busy corner store was the initial headquarters of the Ball Watch Company, which also sold jewelry and silverware.

ABOVE: Archival advertisement of c1880s, announcing the opening of the small W C Ball repair shop, using his former employers Whitcomb and Metten as references.

WATCHES

BELOW: In 1974 Omega released their 'Marine Chronometer'. It was the world's first wristwatch marine chronometer, with a routine variation of less than 2/1000 seconds per day.

But the Americans understood the power of advertising and brand names. They began to purchase franchises on quality Swiss names, believing established reputations would sell their quartz watches. However, the Americans made a few errors of judgment. They assumed everyone would be delighted by lit-up digital time. The Japanese recognized wearers like to see the hands moving on their watch, so-called analogue time, and sales in their analogue watches were high.

Also, the US manufacturers, and perhaps the Japanese too, underestimated the attitude of the public. The masses continued to value the history and traditions of horology; they felt admiration for, even if they were ignorant of the traditions of watchmaking. The grander Swiss companies sensed this and maintained tradition, selling mechanical watches to the rich who could afford to feed nostalgia. But in the late 1970s, the quartz watch became affordable and its accuracy was unrivaled. Despite sentiment, the public bought them, and seemed to show a preference for a conventional design.

LEFT: The Omega Megaquartz 2400 became the undisputed, the most accurate and the most technologically advanced wristwatch in the world. This accuracy resulted from a specially designed tiny disc-shaped resonator, sealed in a capsule, which vibrated at the incredible rate of 2,359,296 times a second!

180

1970s – Design and Opportunity

Above: The Lip Company, were at one stage the largest watchmaker in France. By the 1970s, like many other watchmakers, they were in financial trouble. After securing finance they commissioned several designers, including Roger Tallon, to create new designs for their watches, whilst at the same time securing orders for the new watches with Dugena of Germany. The resulting watch was the quartz Lip-Dugena, which sadly did not sell well, although it was an exciting and different design.

Left: The quartz watch by Lip-Dugena of France, was produced in c1975. The design was by Roger Tallon. It has a central seconds hand and a day/date window at 3 o'clock.

181

WATCHES

The Tourbillon

Abraham-Louis Breguet (1747-1823) turned the watch from a timepiece kept in a separate case into a slim pocket watch, then improved the accuracy of the watch with his invention of the tourbillon. He mounted the escapement on an epicyclic train; this means the centre of one circle is carried round the circumference of another circle. The circles are wheels – called 'trains' by watchmakers. He fitted it all into a 'cage'. This rotates completely on its axis over a regular time period, usually one minute. The trains' rotation controls the hands; before the tourbillon, the trains worked inadequately in half rotation. Aficionados like watches with a tourbillon movement because, as one commented, 'It is difficult to love a quartz controlled watch … whereas a fine movement has the art and grace of a living thing.' Jaeger-LeCoultre includes a tourbillon in their splendid new 'Gyrotourbillon1'.

ABOVE: Seen from above, this is an oversize model of a tourbillon, which was used to instruct apprentices in the understanding of the tourbillion movement and construction

The Tourbillon

LEFT: Clearly seen here is the tourbillion used in this watch that was produced by William Harling of Dessau in 1943.

183

WATCHES

LEFT: During the 1970s, Girard-Perrigeaux, like many other watchmakers moved towards quartz movement for their watches. The company launched Switzerland's first industrial production of quartz watches in 1970.

Of course, designers were excited by the modernity of quartz watches and the opportunity to 're-design' the watch. Pierre Cardin, primarily famous as a fashion designer, offered his 'Espace' creation with a space age theme: he conjured visions of flying saucers through the use of lucite and metal discs. The Bulova 'Accruton' was made of stainless steel. It allowed for adjustments to Greenwich Mean Time, carried names of locations across the world, and showed luminous digital and analogue time. Also, it could be worn without damage to a depth of nearly 700 feet underwater.

LEFT: In 1973, Seiko managed another first in the watchmaking world, with this LCD quartz wristwatch, which was the first to have a six digit digital display.

1970s – Design and Opportunity

Above: Pierre Cardin was known for his avant-garde style and his 'Space Age' designs. This beautiful ladies wristwatch, which he introduced in 1972, could be seen as an extension of that style.

Left: The wristwatch case is made of plastic and has extensions coming out either side in blue plastic. The dial is simple and clean with just the makers name inscribed on it.

185

WATCHES

Quartz Crystal and Liquid

Movements – springs, wheels and so on – were made redundant by the quartz crystal. Used in watches, the crystal is shaped as a tiny bar, or a flat fork that flexes when it vibrates. A small, integrated circuit provides an oscillator to vibrate the quartz crystal, and a divider to break the resulting high frequency into one pulse a second. In an analog watch, this divider drives an electric motor that rotates to operate hours, minutes and seconds. This integrated circuit is more complicated in a digital watch, but the basic principles are the same. The early quartz watches needed a switch to light the time display, but liquid quartz improved this. The liquid was trapped between thin sheets of glass; an automatic electric charge changed the display from opaque to visible. Quartz made timepieces completely accurate, and quartz watches are, in this sense, superior to the best of precision watches that preceded them.

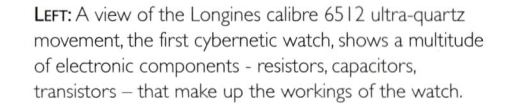

LEFT: A view of the Longines calibre 6512 ultra-quartz movement, the first cybernetic watch, shows a multitude of electronic components - resistors, capacitors, transistors – that make up the workings of the watch.

ABOVE: This is the 1969 Longines Ultra-Quartz timepiece, the movement for which is depicted in the picture on the left.

Quartz Crystal and Liquid

- Coil set
- Microchip
- Electric stepping motor
- Circuit connects microchip to other components
- Tiny central shaft holds hands in place
- Battery
- Quartz crystal oscillator
- Gears turn hour, minute and second hands at different speeds
- Crown screw for setting time

Left: The basic components of a simple quartz watch

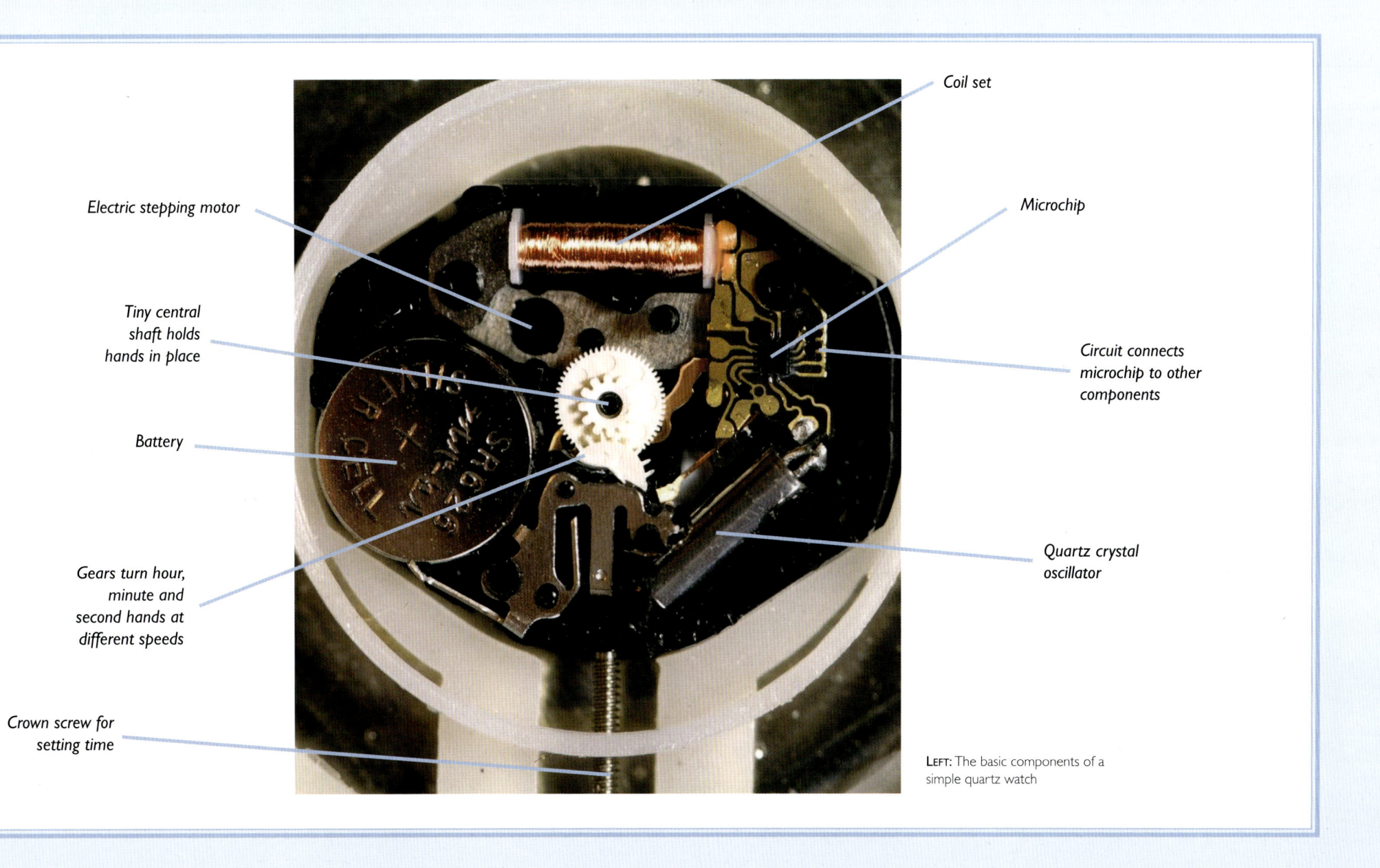

187

WATCHES

Other iconic timepieces were made in the 1970s. Rolex made their Explorer I in 1972, followed by Explorer II in 1973. Sir Edmund Hillary bought the Explorer II to celebrate the twentieth anniversary of his ascent of Everest. Gerald Genta, a trained artist turned watchmaker, was responsible for some of the classics from this era. In 1972, he produced for Audemars Piguet the great 'Royal Oak' to serve deep-sea divers. It was distinctive in its appearance – the case and the strap were integrated as a single entity, and Genta claimed its shape was inspired by a diver's helmet. Nearly 40 years later, 'Royal Oak' continues to be a highly appreciated, highly desired wristwatch. Genta went on to design Patek Philippe's 'Nautilus' and Omega's 'Titanium Polaris Seamaster', while under his own company name he produced the '1974 Perpetual Calendar'.

LEFT: Rolex are often seen as being just status symbols. Their timepieces go much deeper than that though. The Explorer and Explorer II (shown here), for example, were developed specifically for explorers who would navigate rough terrain, such as the grueling Mount Everest expeditions.

ABOVE: In 1972 Audemars Piguet launched the world's first high-end sports watch in stainless steel - the Royal Oak. It was a radical departure from the current watch trends, having a unique octagonal bezel making it a revolutionary shape in watchmaking. This shape was inspired by HMS Royal Oak, the first armoured British warship built in 1862. A small detail of this ship was the octagonal portholes with exterior frames secured with visible bolts.

188

1970s – Design and Opportunity

Left: The Omega Seamaster Chrono-Quartz was introduced in the 1970s, and was one of the biggest men's watches ever made. It was also known as the Albatross.

Below: Launched at the Montreal Olympic Games of 1976, the Omega Chrono-Quartz, was the first "hybrid" watch in the world, with both analogue display for the time functions and LCD (liquid crystal digital) display for the chronograph functions, the two being driven by the same quartz resonator.

WATCHES

Women's watches were sold for their practical, or trendy appearance but the market for jewelry did not abate. Bulova, Cartier, and Tiffany continued to create chic and elegant timepieces, with the designs that were sleek rather than complex jewelry – although Omega presented a white and yellow gold concoction of widely looped, complicated chains holding a gold watch. More typical of contemporary taste was the Piaget 'Polo' produced in a 'His and Hers' combination. On both models, the texture of the gold strap was repeated on the dial, but 'Her' - version had a circular face swelling from the strap while 'His' was rectangular and fit the line of the strap. Both versions were elegant and subtle in appearance.

RIGHT: Seiko have introduced many new ideas to the world of horology and they have contributed many 'first's'. Here though is a simple but pretty lady's watch of the 1970s, which any young girl of the period would have been happy wearing.

1970s – Design and Opportunity

LEFT: The face of the watch is made so that it is a part of the strap, giving it a clean, singular and smooth look. The face gives the impression of being a little cluttered and it has a manual winder at the side.

LEFT: This beautiful Everite lady's watch was given as a 21st birthday present. It has a gold plated case with a semi-rigid 'bark-effect', gold plated bracelet and fold over snap fastener.

Factory pieces were slow to risk high production of 'modern' designs, and pretty wristwatches continued to find sales, even if the 'pretty' now embraced a brighter, freewheeling style. Semi-precious stones were used on the dials. Setting the style for the factory teams, opal made a glimmering appearance on a Cartier dial, and Bueche Girod, renowned for original ideas, made a ring watch with a tiger's eye dial.

WATCHES

RIGHT: : Sekonda is a British brand which was established in 1966 to offer a collection of mechanical watches which were manufactured in Russia. Sekonda quickly became a household name and in the 1970s produced a healthy selection of models, of which this is one. The gold plated strap is robust and matches the gold plated case. The face has simple markings with Roman numerals for the number 12.

1970s – Design and Opportunity

ABOVE: When an explosion crippled the Apollo 13 module, it was an Omega speedmaster that manually timed the precise engine boost required to re-enter the earth's atmosphere and save the lives of the crew. Seen here are three Speedmaster Professional MkIIs

WATCHES

Aeronauts continued to grab attention, and the public was as keen as ever to know which timepieces these heroes wore. The crew of the Russian Soyuz journey in 1975 chose an Omega, and it was the brand selected by the crew of US Apollo 13. There were claims the watch helped save their lives. Omega made their 'Constellation' – usually a chronomatic of a macho-style – in a version for women. This had a mother-of-pearl face and silver arms, with silver dots instead of numbers. Omega made a revolutionary change in their complications watch, 'Speedmaster Mark II', making it not of a precious metal but in stainless steel. It proved another superb offering from this company.

RIGHT: Apollo 11 was the first manned spacecraft landing on the Moon carrying Mission Commander Neil Armstrong, Command Module Pilot Michael Collins and Lunar Module Pilot Edwin Eugene 'Buzz' Aldrin, Jr. Here astronaut Buzz Aldrin is seen on the lunar surface, his watch barely visible, but on his left wrist as you look at the picture.

1970s – Design and Opportunity

Left: This interior view of the Apollo 11 Lunar Module shows Astronaut Edwin E. Aldrin, Jr., lunar module pilot, during the lunar landing mission. This picture was taken by Astronaut Neil A. Armstrong, commander, prior to the moon landing and shows the Omega Speedmaster clearly on Aldrin's wrist.

WATCHES

It was a slow beginning but the watch was moving into the status of a fashion accessory. Men who had no need to check tidal or moon movements yearned for a complications watch because its presence on the wrist brought an authority that could not be ignored, and quartz watches were appearing in many shapes and designs – men adored the up-to-date high tech appearance of a dial that lit up. Such watches gave the wearer an air of modernity.

The Swiss had not crumpled when they missed the great popular surge for quartz watches. True, the great house of Breitling closed; many others faced financial ruin; at Zenith, the management asked for all the old time watchmaking tools to be scrapped. (Luckily, one employee defied this order and stored the equipment.) But the manufacturing complex, Ebauches SA, determined to restore the strength of Swiss production and took to building electronics factories across the country. By the end of the decade one factory was making 10,000 quartz watches a day – even so, production was far behind its competitors. But, the Swiss had another trick to perform that would rock the industry in the next decade.

RIGHT: In the 1970s Charles-Edouard Heuer dedicated this watch, his gold Carerra chronograph, to his chauffer, Kurt Hugi, for the devotion he had shown.

1970s – Design and Opportunity

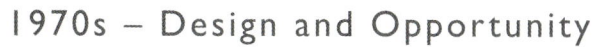

Left: By the 1970s, the Swiss watch manufacturing business was in the grip of a general economic downturn - this was the low point of the Swiss watch industry. Companies were looking to produce products that were attractive and different, like these fine examples form Tissot, a well respected company that had been making watches since 1853.

WATCHES

198

1980s
Time for All

The threat to Swiss watchmaking was very real. The country faced not only the loss of a proud tradition but also the loss of thousands of jobs in what had been a major industry. Two significant watch companies, Société Suisse pour l'Industrie Horlogère (SA) and Allgemeine Schweizerische Uhren consulted leading bankers and economists. They were advised to turn to Nicolas Hayek, the successful leader of Hayek Engineering AG, pleading that he bring his business expertise to their aid.

LEFT: Bright plastic designs have always been at the heart of the Swatch identity and is part of the brand's DNA. The 2010 Colour Codes Collection mirrors this with an array of multicoloured watches in the simple yet eternally stylish plastic watch design that made the brand so famous.

WATCHES

Not being a traditional watchmaker, Hayek did not fret over the time-indication element of watches; these problems had been long solved. He planned the production of an affordable quartz watch – no price over 50 Swiss francs – aimed at the young. In 1982, he launched the Swatch watch. The name was drawn from Hayek's concept of a 'second watch' – not a treasured timepiece, but a cheap, chic and disposable accessory. The case and the strap were made of plastic; designs were stylish, fashionable, and came in bright colors. Within two years, worldwide sales of Swatch reached the ten million mark, and the Swiss were saved.

The new watches from Swatch and later, Seiko along with other companies, were bought for fun. Girls wore them to hold their ponytails; young men wrapped two or three around their wrists, or boldly wore a suit and a Swatch but not a tie. The great fashion houses observed this novel use of the watch, and business houses accelerated their drive to purchase famous brand names to promote quality watches as accessories.

RIGHT: The co-founder and chairman of Swatch Group, Nicolas Hayek, shows Breguet's famous watch, 'Marie-Antoinette,' during the Baselworld trade fair 2008.

1980s – Time for All

LEFT: This picture was taken in 1985 and was entitled: Strap a banana around your wrist - and just smell the time! The Swatch, described as 'a jokey fashion idea', was already sweeping America and about to be launched in the UK. The Swiss-made watch had a strap impregnated with aromas fresh from an Italian ice-cream range. It came in pretty pastels - blue for mint, pink for raspberry and yellow for banana.

201

WATCHES

The 1980s were an era of high economic growth in the west, and fashion became ostentatious; jewelry was designed to be large and eye-catching; people were eager to display their wealth and status. Handbags were showy, boldly carrying logos that fashionistas were happy to display to one and all. The young could not afford the clothes, but they could wear a watch carrying the Dolce & Gabbana logo, or those of Yves St Laurent, Armani, and Paul Smith. But many were just as happy to flaunt the new plastic watches; the novelty brought status – even James Bond was caught wearing a Seiko. The more technology orientated were even able to interact between computer and their hi-tech watches; Seiko had produced the wrist terminal and their UC2000 model – this really was future technology in action!

Above: A simple, step by step view of how a rock watch was constructed, from the basic case through to fitting the movement and finally the finished product.

Left: In 1985 Tissot released the most unusual, and very popular, range of rock watches. The case of the rock watch was made from Swiss granite, millions of years old and no two pieces were the exact same. Different traces of minerals and semi-precious stones can be seen in the watch face, differing according to where the granite was mined.

1980s – Time for All

Left: The 1980s Seiko US 2000 watch, was just one accessory from the 'wrist information system'. It communicated with a pocket-sized keyboard, which offered a spool-fed printer, 4K of RAM and 26K of ROM.

Above: The Seiko, RC-1000 Wrist Terminal was the first Seiko model to interface with a computer, was released in 1984 and was compatible with most of the popular PCs of that time. The watch has six buttons and some interesting functions. In addition to the typical day, date, alarm and timekeeping functions, it also has memo, schedule alarm, weekly alarm and world time functions. There's also a light to illuminate the face.

WATCHES

Fortis

The Fortis Company made an early statement of its interest in innovation and the mechanics of timekeeping. Walter Voight opened Fortis in 1912, then in partnership with John Harwood, inventor of the self-winding watch, issued in 1926, the 'Harwood Automatic'. Fortis had an enthusiasm for aviation, and researched reliable timepieces to function in the skies. The Russians requested a chronograph for their space station, Mir and in 1994 Fortis became official partners with the Russian Federal Space Agency. Fortis consulted with pilots, and created the 'Calculator' containing a classic slide rule, as well as a countdown function and a three time-zone display. Their Flieger Chronograph won the first European Watch of the Year 2004 trophy, and Fortis supply watches for the military in Greece, Germany, and other nations. Their new 'Planet Watch' has received wide respect and now, Fortis is recognized as being among the elite of watchmakers. This Swiss company is privately owned.

LEFT: 1994: After endurance tests on the margins of physics, the Star City Training Center chose the Fortis official Cosmonauts Chronograph as part of their official cosmonaut's equipment. The space mission "EUROMIR 1" crew was the first to be presented with the Fortis Cosmonauts Set and became the world's first automatic chronograph in open space outside the space station.

ABOVE: Fortis produced the world's first Automatic Chronograph Alarm in series production, inspired by the demands of the Space specialists at Star City; it was realized by the Swiss genius watch maker Paul Gerber.

Fortis

Right: The Swiss village of Grenchen was the home of Fortis when the company was founded by Walter Vogt in 1912, and it still is today. An important year in Fortis history was 1924, when Vogt met John Harwood, the British inventor of the automatic wristwatch.

Left: The 2010 Fortis B-42 Stratoliner Chronograph Limited Edition has sapphire crystal with anti-reflective coating on both sides, along with luminous elements. The progression of hours and minutes is marked by gold-plated, partially transparent hands. The seconds are indicated by a slim, gold plated, central hand. Additionally, the dial includes 12-hour, 60-second and 30-minute chronograph counters, featured at 6, 9 and 12 o'clock correspondingly.

WATCHES

Artists were drawn back into the world of horology when they were commissioned to introduce an entirely new appearance to the wristwatch. Keith Haring and Vivienne Westwood, the British punk designer, worked for Swatch while Max Bill, designer for Omega, created radical patterns and colors for dials and straps. The creative spirit behind the Italian furniture company Memphis, Ettore Sottsass, who had designed for early quartz watches found his métier in the new fashion accessory. The dials of these watches were to include Andy Warhol images, and the signature of Bob Dylan appeared on the face of an Oris watch, which would also be reissued in 2010.

RIGHT: Colourful watches seemed to appear from everywhere in the 1980s. Straps were plastic and multi-coloured, whilst the watch cases too were plastic and the faces were decorated in a multitude of patterns and colours.

1980s – Time for All

LEFT: During the 1980s, watch makers were trying all kinds of experiments to brighten up watches. Not unlike the 1980s, Oris have launched their Bob Dylan watch in limited edition for 2010; just 3000 pieces worldwide.

BELOW: The 2010 Bob Dylan watch has a rectangular face and is a tribute to the multi-talented living legend. The stainless steel case carries his portrait on the case back and his signature adorns the dial. The special presentation set includes a Hohner Marine Band harmonica – the instrument for which Dylan is best known.

WATCHES

The highly successful launch of the watch as a fashion accessory caused some deep thinking among the grand names in watchmaking. The egalitarian mood promoted by Swatch was one they wished to avoid, but they were not averse to using some of the elements behind the brand's success. Cartier, jewelers and craftsmen, spotted the link to artists. In 1984, they opened the Foundation Cartier in Jouy-en-Josas near Marseilles. Here, they pursued a policy of exhibiting the work of contemporary but high-end artistes. The moviemaker, David Lynch was given a show, as was Patti Smith, doyen of rock and roll.

RIGHT: Wristwatch and jewellery set known as Ellipse d'or, shown in the Patek Philippe museum in Geneva, Switzerland. This is dated around 1975 – 1985 and there are earrings to match.

1980s – Time for All

The marketing men sensed art was a high quality commodity and Cartier created a connection between 'Art' and horology in the minds of the sophisticates and celebrities. Now, Foundation Cartier is firmly established as a patron of the arts and, therefore in the consumer's perception, Cartier makes artistic products. In this way, the market for luxury goods was prepared, and it proved a life-giving path of revival for the traditional, elite, and expensive watch.

Left: Shown here is a beautiful, 18 carat gold bracelet set with diamonds. The movement of the watch is a caliber 990 automatic "squelette" and the watch is from the Agassiz Collection. It was produced in 1982 at the occasion of the 150th anniversary of the creation of the first Comptoir Auguste Agassiz in 1832, which later lead to the creation of Longines.

WATCHES

Art was used as a selling point but so, too, was sport. The term 'sports watch' made a shy appearance. Jewelry was not acceptable as an accessory for most men, but a big and beautiful watch brought some compensation, especially if the timepiece had an aura of rugged, sporty masculinity. A chap may prefer a gin and tonic on a yacht deck to any bold adventure on the high seas, but who could tell? He wears a large complications watch, waterproof and fit for deep sea diving or another rugged sport: ergo, he is a brave sportsman.

RIGHT: In 1972 Audemars Piguet introduced the Royal Oak, a high-end sports watch made of steel. For 1983 the highly recognisable Royal Oak was upgraded as the self-winding Royal Oak with perpetual calendar. An impressive watch that stood out from the rest, with its octagonal bezel and eight hexagonal screws.

1980s – Time for All

BELOW: The Manufacture Audemars Piguet has a well-established tradition of commitment to sailing. In 1985, it supported the UBS Switzerland and Pierre Fehlmann in his round-the-world team race.

211

WATCHES

Oris

This company was established in 1904 in Holstein, Switzerland. Over the years, it has focused on making watches dedicated to aviation, diving, motor sports and culture, and timepieces are designed to suit each particular category. Strongly linked to the BMW Williams Formula One group, Oris also formed a partnership with the small, elite sports car manufacturer, Alois Ruf. Whenever a RUF CTR3 is sold, the buyer will find an Oris ProDiver Chronograph in the glove compartment. This titanium watch has a ceramic bezel and withstands water pressure up to the 100 bar. And Oris has a 'jazz' collection of watches honoring Charlie Parker, Frank Sinatra, and Bob Dylan. International recognition of Oris has been growing, particularly because it manufactures mechanical watches but presents them in modern designs. These are high quality watches but available at very reasonable prices. The company remains in private hands, and the Managing Director in 2010 is Ulrick W Herzog.

RIGHT: Be it on land, in the air or deep down in the sea; the Italian 9th Parachute Assault Regiment has tested the Oris 'Col Moschin' watch to the extreme.

Oris

RIGHT: Williams Formula One driver for 2008, Nico Rosberg, checking data on his Oris watch.

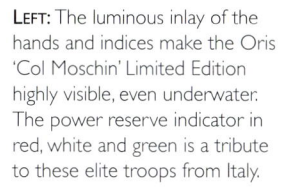

LEFT: The luminous inlay of the hands and indices make the Oris 'Col Moschin' Limited Edition highly visible, even underwater. The power reserve indicator in red, white and green is a tribute to these elite troops from Italy.

RIGHT: Hölstein in Switzerland has been home to Oris Headquarters since it was established in 1904.

WATCHES

An indication of this trend showed in the revival of Breitling, and the company's claim to expertise in 'compteurs de sport'. Cartier's produced their steel and gold 'Santos' while Chopard gave the motor racing world the 'Mille Miglia'. Omega made the stainless steel and gold 'Constellation Marine Chronometer', a tough, unadorned timepiece. In an interesting development, Chanel presented the J12, a man's sports watch in a woman's version. This was an indication that women were firmly established in the world of work and sport.

RIGHT: Brescia in Italy is where the Mille Miglia always starts and finishes. Here, the Mercedes-Benz of Stirling Moss attracts a great deal of attention while it waits for its drivers to be checked in. The race, although many would say it is not a race, travels down one side of Italy to Rome and then cuts back up the other side to Brescia. All this mileage (as the title of the event notes: 1000 miles) is covered between the Friday evening and the Sunday afternoon; precision timing is paramount for the drivers.

1980s – Time for All

BELOW: Like many of the wonderful cars that participate in the Mille Miglia, the Chopard Mille Miglia Grand Turismo line of watches have performance, passion and precision. Each of these beautiful timepieces has an engine that drives a variable number of displays and functions, many of which are used by the competitors for their sport. Chopard have sponsored the event for many years now and they understand what is required by the drivers attempting to get the most from their timing.

WATCHES

Women were seeking a modern, even severe look on their wristwatches. Yves St Laurent designed a black face barred with gold stripes, but Omega's 'Sapphire Art Series' conjured up the utmost in simplicity: on one version, the face was circled by a narrow black strip enclosing a white dial without numbers. The hands were black. Pulsar Quartz used steel to form an unusually large, irregular shape for their analogue watch. It had a masculine, but chic appearance that appealed to the career woman.

Of course, Swatch did not ignore the grown-up women's market and sold a steel watch with a plain, conventional face, then gave it an interesting large-linked steel strap. Formerly THW, the Timex Company continued the former company's policy of making affordable watches, and was very successful with international sales although their designs were not as radical as those of Swatch. Their women's watches tended to be small in size, but functional in appearance. So-called 'cocktail watches' increased in popularity for eveningwear. These often had complications, a bright dial of one color and a decoration of rhinestones or precious stones. The Reverso-style watch continued to be a popular seller.

RIGHT: Portrait of American actress Candice Bergen as she poses in front of a window that overlooks Central Park, New York, in the mid 1980s. The watch is stunning and 'in your face' but hey, she will never turn up late to the studio!

1980s – Time for All

Left: Made by Pulsar Quartz of Switzerland, this wristwatch is powered by an amorphous silicon photocell (which surrounds the dial), and has reserve power provided by a capacitor.

WATCHES

Swatch

The Swatch is a triumph of democratic consumerism. After centuries of a minority carefully guarding their expensive timepiece, a consortium, the Société Suisse de Microcelectronique et d'Horologie (SMH) under the leadership of Nicolas G. Hayek produced a watch that was cheap, and accurate. The Swatch was made possible by the introduction of quartz and plastic into watchmaking and was the Swiss's triumphant answer to the watches imported from post-World War II Japan. The clever promotion of Swatch as a cheap fashion accessory ensured its success. The brand had five major ranges: 'Irony', made with metal; 'Scuba' for divers; 'Skin', thin, light watches; 'Beat' connects to the internet to read stockmarket prices, and 'Bijoux'. The Swatch Group—which owns Swatch—promotes sport and athletes across the world, and has become the world's biggest watchmaker, having bought luxury brands Longines, Tissot, Tiffany, Flik Flak, and many others into its corporation.

Above: Flik Flak's entire brand life is expressed in the word 'Passion'. Created in 1987, Flik Flak was designed to be more than just a simple children's watch. It is notably the first ever brand of children's watch to introduce the concept of teaching the time, allowing this learning experience to be transformed into something amusing for children. Synonymous with unique quality, Flik Flak quickly became the world's best-selling children's watch.

Left: Each of these tiny hands will have to be fitted to a Swatch watch. The technician uses tweezers to select which one's he needs next.

218

Swatch

LEFT: For 2010, Swiss fashion watch and jewellery maker Swatch presented the 'Swatch New Gent Collection'. Ten trendy models in understated, yet bold colours introduce a new, much bigger Swatch watch inspired by the legendary Swatch Gent Originals.

RIGHT: The person in the picture is shown removing dust from glass with a small air compressor before applying the protective sticker.

ABOVE: In 1978, the Japanese challenged the Swiss watchmakers by launching a watch with a thickness of just 2.5 mm. The Swiss naturally respond by developing a still flatter watch which could not exceed 2mm - the thickness of a matchstick. After five months of arduous development and production work, ETA SA, a subsidiary of ASUAG, launched "Delirium Tremens" at the end of 1979. Officially known as calibre 999, it has a thickness of just 1.98 mm and remains the flattest wristwatch in the world today!

WATCHES

Watches for children proved successful because of the low cost and cheerful designs. These appeared decorated with cartoon characters, flowers, animal images and the like. The cheapness of these watches made them suitable for little people who might easily lose the timepiece.

Fashion and watches were now inextricably linked. The great houses of haut couture – Gucci, Chanel, Dior, Yves St Laurent, Hermes and the like – were advising that watches were an essential accessory, and they were selling their own luxury brands. Fashion designers were the new celebrities. Their designs showed the influence of Swatches in the use of color and design but, where inexpensive fun watches used plastic, high fashion used colored metals, gemstones; straps were intricate chains, expensive leathers, or etched silver.

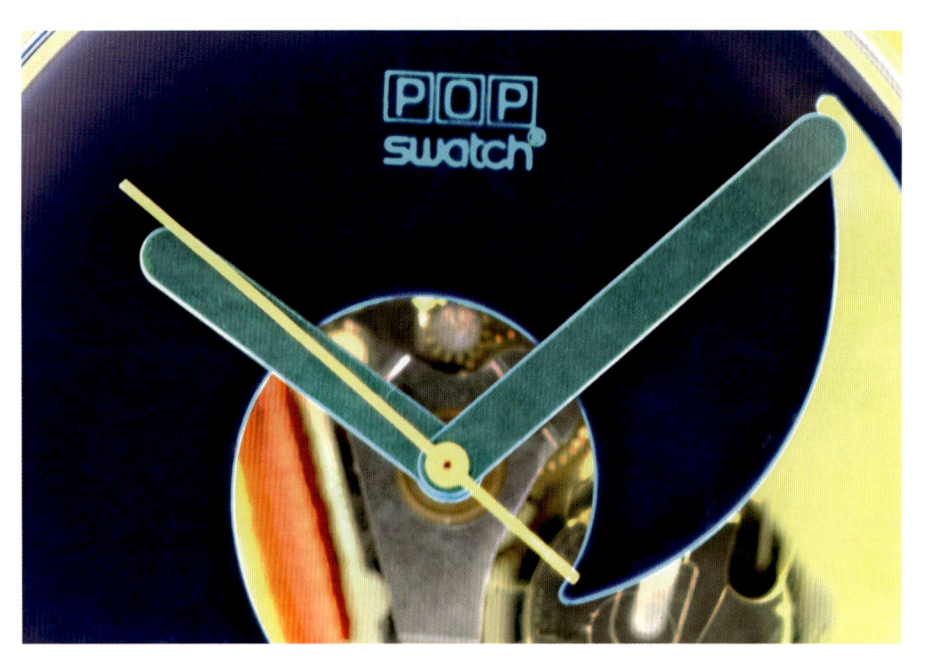

ABOVE: Swatch watches enjoyed their peak popularity during the mid-1980s. Such fads included wearing two Swatches and using a Swatch as a ponytail band. Some models, like Pop Swatch, allowed wearers to attach the watch directly to clothing.

LEFT: The first Swatch Pop watch came out in 1986 and was seen as a new fashion item. Its simplicity and colorfulness was exciting and attractive. It didn't take long to catch on.

1980s – Time for All

Consumers did not perceive obvious logos as cheap advertising for the maker but believed a famous name brought the wearer respect and status. Sadly, many of the logo branded watches were uninspiring; the old traditions of watchmaking and formal design were ignored in the rush for mass sales of watches in colorful, quirky designs. A small band of Swiss makers kept the old traditions, and there were watchmakers who did not lose their passion for the mechanics of watchmaking. Gerald Genta, passionate about horology, did not stop his research and in 1981, devised the world's thinnest minute repeater.

RIGHT: Gerald Genta's designs include a sonnerie, the Gérald Genta Octo Granda Sonnerie Tourbillion, which has four gongs and rings the Westminster Quarters melody at each quarter and on the hour, and costs in the region of US$810,200. In 1994 he designed the "Grande Sonnerie", the world's most complicated wristwatch, price approximately one million US dollars.

WATCHES

Others pretended to follow tradition but brought out modified versions of old favorites fitted with modern quartz technology. Ralph Lauren colored his watches to give them a reassuring old, classic appearance, and made them with thin, square old-fashioned dials. Patek and Audemars Piguet did not succumb to radical chic design but maintained a steady conservatism in the appearance of their products.

LEFT & ABOVE: In the late 1970s, the Swiss watchmaking industry was in deep crisis. Girard-Perregaux was one of the first prestigious watch companies to take up the challenge of a return to traditional mechanical timepieces. Girard-Perregaux's master-watchmakers set about remaking twenty of the famous Tourbillon with three gold Bridges pocket watches; Number one was unveiled in 1981. Ten years later, to celebrate its bicentenary, the Manufacture achieved the feat of producing a version of the Tourbillon with three gold Bridges miniaturised to wrist watch size.

WATCHES

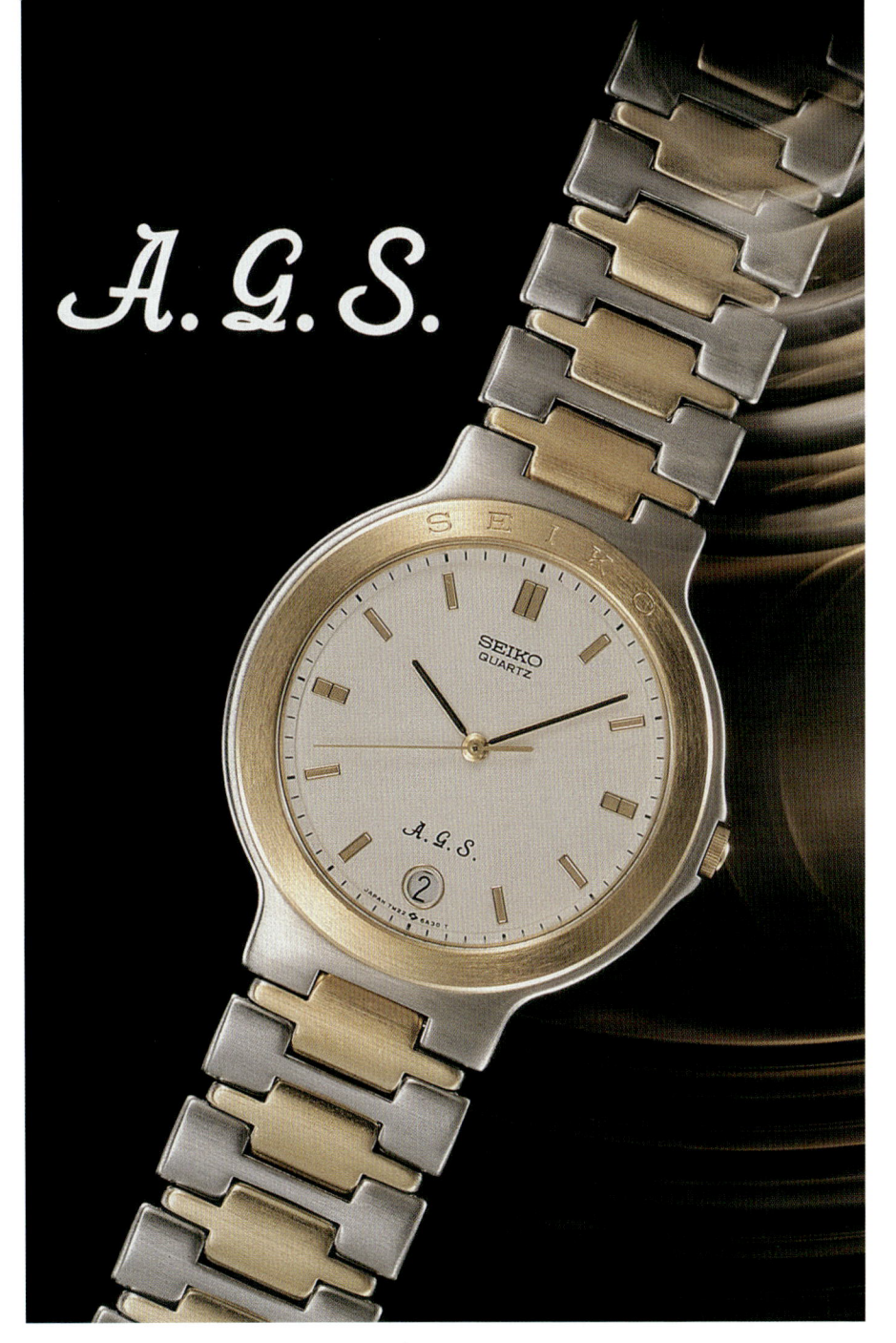

1980s – Time for All

The Swiss traditionalists were encouraged by the growth of a small but significant market in old watches. Toward the end of the decade, auction houses realized much higher bids than they ever expected for mechanical watches. Watches had become, it seemed, part of the west's artistic heritage.

LEFT: It was at the 1986 Basel Fair that Seiko unveiled its first Kinetic prototype. Introduced under the trial name of 'AGM', it was the first watch in the world to convert kinetic movement into electrical energy. It was the first step in a development that, 20 years later, has made Kinetic synonymous with environmental friendliness, high performance and long-lasting convenience to a generation of users worldwide.

WATCHES

LEFT: TAG Heuer is proud of its 'Searacer' series. The watch is waterproof to a depth of 200 meters, and the wearer can move the bezel to read 1/10th of a second. This watch is peculiarly suited to sailing, and the company manages the TAG Heuer Maxi World Cup, a major yacht race. The colorful sails of this yacht are part of the promotion for the event.

1990s
Outside the boundaries

The determined marketing of the watch as an accessory helped the industry. The watch became an essential part of an outfit, and because of Swatch and other inexpensive lines everyone could own one – or two or three. The division between the low priced and the timepieces sold under the name of quality houses was defined by the status of the brand, and not the superiority in timekeeping, so the big brands pursued the famous as a way of marketing the luxury watch.

WATCHES

RIGHT: For his personal satisfaction, Garry Kasparov, world chess champion, chose the Audemars Piguet '1998 Millenary'.

In the 1990s, celebrities sought high-level publicity, making themselves into major brands. Consumers were deeply interested in the lives of the famous and wanted to know every detail of the 'celeb's' life, including the watches they wore. It was important to learn what the young star Madonna preferred, or even to learn Anne, the Princess Royal, wore an Accurist. But this mass marketing technique, one that created a yearning for fashion status, had its drawbacks as was clearly demonstrated by the new watchmaking industry in the Far East.

1990s – Outside the Boundaries

Left: There are standard time controls in chess grandmaster tournaments – each player must take a number of moves within a specific time. Timing clocks are now digital, but they were once stopwatches that clicked throughout the game. Technology has changed other aspects of the game. Here Kasparov plans his moves against the IBM computer known as Deep Blue.

WATCHES

RIGHT: This is the Patek Philippe model chosen by the Russian space authority for their Soyuz exploration in 1992.

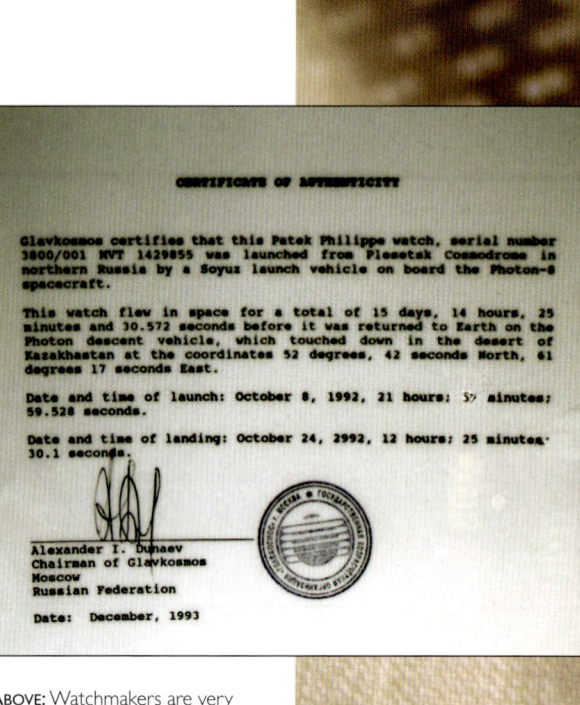

ABOVE: Watchmakers are very proud if their timepieces survive when used during extreme sports or unusual explorations. This certificate of authenticity was important to Patek Philippe because it confirmed their official status as suppliers of watches to Russia's space program.

1990s – Outside the Boundaries

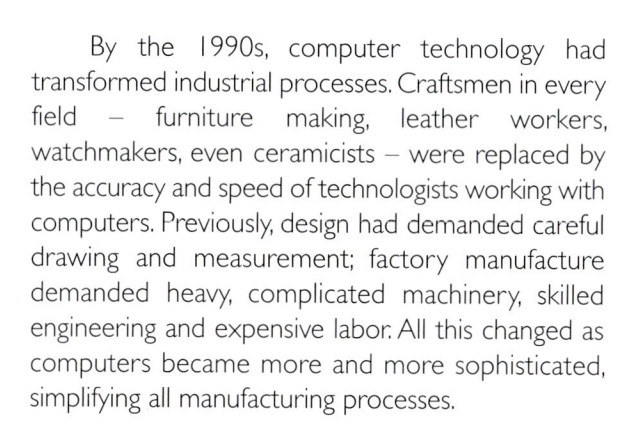

By the 1990s, computer technology had transformed industrial processes. Craftsmen in every field – furniture making, leather workers, watchmakers, even ceramicists – were replaced by the accuracy and speed of technologists working with computers. Previously, design had demanded careful drawing and measurement; factory manufacture demanded heavy, complicated machinery, skilled engineering and expensive labor. All this changed as computers became more and more sophisticated, simplifying all manufacturing processes.

LEFT: Tissot used ceramic in making their 'Ceraten' in 1991. The ceramic was an important innovation because it was much tougher than any produced before, and so could withstand rigorous conditions.

229

WATCHES

Audemars Piguet

In 1875 Jules-Louis Audemars and Edward-August Piguet started a watchmaking business. They set a standard of meticulous production, with careful attention to the use of appropriate materials, maintained to this day. In the 1920s, its timepieces were marketed by Tiffany, Cartier, and Bulgari. Despite its attachment to traditional methods, Audemars Piguet was the first to produce a serial range using the tourbillon, and has experimented with silicone escapements, and steel and ruby jewel bearings. Audemars Piguet modified an escapement designed by Robert Robin (1742-1799) and the new design eliminated the need for oil lubrication in the movement. In its famous 'Royal Oak' range, forged carbon was used to construct the 'Offshore', a model within the range. All the watches are handmade, and well known for their thin, robust construction. The company, based in Geneva, is a major Swiss maker of luxury timepieces. The descendants of the founders are on the Board of Directors.

ABOVE: Audemars Piguet and Cie proudly advertise their status as horologists confirming their reliability by mentioning the international extent of their market.

BELOW: A special edition of 'Royal Oak' was made for the grand yacht race, America's Cup when the finishing port was the 'City of Sails' as the New Zealand harbour, Auckland is known. The back carries a commemorative engraving to suit the occasion. The 'Royal Oak' is a long-enduring and famous range from Audemars Piguet.

Audemars Piguet

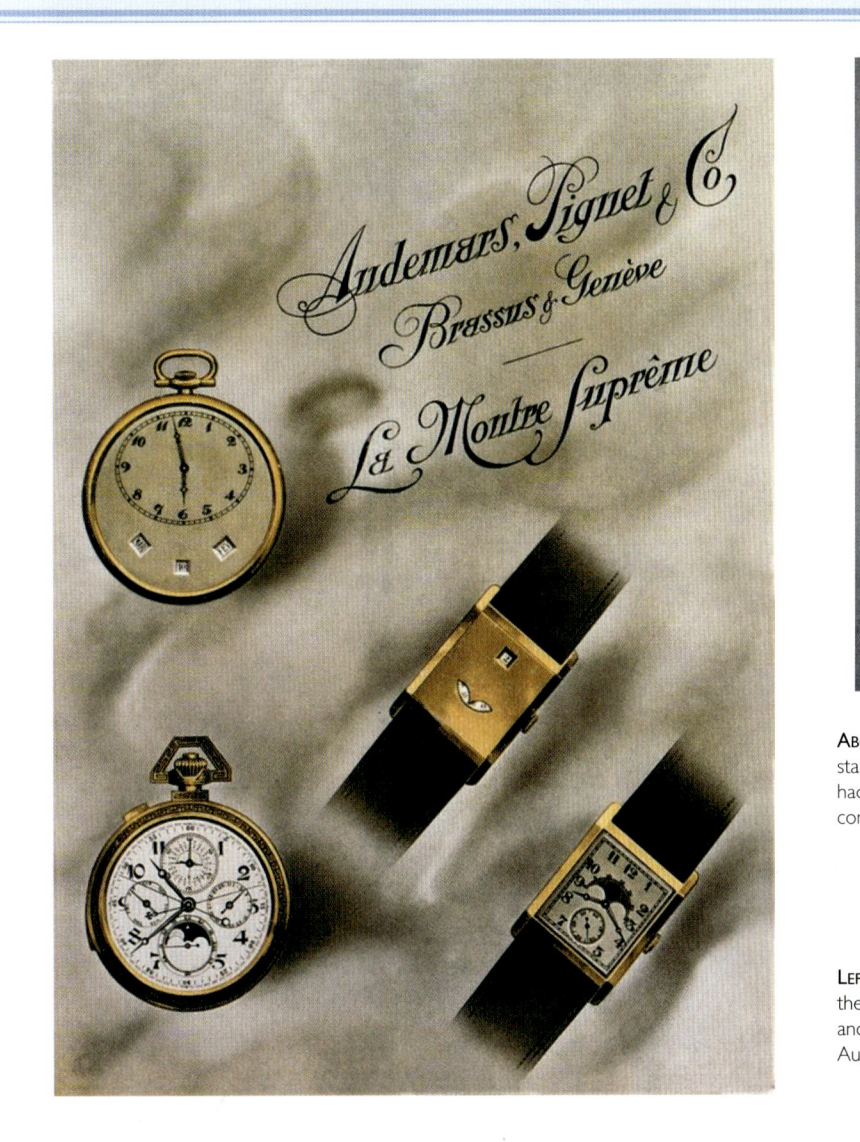

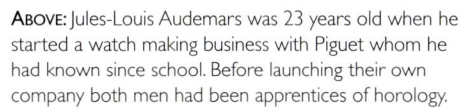

Above: Jules-Louis Audemars was 23 years old when he started a watch making business with Piguet whom he had known since school. Before launching their own company both men had been apprentices of horology.

Above: Edward-Auguste Piguet was 21 when he joined Audemars in business. Despite their youth, within 20 years their company became the biggest watchmaking employer in the district of Vaud, southwestern Switzerland.

Left: This sophisticated advertisement is a far cry from the billboard of the 19th century. It dates from the 1920s and simply presents images of elegant timepieces from Audemars Piguet.

WATCHES

During the 1980s, Western manufacturers moved their businesses to China, Vietnam, and Korea. Here, labor was cheap and traditional skills rendered unnecessary by the new technology. Far Eastern traders also saw advantages in these changing methods and developed their own companies to supply the masses with cheerful, accurate watches. But they watched the great trading houses of the west stress the quality and status of expensive high-end timepieces. Some Asian manufacturers found a way to break into this corner of the market. They began to copy the appearance of the luxury brands, not only in design but also, in the blatant use of logos.

RIGHT: This lavish luxury watch has the Central Tourbillon developed by the company in 1994. All Omega Central Tourbillons are hand assembled and hand decorated. The movements and case components are made specifically for each watch.

1990s – Outside the Boundaries

Counterfeit watches began to appear in the west. Sales were in outlets that were difficult to police. They were sold in street markets and at boot sales; suddenly, even those on low incomes were apparently sporting a Rolex, a Gucci or a Patek Philippe. The counterfeits were meticulously produced, and accurate in their imitation of other people's work. Of course, they were made of inferior materials, gilt and cheap metals, and many were not even reliable timekeepers. Customers were disappointed to find their so-called Rolex stopped working within days, or quickly became scratched and tarnished.

Legally, companies and designers have copyright over their work, but the laws of ownership were not the same in every country. It was difficult to enforce the law, although police forces and customs officers in the USA and Europe tried their best. Cargo consignments were confiscated, and street markets raided, but the customers and the sellers did not help the legal forces. Both were happy with the counterfeits that looked so like the real thing. Colin McDowell, writing in Vanity Fair, commented that the person who wanted his Rolex to be noticed was the person wearing a fake. "Wearers of the real thing," he claimed, "are far less ostentatious."

RIGHT: Counterfeit products were such good imitations, that luxury brands were compelled to find distinctive ways of identifying their watches, whether through use of precious gems or secret markings. The watches above are counterfeits and traders in these illegal products refer to them as 'same-same watches'. Two copies of Rolex watches flank the Louis Vuitton fake.

233

WATCHES

However, the flamboyant leader of the Italian Fiat car company, Gianni Agnelli did not bother with the subtle but strapped his expensive watch over his cuff.

Watchmakers of the genuine product did not sink under the counterfeit onslaught, and new luxury watches appeared. Perhaps taking a cue from Fiat's leader, one designer, Angelo Galasso, created the 'Polso Orologia' that was designed to fit over the cuff, allowing the wearer to check his watch at a glance.

RIGHT: Angelo Galasso models his watch wrapped over the specially modified shirt cuff. As stylish a dresser as he was a designer, Glassi was pleased to sport this novel way of wearing his timepiece.

LEFT: The idea never swept through the fashion world, but Angelo Galasso presented his cuff watch shirt with great confidence. The cuff is cut away to give space to the watch face.

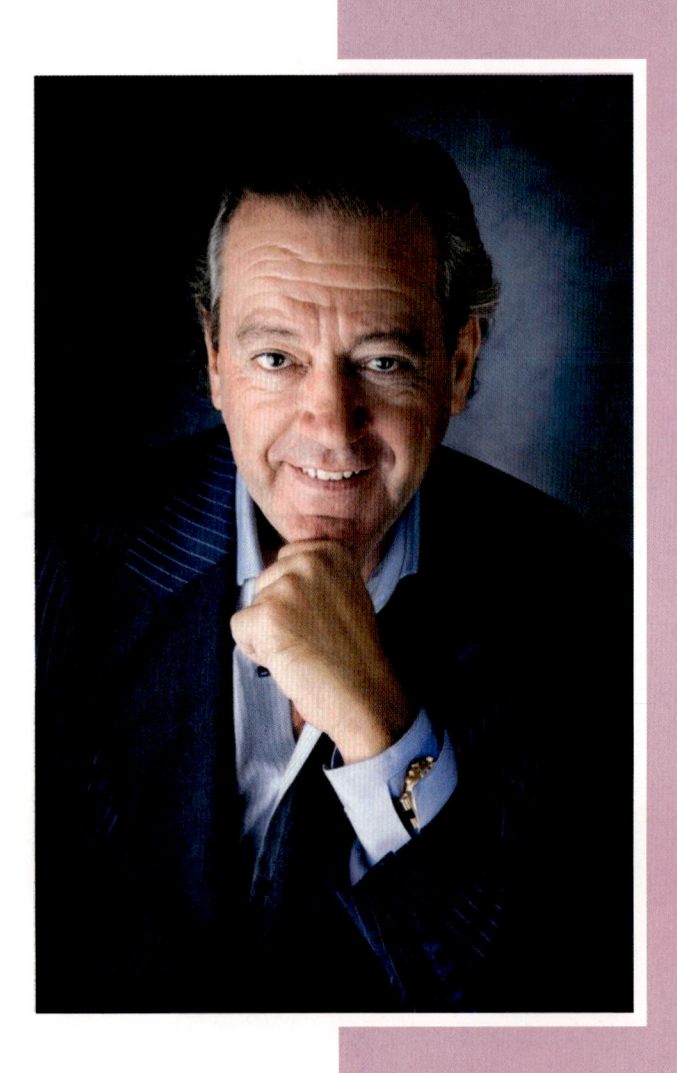

1990s – Outside the Boundaries

Neither were rap singers, super models and movie stars shy about their timepieces. James Bond, now represented by Pierce Brosnan in *Golden Eye* wore an Omega 'Seamaster Professional'. The public wanted to know what the movie actress, Uma Thurman or the Wimbledon champion Steffi Graf preferred to wear on their wrist.

RIGHT: Pierce Brosnan enjoyed great fame when he played the coveted role of James Bond. This made him a fine ambassador for the Omega 'Seamaster' and here he is exuberant at the launch of the range in 1999.

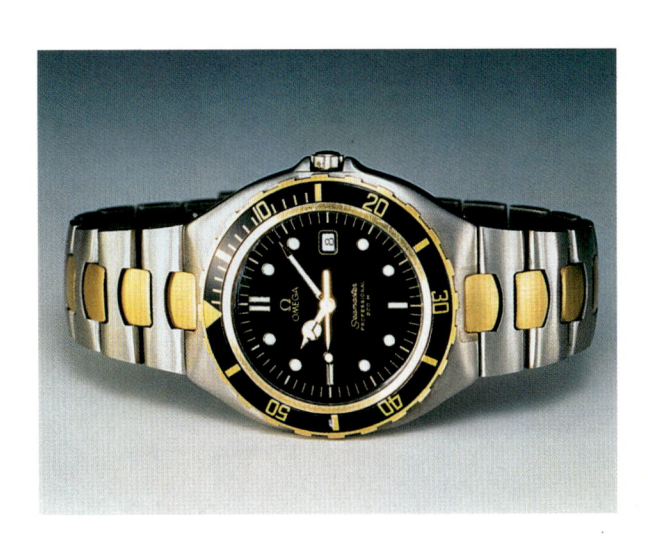

LEFT: The 'Seamaster' range is an automatic, and its functions cover hours, minutes, sweep seconds, and the date. The band is stainless steel and red gold. It has proved a popular range and it embraces many models.

WATCHES

BELOW: Seven times world Formula One motor racing champion Michael Schumacher and technician Ross Brawn, examine lap times on the TAG Heuer computer. Michael Schumacher also wears a TAG Heuer watch and the Ferrari Formula One team has a long relationship with the watch maker.

1990s – Outside the Boundaries

Other watchmakers continued to produce innovative designs, and in keeping with contemporary attitudes, sports watches were marketed for women. TAG Heuer introduced their 'Kirium' with a severe gold face and a chunky silver strap, aiming it at women. They claimed this new watch represented "the spirit of sport," and perhaps, hoped the dashing Formula One motor racing champion, Michael Schumacher and the Ferrari team he raced for would inspire their customers - he wore the Heuer brand and the timing equipment was TAG Heuer.

Gucci, who never relaxed in their pursuit of excellence and beauty, presented a heavy, gold square surrounding a black unnumbered face. The 'Classic Watch Collection' was launched by Mont Blanc, featuring automatic and quartz movements as well as a traditional manual-winding watch. Tommy Hilfiger was happy to make chic, sensible, and stylish watches for the men and women who bought his clothes and perfumes.

LEFT: The TAG Heuer SEL 1990 is a sports watch with a quirky design. The ornate metal curving recalls old-time cowboy spurs and boots but the complications include chronograph and date. And a woman could happily put this watch with its elaborate decoration on her wrist.

WATCHES

Ebel

A Swiss couple, Eugene and Alice Blum opened the Fabrique, Ebel, Blum et Cie (Ebel) in 1911 concentrating on ladies' and jewel watches. The company designed a crown to fit on the case back so as not to disturb the flow or aesthetics of their jewel watches. But they revealed an understanding of sturdy, accurate timepieces, leading to a British Royal Air Force commission in World War II. It took time for Ebel to acknowledge the growth in sports watches but then approached this market with gusto. In 2007, it allied with FC Arsenal, the English football club, making the 'Gunners' watch. It is also associated with Real Madrid, and for FC Bayern made an edition of the 'Classic Hexagon Chronograph' displaying the extra time granted during a football match. Ebel sports watches are characterized by a domed glass and curved hexagonal shape. The company is part of the American MGI Luxury Group.

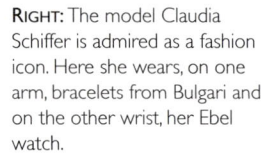

RIGHT: The model Claudia Schiffer is admired as a fashion icon. Here she wears, on one arm, bracelets from Bulgari and on the other wrist, her Ebel watch.

Ebel

LEFT: The French Arsenal Football club player Thierry Henry appears at the public announcement when the luxury Swiss watch brand, Ebel told the world that they were the official timing partner for Arsenal. The footballers and the watchmakers signed a five-year deal that allows Ebel to time reference critical moments of Arsenal football matches and display them on giant screens at the Arsenal Emirates stadium. Gisele Bundchen, a model is at Thierry's side.

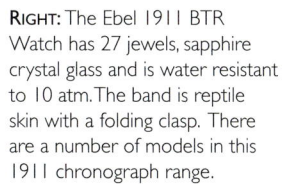

RIGHT: The Ebel 1911 BTR Watch has 27 jewels, sapphire crystal glass and is water resistant to 10 atm. The band is reptile skin with a folding clasp. There are a number of models in this 1911 chronograph range.

WATCHES

ABOVE: This advertisement emphasis the edgy design and acknowledges the designer Ettore Sotssass. This was unusual, but certainly designers deserve to be recognized.

RIGHT: Tissot long associated with fussy if sophisticated jewel watches or sleek sport watches delighted the market with this bold graphic design.

Professionals were tempted by the styling of the 'Metropolis' and 'Spirit' lines issued by Hugo Boss and advertised as suitable for men and women. The 'Lady J' from Breitling was for 'the sport-spirited' female.

1990s – Outside the Boundaries

LEFT: This workman-like Tiffany watch was bound to appeal to a professional woman. It would give the wearer an air of practicality combined with elegance and a no-nonsense attitude to her – and anyone else's – gender.

WATCHES

Left: The 'Kinetic' range from Seiko was given a chunky appearance, but it was decorative enough to appeal to women as well as men.

Seiko introduced their 'Kinetic' quartz watch powered by the movement of the wearer's wrist. Their advertisements announced the timepiece ran on carbohydrates and so advised their female customers not to forget to eat! The jewelry houses were not afraid to make watches that did not look like jewelry, although the Piaget 'Polo Mini' circled the dial with a lavish use of diamonds, and the strap was 18 karat gold.

1990s – Outside the Boundaries

Left: This company is daring in its designs. This brilliant arrangement recalls the dashboard of a motorbike or perhaps a flying machine. The watch is the 'Spartura' one of the Kinetic range.

WATCHES

Jaeger-LeCoultre

Antoin LeCoultre started a watchmaking business in 1833; his son, Elie took over in 1866 and, having housed all his workers under one roof, in 1870 installed factory machines. In 1903, Edmond Jaeger began working with the company. The two men were dedicated to making slim, small watches but the company's most famous design is the 'Reverso'. The Neuchatel Observatory gave an award in 1941 for the tourbillon 'Caliber 170'. The company registered as Jaeger-LeCoultre in 1937, but changes of ownership and confusion over US copyright, make it tricky to identify some mid-20th century models of its watches. In 2009, it presented the 'Master Grande Tradition', presenting a new combination of the tourbillon and perpetual calendar, and also the 'Hybris Mechanica a Grande Sonnerie', a watch with 26 complications. Both are masterpieces in their combination of high technology and traditional methods, and this company has a high status in luxury brands.

ABOVE: Antoine LeCoultre was an inventive man, and was awarded a gold medal for precision and mechanisation at the Universal Exhibition, London in 1851.

ABOVE: This is LeCoultre's first workshop at Le Sentier, Switzerland.

Jaeger-LeCoultre

Right: The most famous of Jaeger-LeCoultre's timepieces is the Reverso. This dainty version was made in 1933 and was intended for the company's female customers.

Left: This is a model of the Master Compressor Extreme Tourbillon. It displays the moon phases, weekdays and date as well as the usual time functions. The strap is reptile and there is a folding clasp. It represents the finesse and functionality typical of Jaeger-LeCoultre.

WATCHES

RIGHT: Winnie the Witch, a favourite character in contemporary children's literature, gives her mad grin as the head of her cat, Wilbur serves as a seconds hand. These cartoon watches are popular with children although grown-ups like wearing them to make a subversive, but fun statement.

1990s – Outside the Boundaries

The mass market sold watches in boxes of six, each with a different design and color scheme. Many of these sets sold for less than 20 dollars, or about 10 pounds. Images of cartoon characters, Bob Marley, Che Guevara, and similar famous folk decorated dials. The children's market was fully exploited, with large, friendly, and ever-more colorful products. Swatch had outlets everywhere. The quartz watch had become an everyday, disposable consumer item even as the 'logo' watch grew more expensive and elite.

ABOVE: When Swatch made this watch in 1997 it was the thinnest watch in the world – and perhaps also it had the most lurid color scheme.

ABOVE: This watch was aimed at the niche market of the religious Rastafarians who were followers of Haile Selassie, the late Emperor of Ethiopia. His cap, badge, and epaulettes make for a decorative display.

WATCHES

ABOVE: Junghans Mega wristwatch, introduced in 1990, was the world's first radio-controlled wristwatch. It was given an offbeat modernistic shape to complement its radical source of energy.

1990s – Outside the Boundaries

There remained one indication that some people continued to appreciate the traditions of craft watchmaking, and this was the ever-growing number of auctions offering classic mechanical watches. Aficionados knew to look for the lettering on the dial, the serial numbers, and the slightest change in size or line; counterfeits did not fool them, and prices for the genuine article began to reach giddy heights. But this was of little help to the watchmakers. Their market continued to be eroded by the black market in fraudulent products, and the counterfeits sullied the reputation of the real thing.

But the contemporary world is one of constant change, and the world of timekeeping is not exempt. Just as the pocket watch was made obsolete by the early 20th century wristwatch, so a new invention was to threaten the wearing of a watch. The cell phone, also known as the mobile phone appeared initially as a clumsy, brick-sized object but soon assumed a neat, pocket size that not only made phone calls but also gave the time in a continual digital display. Yet again, watchmakers faced a crisis in their industry, and the new century opened to a serious situation, demanding ingenuity and a cunning, persuasive approach to marketing techniques.

WATCHES

RIGHT: Inma Shara has already conducted some of the world's greatest orchestras. Sharing the same values, she and Vacheron Constantin do not exercise their art without exploring new horizons, challenging accepted standards, and continuous re-orchestration. One sublimates and deciphers time, the other transcends and interprets music, and both draw their raison d'être from surpassing themselves and being exceptional.

2000s
The Artistry of Time

Despite the high technology of horology, it remains a wonderful thing that a small, crafted object can hold, within itself, measures of the time, the calendar, the movement of planets and world time. The marketing departments understood this, and knew the great houses should not compete with plastic quartz watches or mobile telephones; instead, the crafting of luxury watches was promoted as something very close to 'High Art'.

WATCHES

Promotions allied the luxury watch with painting, photography, sculpture, and music, and the contemporary association of the arts and horology is now a major factor in bringing recognition to the value of the 'crafted' wristwatch. Cartier set up an annual art prize, the presentation being part of the highly prestigious Frieze Art Fair in London. Vacheron Constantin sponsors classical musicians, and like Jeager-LeCoultre, they present an annual photography award. In 2009, Swatch launched the CreArt collection with panache typical of the brand. In New York, street and installation artists, musicians, and poster designers gave a lively, noisy exhibition.

2000s – The Artistry of Time

Left: Singers Constantine Maroulis and Savannah Wise (on top) and the musician Joel Hoekstra, attend the Swatch CreArt Collection Launch Party in 2009 in New York City and display some of the new Swatch creations. Musicians, artists and the like gathered to see the work created by Billy the artist, who describes his work as urban primitive reality, a kaleidoscope of puzzle-like images that celebrate the diversity and joy of the human spirit.

WATCHES

2000s – The Artistry of Time

Luxury products are beyond the reach of the great majority. And in reality, the folk of this new century, rich or poor, are not inclined to brood on the old enigmas surrounding the movements of the sun, the seasons, and the moon, or the mystery of measuring time. Nowadays, the tracking of time is as commonplace as eating a sandwich. Millions own tiny telephones, carried in a pocket or purse, and showing accurate time in digital; inexpensive plastic watches, accurate in their timekeeping, continue to be sold, but as novelty items or to add color to an outfit.

LEFT: Attractive, easy to wear watches in a multitude of colours and shapes can often be purchased in markets as well as shops. They are a great extra that will brighten up any grey day. These watches are non-expensive and will last practically forever.

RIGHT: Simple shapes and simple electronics allow watches to be made in many different shapes and sizes. These particular ones come from a company in China, where they are turned out by their thousands.

WATCHES

As the columnist, Nick Foulkes observed, "They (watches) have in effect ceased to be timepieces and have become something that is part accessory, part fashion item." Young people may use their cell, or mobile phone when they check the time, but they continue to be fascinated by a grand watch worn by an artist or an athlete.

RIGHT: There is much discussion regarding watches and the mobile phone. It is true that the modern mobile phone will do everything a watch can do, but it doesn't have the charisma or the delicate details and beauty of an exquisitely made watch.

2000s – The Artistry of Time

BELOW: The face of Formula One is constantly changing and Oris' motor sports model has evolved with it. With its lightweight, pared down appearance the Oris Williams F1 Team Skeleton Engine Date is a high-tech piece of machinery, just like the team it sponsors. The movement and the design are pure Oris, the dynamic racing style pure Williams F1.

Sport heroes are perceived as inspirational, as they have been since Mercedes Gleitze swam the English Channel. Consequently, the designation 'sports watch' stimulated sales. The famous celebrity sportsmen wear luxury brands because they are status accessories; the timepieces are impressive in size and carry information such as global time and the calendar; they are waterproof and impervious to temperature change.

WATCHES

ABOVE: The pilots of the Breitling Jet Team are all extremely experienced professionals from the French air force, or the Patrouille de France. Trained to make precision-like movement at lightning speed, these pilots rely on their Breitling chronometer to keep them up to speed.

2000s – The Artistry of Time

ABOVE: The Breitling Jet Team is made up of six L-39C Albatros Czech-built twin-seater military trainers. These are no ordinary aircraft. They are decorated and styled with great care and attention. The tiniest of details is calculated and refined until it is perfected. Little wonder Breitling are happy to have their name on these aircraft.

WATCHES

LEFT: Citizen Eco-Drive Thermo watches were introduced in 1999 and use the temperature difference between the wearer's arm and the surrounding environment as a power source, so it should never need winding up. England batsman, Kevin Pietersen understands precision timing; a double century in the Ashes tour of 2010 demonstrated that.

2000s – The Artistry of Time

The watches are designed for robust activity but, actually, consumers (and players) are not prepared to risk their expensive sports watches on the football field, or while playing basketball.

Men feel a sports watch gives a fit, healthy aura; women want these watches because they signal youth and vitality.

Left: The Grand Seiko was born in 1960 and the goal that inspired its makers was never modest. They would create the best luxury watch in the world. Fifty years on, the watch has without doubt stood the test of time and although Seiko's watchmaking technology has evolved rapidly, the spirit and the essence of the Grand Seiko remains the same.

WATCHES

RIGHT: Victoria Beckham, wife of England footballer David, is caught during an outing in Los Angeles. Shading her face from the opportunist photographer, she seems unaware of showing off the 'bling' she has hanging from her wrist.

2000s – The Artistry of Time

Left: In 2010 Girard-Perregaux celebrated a double anniversary. Thirty-five years of its 'Laureato' collection and forty years since its first quartz watch was introduced. It was Gerard-Perrigeaux that set the decisive frequency of 32,768 Hz, since adopted by all manufacturers as the universal standard. The company has an extraordinary heritage, a part of which is celebrated by this commemorative model.

WATCHES

Ulysse Nardin

This company opened in 1846 in Le Locle, Switzerland and specialized in marine chronometers. It was successful in supplying these timepieces to merchant ships and naval services including the Japanese among their customers. The invention of quartz crystal and its high accuracy in chronometers scuppered the business. Rolf Schnyder and Ludwig Oechslin bought Ulysee Nardin in 1983. They retained the artisan employees and concentrated on watch making, and are proud of their 'Trilogy of Time' range. The first model that came out in 1985 was the 'Astrolabium Galileo Galilee' and was described as the world's 'most functional watch'. It shows local and solar time, as well as the orbits and ellipses of the Sun and the Moon. The second model in the Trilogy is the 'Planeterium Copernicus' and the third, 'Tellerium Johannes Kepler'. These names reveal the serious purpose of these complication watches. Ulysse Nardin remains in private hands, and is an elite watchmaker of superb timepieces.

RIGHT: Genghis Khan by Ulysse-Nardin - The first ever Westminster Carillon Tourbillon Jaquemarts Minute repeater. The visible one minute Tourbillon is integrated into the black onyx watch dial. The Westminster has four gongs, each with a different tone (Mi-Do-Re-Sol). All four gongs sound in three different sequences for the quarters. The figures on the black onyx dial are hand-carved in 18 ct gold.

LEFT: Ulysse-Nardin has been dedicated to excellence for over 164 years in manufacturing mechanical watches. This is their headquarters in Le Locle, Switzerland.

Ulysse Nardin

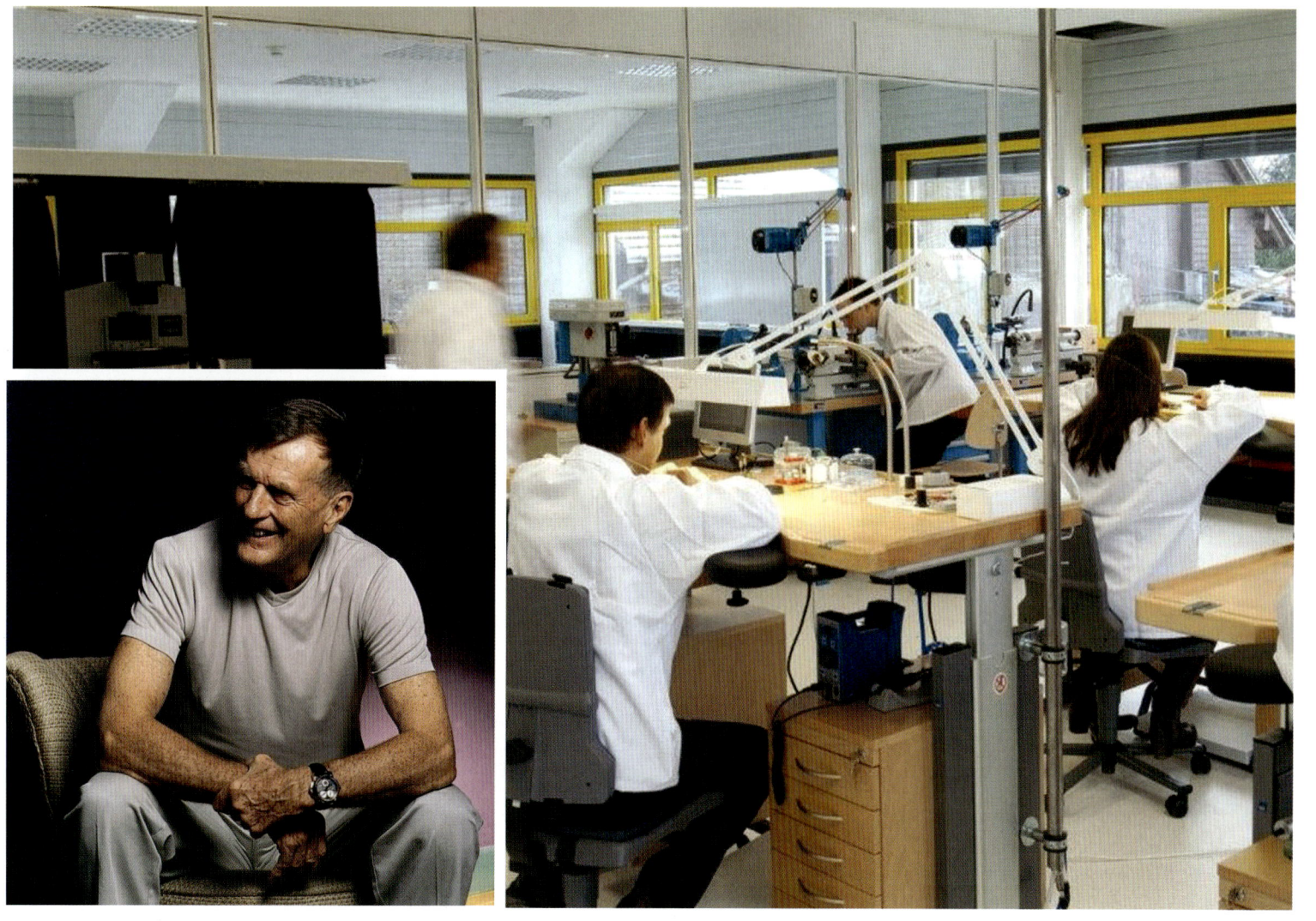

LEFT: Since the manufacturer's earliest days more than 160 years ago when its founder, Ulysse-Nardin, began making marine chronometers in a mountainous location in Neuchâtel, Switzerland, the watchmaking powerhouse has continually proved that challenges present intriguing opportunities worthy of exploration. This is the current Ulysses-Nardin workshop in Le Locle.

INSET: Behind the exceptional brand of Ulysse-Nardin is Rolf W Schnyder, a Swiss with over 40 years of experience in various aspects of wristwatch production. He describes himself as a businessman with a lot of creative feelings and maintains that Ulysse-Nardin is not a fashion brand.

265

WATCHES

The 'J12', from the house of Chanel, formerly sold as a practical looking woman's sports watch now appears in pink gold, its figures and complication dials prettily arranged on the main dial. This is not a watch to wear on the tennis court. But women like the designation of the watch, knowing that the beautiful Wimbledon champion, Maria Sharapova wears a sports watch, the 'Ladies' Carrera' from TAG Heuer. Another female icon is Ellen MacArthur, who sailed solo around the world, has a sports watch, the Omega 'Seamaster Aqua Terra.'

Right: Maria Yuryevna Sharapova, a former world number one professional tennis player, serves in a match against Kimiko Date Krumm of Japan at the Toray Pan Pacific Open in 2010.

2000s – The Artistry of Time

LEFT: Sharapova's tennis success and appearance have enabled her to secure commercial endorsements that greatly exceed the value of her tournament winnings, including being an ambassador for TAG Heuer.

267

WATCHES

Many great athletes of the world wear sports watches: The Formula 1, McLaren drivers Jensen Button and Lewis Hamilton wear TAG Heuer watches. The French footballer, Zinedine Zidane, owns a special edition Ingenieur Automatic Edition; the Chelsea player, Didier Drogba, swans around with an Audemars Piguet 'Royal Oak' – it is customized with over 450 diamonds. Few can aspire to this level of exclusivity, but many will yearn to imitate the sports heroes by owning a heavy, impressive complications watch.

RIGHT: Jenson Button finds a moment of relaxation. On his wrist is his trusty TAG Heuer Silverstone chronograph, named after the race circuit of the same name. The circuit has a special place in TAG Heuers' heart because many of its racing ambassadors and F1 team partners have scored career-making victories there. From Emmanuel de Graffenried, the very first ambassador in 1949, to the 2009 World Formula One champion Jenson Button.

2000s – The Artistry of Time

Left: Design has always been an essential component of TAG Heuer DNA, but the company has become the world leader of prestigious sports watches and chronographs by breaking its rules and challenging its conventions. The Silverstone's distinctive and vintage design – a squared case with rounded edges in polished stainless steel – was based on another breakout timepiece of the period, Steve McQueen's 1969 Monaco. Softer edged, graced with a colourful dial, totally new shape, and fully loaded with leading-edge chronograph functionality, the Silverstone is one of TAG Heuer's purest designs and most emblematic creations ever.

WATCHES

Right: The 'Carrera Panamericana' was an epic race that was started in the 1950s and attracted many of the leading drivers of the time. Juan Manuel Fangio, the famous Argentinian driver who was Formula 1 World Champion five times, won the race in 1953. To pay tribute to this unique adventure, in 1964 TAG Heuer launched the Carrera Chronograph that combined refinement with the spirit of sport. It was an immediate success. It has been modernised but still retains its sober elegance. The Carrera perfectly embodies the vibrant memory of the era of 'Gentleman drivers'.

Above: Lewis Hamilton, 2008 Formula One world champion, shows off his TAG Heuer Carrera Calibre 1887 Chronograph, which comes with Black or silver dial with 3 counters and 5-row alternate fine-brushed and polished steel bracelet.

2000s – The Artistry of Time

LEFT: From the Olympic Games in the 1920s to its role as official timekeeper to within 1/10,000th of a second for the legendary Indy 500 car race, TAG Heuer, in a constant quest for innovation, excellence, performance and prestige, continues to aim ever higher. This is reflected in its quarter-century partnership with F1 team Vodafone McLaren Mercedes, its 7-year partnership with 2008 Formula 1 World Champion, Vodafone McLaren Mercedes driver Lewis Hamilton, and his new teammate, 2009 Formula One World Champion Jenson Button. Both drivers have reached the pinnacle of their sport by becoming world champions.

271

WATCHES

RIGHT: Dedicated to the automobile world, the Breitling for Bentley line unites the best of two worlds - elegance and expertise; British chic and Swiss tradition. Embodying the perfect combination of technique and aesthetics, it is designed to appeal to connoisseurs and to all those with a love of rare and exclusive watches. Beautiful motors encased in beautiful bodywork.

Watchmakers widened their promotions from individual celebrities and began to ally themselves with an entire club, major event or another luxury brand. Breitling is partnered with the manufacturers of the Bentley car; with this twinning, they imply the consumer should own both luxury products. Ebel launched the 1911 Tekton Real Madrid in association with the famed football club. This partnership persuades fans that both brands are very important in the world of football. These and similar twin-branded watches are sold through superior outlets such as Harrods in London, Saks Fifth Avenue, New York, and boutiques in expensive malls across the world.

2000s – The Artistry of Time

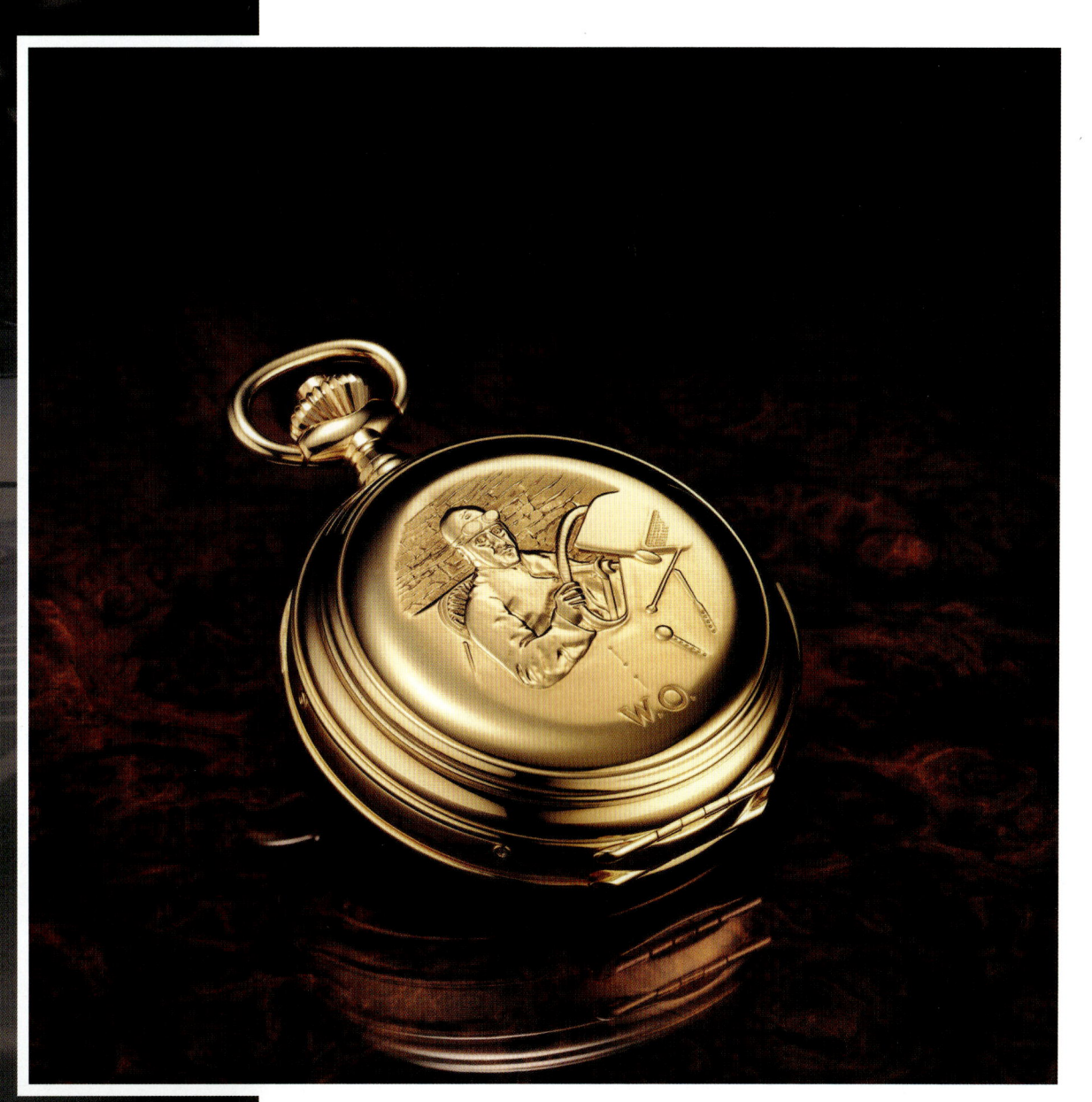

Left: The Breitling for Bentley collection welcomed a new one-of-a-kind model in 2010, dedicated to the founder of the prestigious British car manufacturer. The 2010 Bentley Masterpiece is a pocket-watch combining two of the most sophisticated complications in the horological repertoire - a perpetual calendar (displaying the date, day, month, leap years and moon phases) that takes account of the quadrennial occurrence of February 29th, and a minute repeater striking the hours, quarters and minutes on demand. In tribute to Walter Owen Bentley, the cover of the 18-carat yellow gold case is adorned with an engraving depicting him at the wheel of one of his racing models, accompanied by the famous 'W O' initials.

WATCHES

RIGHT: To celebrate Bentley's autumn 2010 launch of their new Continental GT, Breitling for Bentley issued an exclusive version of its Bentley GMT chronograph in a 1,000-piece worldwide edition. This limited series is distinguished by its inner bezel and rubber strap clad in the famous British Racing Green colour, characteristic of the finest English racing cars. Equipped with an ingenious multiple timezone display system, it proudly serves as an international ambassador of the time-honoured British automobile tradition.

RIGHT: The case of the special edition Bentley GMT chronograph is made of steel. It is water-resistant to 100 metres and has a screw-locked crown, rotating pinion bezel with British Racing Green inner ring carrying the 24-city timezone scale. Cambered sapphire crystal, glareproofed on both sides and has personalisation marks on the rear.

2000s – The Artistry of Time

RIGHT: The dashboard of the Bentley coupe, showing the Breitling clock beautifully fitted into the polished, wood-finished instrument panel.

WATCHES

RIGHT: Nicole Kidman has been an ambassador for Omega since 2005. Here she is putting her name to a 2010 constellation model. The dial is surrounded with white mother of pearl diamonds and the case is of yellow gold, in which there is a quartz precision movement.

NICOLE KIDMAN. MY CHOICE.

Ω OMEGA

2000s – The Artistry of Time

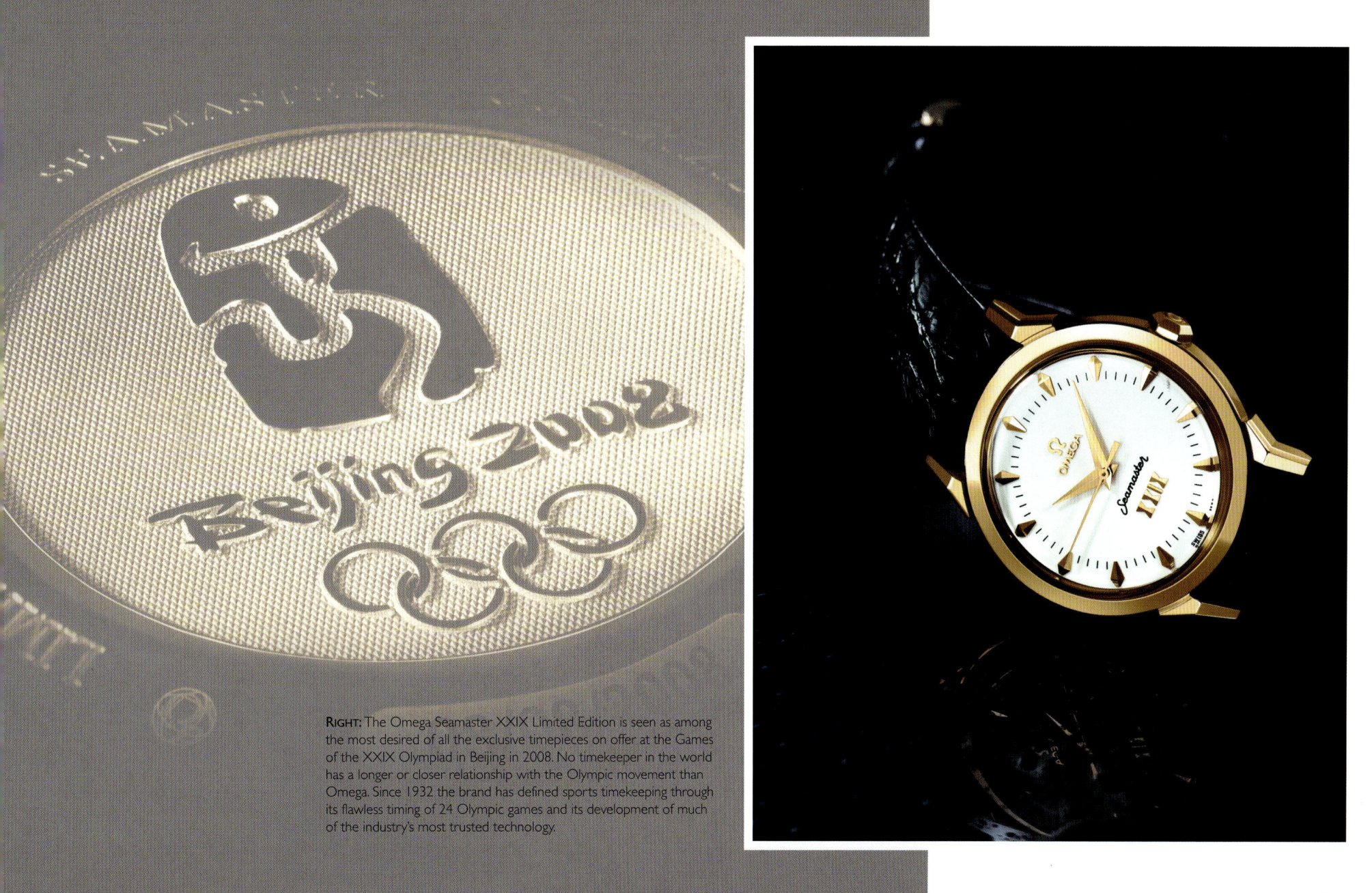

RIGHT: The Omega Seamaster XXIX Limited Edition is seen as among the most desired of all the exclusive timepieces on offer at the Games of the XXIX Olympiad in Beijing in 2008. No timekeeper in the world has a longer or closer relationship with the Olympic movement than Omega. Since 1932 the brand has defined sports timekeeping through its flawless timing of 24 Olympic games and its development of much of the industry's most trusted technology.

WATCHES

Right: Van Cleef & Arpels has also introduced a system where the owner can decide on which strap they would like to wear with their 'charms' timepiece. With this new creation, that is both charming and delightful, Van Cleef & Arpels have shown that a delicate and refined timepiece also allows a hint of mischief. Interchangeable straps allow the owner to decide on different colors that might suit their mood, their outfit or inspiration for the day.

Right: Van Cleef & Arpels explain that their 'Charms' collection, find their roots in the verb 'to charm', which means to attract or to seduce. These charming talismans, which flourish on their timepieces, are a reminder of the ancient amulets, trinkets and good-luck pendants whose existence date back to the dawn of time. Their beauty and exquisite finish is enough to seduce any woman.

2000s – The artistry of time

Of course, women's love of jewelry ensured the supply of exquisite timepieces. Van Cleef & Arpels designed the 'Charms Mini Watch'. It has a diamond-studded charm attached to the pink gold case set with three rows of diamonds. Patek Philippe made a minimalist design in steel, and lined with diamonds. Bulgari produced a gold snake bracelet, the watch forming the reptile's 'head'.

ABOVE: Watch and jewelry making unite in perfect harmony to produce a new version of the Van Cleef & Arpels Alhambra timepiece. The marriage of white mother-of-pearl, naturally grey mother-of-pearl and onyx, confer an ever changing iridescence upon the timepiece. A Swiss quartz movement ensures the smooth rotation of the two polished and brushed Dauphine hands, which circulate elegantly around the mother-of-pearl dial.

WATCHES

BELOW: The Ball company is one of the most respected and established watch brands in the United States. Their history is of precision and robust accuracy of time, and nothing has changed. The new Engineer Hydrocarbon Spacemaster timepiece is shock resistant to withstand a 7,500Gs shock test and is water resistant to 333m.

2000s – The Artistry of Time

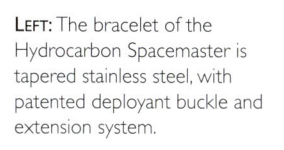

Left: The bracelet of the Hydrocarbon Spacemaster is tapered stainless steel, with patented deployant buckle and extension system.

Right: The movement of this chronometer is enclosed within a stainless steel case, which has a luminous, unidirectional rotating bezel. The dial also has a night-reading capability.

These luxury watches are marketed as 'heritage' pieces and the Ball Company issued a watch with authentic historic associations. Their 'Engineer Hydrocarbon Spacemaster' is a refinement of their railway pocket watches, made to meet demanding standards set by the US government in the 19th century. This new model was tested in the world's first private manned spacecraft, and has self-powered micro gaslights on the hands and dial; the lock resists powerful pressure and is virtually unbreakable.

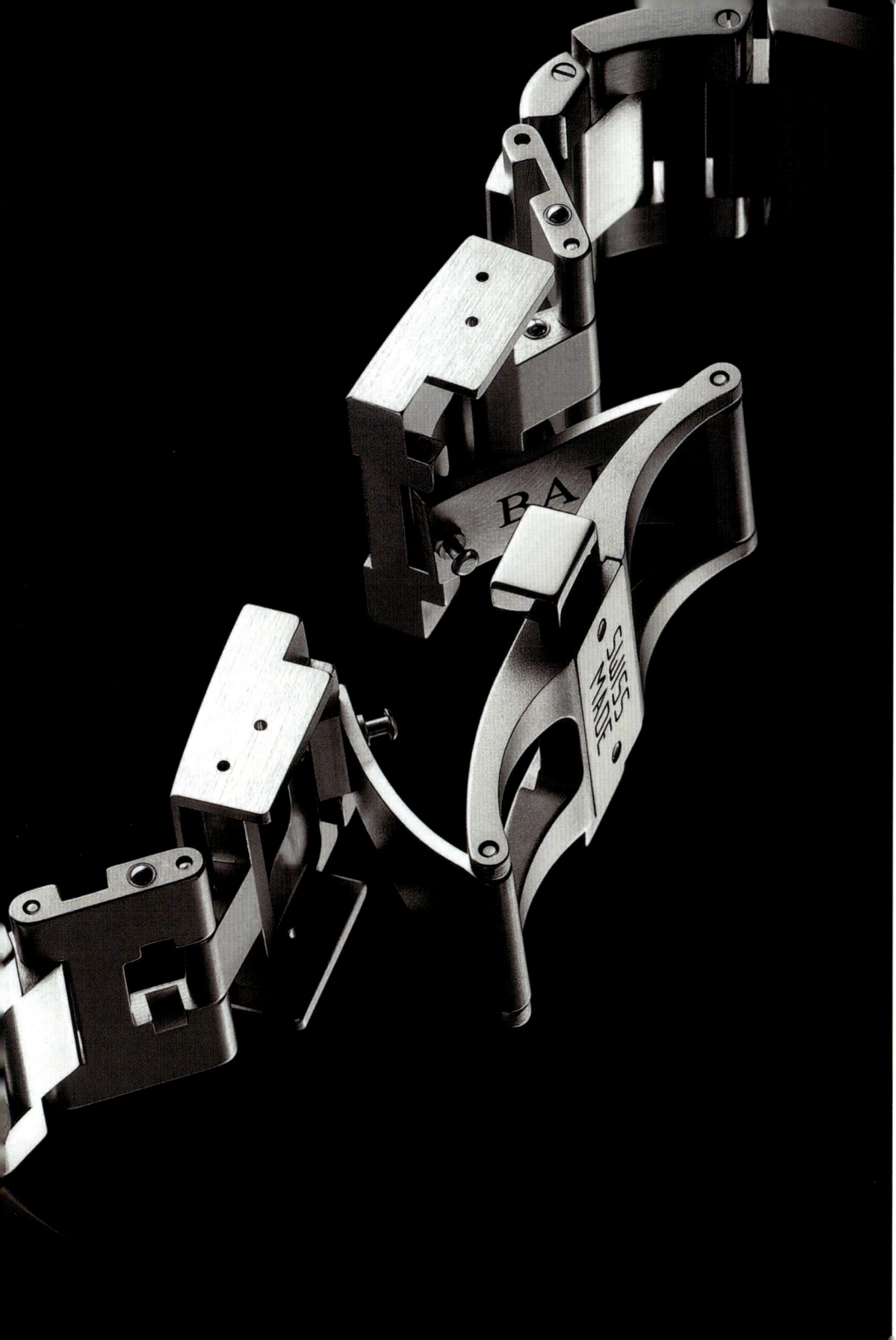

WATCHES

Accurist

This independent English watch company weathered all the trade problems of the 20th century, and is now a major supplier. Asher and Rebecca Loftus opened in London in 1946, importing mechanisms from Switzerland. In the 1960s, Accurist sensed the growing perception of the wristwatch as an accessory, and issued the 'Old England' range, worn by contemporary celebrities such as the Beatles and Twiggy. It became officially associated with the Greenwich Observatory in the 1990s and were timekeepers for the Millennium celebrations, 2000. In the new century, Accurist counts its 'Bling' jewel watches as a success, as is the 'Charmed' series that supplies different straps of Swarovski bead crystals to change the look of its watch with a mother-of-pearl face. It designed for the Football Association, issuing limited editions of the Sports Chronograph bearing the FA crest. Accurist has won many awards, and works out of Switzerland and London. In 2010 the Chief Executive is Andrew Loftus.

ABOVE: The Accurist 2010 'Pretty in Pink' ladies silver plated charmed watch, has an elegant mother-of-pearl dial and decorative Swarovski crystal set bezel. The watch also includes all the beads and stoppers that can be seen.

Accurist

LEFT: The 2010 collection of men's watches from Accurist include this chronograph, with stainless steel bracelet and case. It is water resistant to 100m and comes in a selection of colors.

ABOVE: In 1998 Accurist launched its innovative 'Put some weight on' campaign to promote its range of solid silver watches. The campaign set about highlighting the fashion industry vogue of using unnaturally thin models, stimulating public debate about the danger of using such images.

WATCHES

LEFT: Model Melania Trump, attends the 250th anniversary celebrations for the luxury watch brand Vacheron Constantin, in New York City. Melania Trump was the hostess of the evening at the New York Public Library and is showing a stunning Kallista watch from the company.

2000s – The Artistry of Time

LEFT: The Manufactory, Vacheron Constantin, presented a unique, exceptional and fabulous watch, called Kallista, which in Greek means 'the most beautiful'. Its creation and realization was the achievement of several talented artists, among others the painter Raymond Moretti. Many challenges had to be overcome to select the 118 emerald-cut brilliants between 1, 2 and 4 carats (130 carats), matching perfectly and dressing the bracelet, the dial and the back of the case.

WATCHES

However, Chopard nursed a revolutionary design. The company commissioned, the designer, Alberta Ferretti who presented the concept of a watch not attached to a strap, but to fabric twisted like a small scarf around the wrist. The watch of precious metals and gems seems to be casually tucked into the fabric's folds. The 'scarf' can be changed to match the wearer's dress. (These are not yet in major production.)

Left: The DolceVita collection by Longines, melds the neat, trim lines of the 1930s with the glamorous 1950s. This stylish timepiece expresses enjoyment of life in the finest Italian spirit, with its inspired refinement and unique way with style. The results are delightfully inventive, an unfailingly stylish collection called Longines DolceVita.

Chopard
ALBERTA FERRETTI

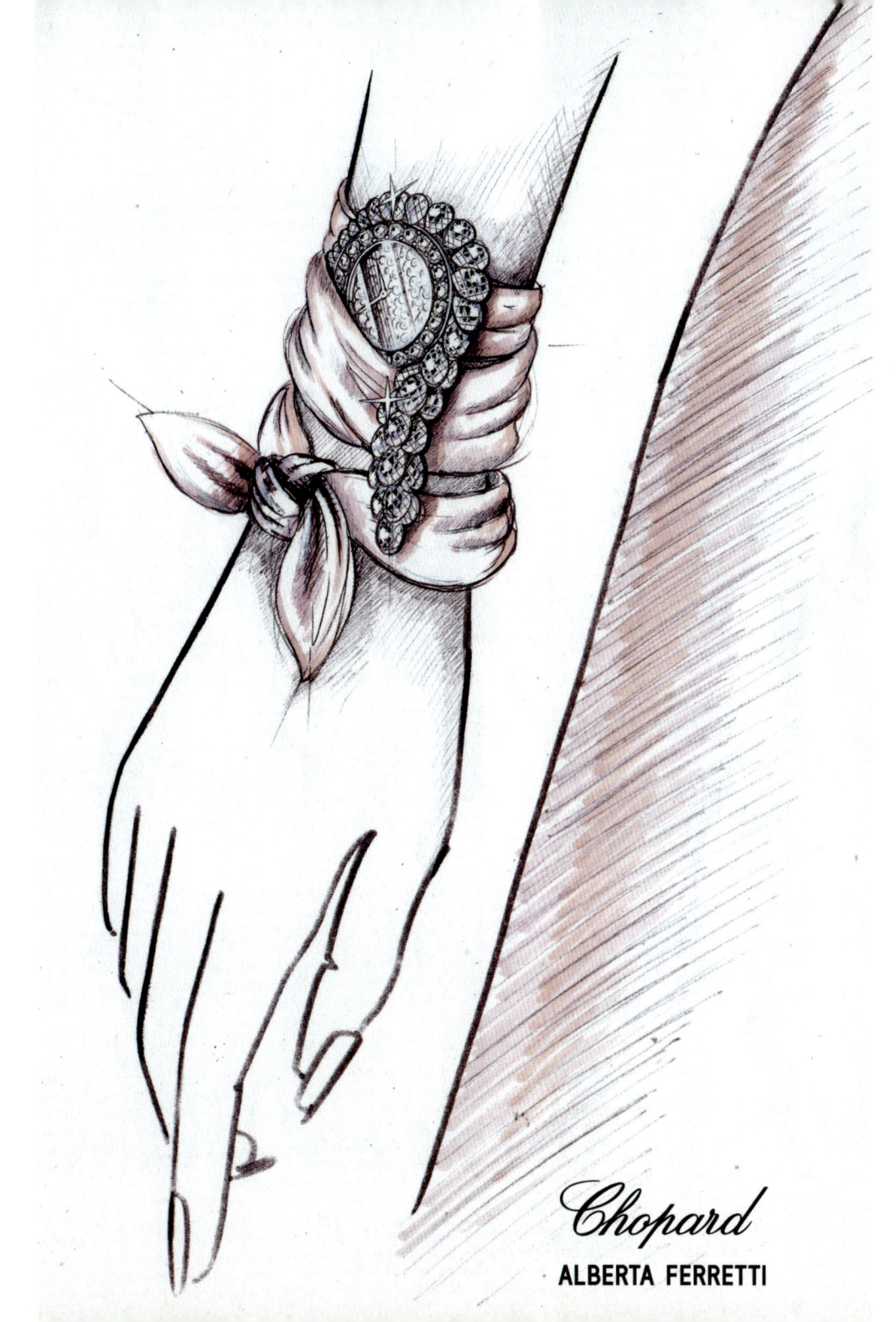

Left: From the very concrete feminine sensibilities of Alberta Ferretti and Caroline Gruosi-Scheufele, a new kind of watch is born. Precious, unmistakable, custom-made, it is the first version of a new expression of glamour, the 'WatchCouture'. This unique watch is entirely made of white gold and diamonds, embellished by delicate briolette cut diamonds and tied to the wrist by a skin pink satin bow. (At the time of writing this watch is not yet on the market).

WATCHES

ABOVE: This is no ordinary Rolex Milgauss, look closely and you will see the name Bamford, discretely marked at the bottom of the watch face. This is one of many watches that have been personalised for its owner by Bamford Watch Department of London.

RIGHT: One person that did have a watch uniquely personalized by Bamford was Jennifer Aniston. She can be seen, together with Owen Wilson, wearing her Milgauss in this promotional picture taken for the film *'Marley and me'*.

2000s – The Artistry of Time

Then the watchmakers found other ways of pleasing keen horologists: the customized watch, or the limited edition of a particular model. There is an old story that, many years ago, the South African Army asked Rolex to darken the dials on some of their watches so the glass would not reflect the sun. (Rolex declined the offer.) A luxury goods shop in London, Bamford and Sons, were inspired by this tale. Could they make changes to watches, and thus personalize them for their customers? Now, Bamford will customize the watches they retail, changing the dials, numerals and dates, or altering colors to suit individual taste. One client asked for a color to match that of his luxury car.

LEFT: Each watch created by the Bamford Watch Department can be unique to the specific request of the client. The Bamford website gives the possibility of personalising your watch but it would probably be better if you made a visit to their shop in London, England.

WATCHES

Right: Ulysse-Nardin introduces the San Marco Cloisonné collection. The HMS Victory was constructed in 1759 and is the only surviving naval warship that represents the skill of naval dockyard shipwrights, ship designers and the industrial power of Britain during the mid 18th century. A miniature reproduction of the ship adorns the enamel cloisonné dial of the San Marco Chronometer. The Victory is available in a limited edition of 30 pieces each in 18 ct rose gold and platinum.

2000s – The Artistry of Time

Ralph Lauren issued a limited edition of his famous 'Stirrup' watch in platinum, each model engraved with its own number and having an enamel dial.

The consumers' search for the elite, even unique timepiece revived that almost forgotten craft, that of the enamelist. An elderly and great miniature enamel painter, Carlo Poluzzi, introduced a young enamelist, Suzanne Rohr to Patek Philippe who were excited by the possibilities this craft offered. Ulysse Nardin coaxed an old master, Michel Vermot, to return to work and so, the trend for this distinctive decoration began. Now, all the major houses have enameled watches as part of their repertoire.

Designs may be a copy of an Old Master painting, a map, flowers, a horse or an abstract image. The artist, Vanessa Lecci, widely celebrated as a master of the art, prefers to give a unique decoration to each watch, and avoids working on a series if she can. Whether one original, or a limited series, the work is slow and demands the concentrated efforts of a skilled craftsman, but these decorative products are highly valued, and consequently highly priced for the luxury market – and very difficult to counterfeit.

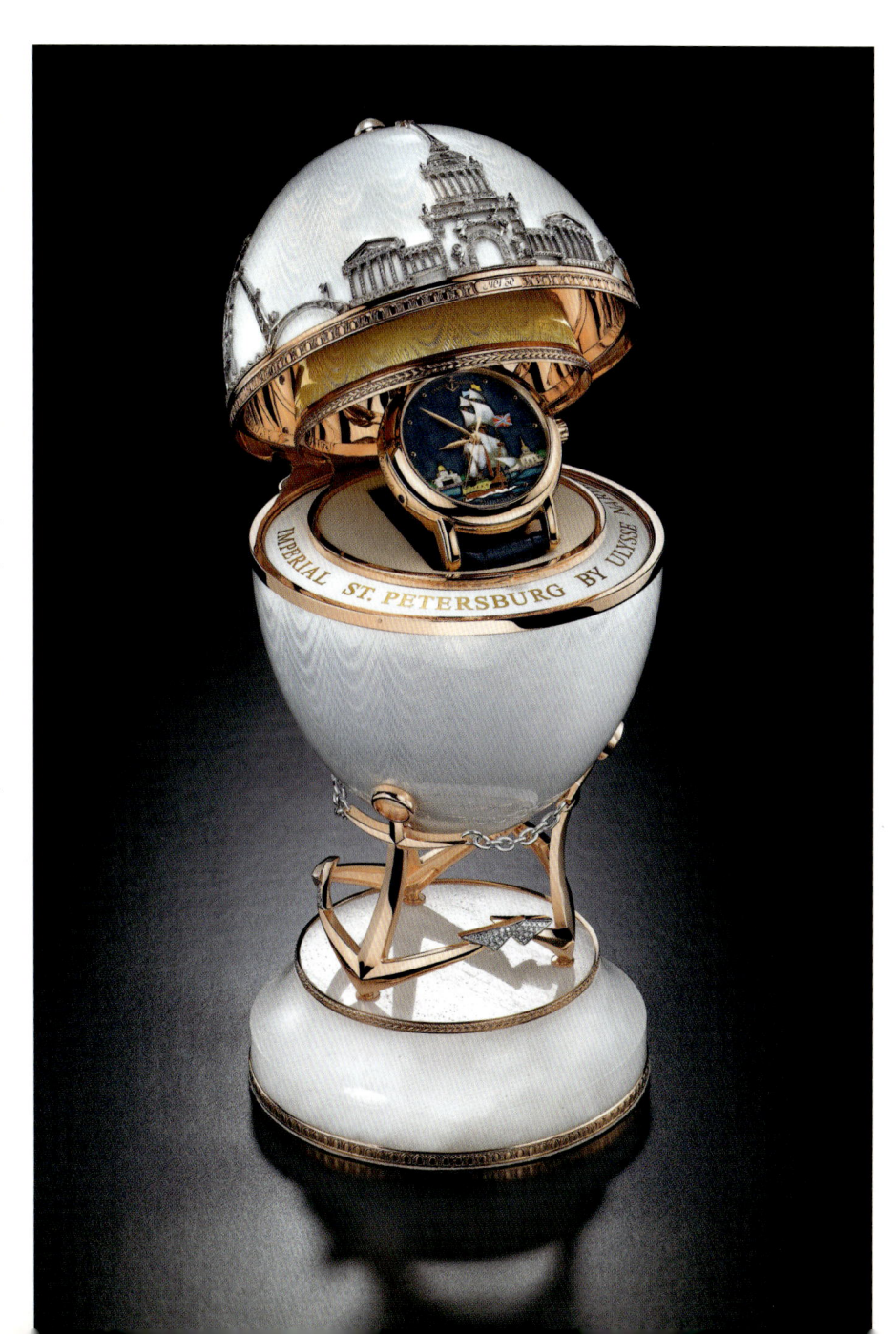

LEFT: The Ulysee-Nardin Imperial St. Petersburg is presented in an elaborate multi-layer white translucent enamel Egg of the Tsars, decorated with 4.25 carats of diamonds. The diamonds have been employed in recreating legendary symbols of St. Petersburg. Ulysse-Nardin's anchor serves to link the egg to the white marble base.

WATCHES

Roger W Smith

Roger W Smith was born in Manchester, England in 1970. At the age of 16, his father enrolled him on a course at the Manchester School of Horology. Roger was hooked from day one, and passed out top of his class, winning the British Horological Institute's Bronze medal. During this time, Dr. George Daniels, a man who is widely regarded as the greatest living horologist, was a visiting speaker, and from that moment Roger knew that he wanted to make watches.

Using Dr. Daniel's book 'Watchmaking' he set about making his first pocket watch in his spare time in his bedroom at home. Two years later, Roger took the watch to Dr. Daniels, who told him to go back and start again because it looked 'handmade', not 'created'. Not deterred, Roger returned to his bedroom, and spent the next 5 years refining his pocket watch, which he took back to Dr. Daniels. After close examination, it passed the test and shortly afterwards, Dr. Daniels invited Roger to work with him on the now legendary 'Daniels Millenium' series.

Roger set up his own workshop in the Isle of Man, and produced his 'Series 1', a series of 9 rectangular cased watches fitted with a retrograde calendar complication. He then turned to creating his own handmade production wristwatch. The Series 2 was launched in February 2006. Almost all of the watch's 225 parts were created in the R W Smith workshop, including the most technically advanced escapement in 250 years – the Daniels co-axial.

Roger is now collaborating with Dr. Daniels to produce a Series of 35 wristwatches, to commemorate his invention of the Co-axial escapement. The prototype is currently in progress, with the first watches expected to be launched in 2011.

LEFT: Roger W Smith series 2 wristwatches are made to the same exacting standards expected of a commissioned watch. All watches are fitted with the Daniels co-axial escapement, the first production English watch to do so.

…

Roger W Smith

Left: The delicacy that can be created when working by hand is remarkable, so it is no surprise that the true collectors and connoisseurs have long known the attention to detail that is to be found in a hand made creation.

Right: This 18 carat gold, 42mm cased wristwatch, displays a Grand Date aperture at the 9 o'clock position with minutes, hours and seconds with 18 carat red gold hands. The manually wound mechanism is fitted with a one minute 'flying' tourbillion containing the Daniels co-axial escapement.

Right: All watches are beautifully finished, right down to the R W Smith name placed on the gold buckle.

WATCHES

RIGHT: The Van Cleef & Arpels 'Midnight in Paris' timepiece adds a new dimension of reverie and poetry to mechanical complications. Stars rest on a midnight blue, aventurine dial. The calendar at the back of the pink gold case is set with genuine meteorite, and the movement ensures the barely-perceptible rotation of the stars disc plate over a cycle of 365 days.

2000s – The Artistry of Time

Left: The OMEGA 'Ladymatic' reintroduces a name from the storied brand's illustrious past. Originally launched in 1955 and continuing for the better part of a generation, the 'Ladymatic' wristwatch line defined feminine grace and elegance in another era. These are timepieces that have been created to address women's desire to own wristwatches that make profound fashion statements but which are also equipped with the best series-production mechanical watch movements in the world.

WATCHES

Right: This Oris special edition timepiece is for lovers of the good life. Everything about this homage watch is pure luxury, from the rose-gold case, numerals, and indices to the black guilloche dial, the sapphire crystal to the dark-blue stingray leather strap. Individually numbered and certified as a chronometer, the watch also has an engraving of Sinatra on the case back.

2000s – The Artistry of Time

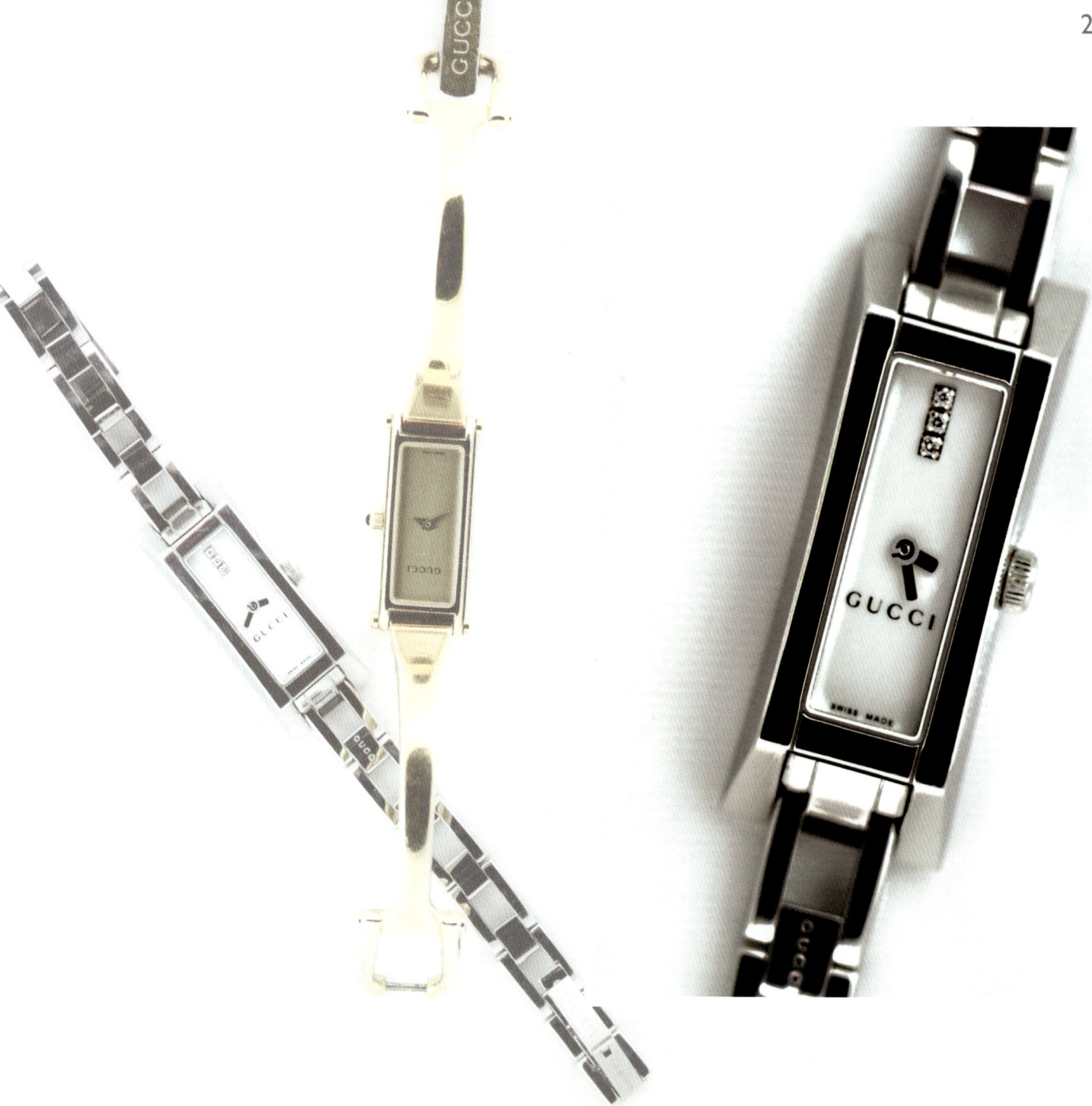

Left: When it comes to designer watches, there is nothing more luxurious than a Gucci women's watch. Breathtaking women's watches shine with diamonds and sparkle with a lustrous gold and platinum finish.

297

WATCHES

RIGHT: In reinterpreting the historical model designed in 1972, Vacheron Constantin is offering today's women, always on the lookout for a rare, precious and exclusive object, renewed proof of its attachment to ladies' collections. The current 1972 Cambrée is crafted in 18-carat white or pink gold, clothing a smaller and exquisitely cambered case.

298

2000s – The Artistry of Time

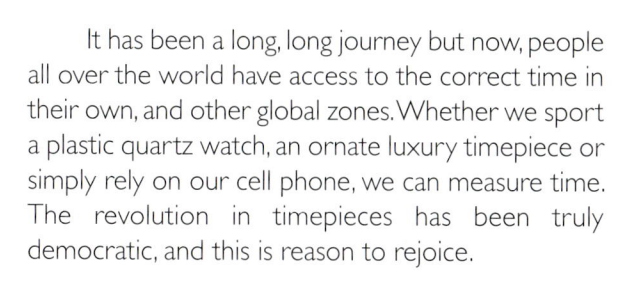

It has been a long, long journey but now, people all over the world have access to the correct time in their own, and other global zones. Whether we sport a plastic quartz watch, an ornate luxury timepiece or simply rely on our cell phone, we can measure time. The revolution in timepieces has been truly democratic, and this is reason to rejoice.

LEFT: The Patek Philippe Ref. 5951P shown at Baselworld 2010, was the thinnest split-seconds monopusher chronograph ever made with a perpetual calendar. Right down to its hand-stitched alligator strap with platinum prong buckle, this timepiece is a show window on a magnificent movement. It reveals many hand-finished components, the elaborate rattrapante mechanism, and the rhythmic beat of the Gyromax balance wheel. It is a sight that will never bore the true watch enthusiast even though the ballet repeats itself infinitely.

WATCHES

Novelty Watches
In Disguise

LEFT: This ostrich-feathered fan represents the style of the wealthy industrial classes of the mid-Victorian era. This preposterous object is decorated with gold, diamonds and enamel and is shown here with its hinged central section lifted, thus revealing a watch, an incongruous attachment on this showy design. The watch movement is signed 'G & O', possibly for Gogel & Olivet of Geneva, and the fan is kept in the Patek Philippe Museum, Geneva.

As has already been mentioned, the first watches were given a fanfare introduction as timepieces that could "be carried in the bosom or in the purse." The invention attracted craftsmen and jewelers who worked closely with horologists decorating clocks; now they rushed to create interesting watches and cases. Thus their artistic inventiveness has long been associated with watches, leading to some extravagant, even bizarre, designs and embellishments.

In the 17th century watches were encased in wonderful novelty silver skulls, grizzly reminders of time moving inexorably towards death. Some pocket watches were enclosed in respectable cases that opened to reveal a dial painted with naughty little images of loving couples – although such designs were not freely available but supplied privately.

WATCHES

The Victorians, fond of ornate and sentimental design, produced many novelty watches. For instance, they favored a brooch of a silver dog's head, its jaws clamped around the straps of a metal handbag, the watch fitted on its center while another brooch is a finely wrought gold griffin with a hook on the side from which to hang a small watch. A close look at enameled brooches painted with country scenes reveals a watch fitted onto a church tower, or stuck on the front of a gaily-colored steam locomotive. Heavily decorated pendants concealing a watch were also popular.

The 20th century produced some quirky designs. In the 1930s a pendant formed as a little tennis racquet, patterned in black, green, and white enamel had a watch centered on the strings. The mid-20th century designer, Sarah Coventry, made a spotted beetle of silver. The wings opened sideways to reveal the watch. The US jeweler, Tiffany and Co made a slim pen, its shape a long rectangle rather than the conventional cylinder and, at the opposite end from the nib, a neat watch was fit on one surface. Other American designers made walking canes, the gilded tops of which could be unscrewed to expose a watch. And a Japanese craftsman had the ingenuity to fit a watch onto a netsuke, the ornamental fastening used in traditional Japanese clothing.

There was an odd development in the early 20th century when cameras were disguised as watches. They were marketed as 'detective watches'. Then the 1950s saw a flurry of watches designed not for the wrist or pocket but to be fixed onto another accessory. A leather cigarette case from Lederer carried a watch on its outer covering, while Boucherer adorned a gold cigarette lighter with a small watch.

LEFT: It seems certain artists can't resist certain subjects even on a tiny canvas such as a watch face. This 18th century fob watch is one example with its decoration of erotic scenes. Such timepieces were circulated privately, and no doubt shown in gentlemen's clubs. Similar designs can be found in watches of the 21st century but even in these enlightened times, are not flaunted in public.

LEFT: A jeweled panther appears to be crouching over the timepiece as if over prey. The bangle is made by Cartier who, of course, has made the exotic panther its trademark design and even its latest jewel watches, dated 2010, use the panther as an emblem obscuring the timepiece.

Novelty Watches – In Disguise

Rings as timepieces are a real challenge to jewelers who have to add a functional element to a pretty, small jewel. Many watch rings from all ages have a hinged lid to hide the watch. The Georgians wore chunky arrangements with domed, hinged covers to hide the watch, or large enameled surfaces to carry the timepiece. In the Edwardian era many rings made a bold display to detract from the watch, encircling it with seed pearls or small diamonds, or fitting it into an elaborate marquisette setting. Ring watches, made of brightly colored plastic, or richly set with precious gems remain popular with modern customers.

The technology and synthetic fabrics of the late 20th century, and early 21st century have given designers great scope for imaginative, novelty timepieces. High street shops retail earrings with very small watches fitted into a floral design, or pendants shaped like insects, flowers, or hearts but hiding a watch; necklaces dangle a jumbled mixture of charms, beads, and tiny watches. Long neck chains with huge links are held by a key or lock that is a watch. However, a 19th century watch matches this quirkiness: a jeweled, enameled double-barreled pistol has a little watch on its handle and a chirping bird sits on the barrel. It can be seen in the Patek Philippe Museum, Geneva.

ABOVE: Artisans have always been tempted to stretch their work beyond the obvious. This beautiful jeweled watch pistol with a singing bird reveals talented craftsmanship; the timepiece is merely an excuse for creative activity. It was made for the Chinese market. The watch movement is from Les Freres Rochat, Geneva c1810-1815. It is a rich piece of gold, enamel, pearls, and agate and can be seen in the Patek Philippe Museum, Geneva.

LEFT: In the early 19th century watchmakers showed ingenuity in making tiny jewel watches. In 1835, Breguet created a gold ring watch with an alarm. The ring shown here is of the 'navette' shape. The two dials are given an ornamental value, but one shows hours and minutes and the other tells the seconds.

ABOVE: Perhaps this is a novelty design that cannot be bettered. Decorated with gold, enamel, and pearls, it is a fruit knife. It has two blades but incorporated into the handle is music, a magnifying glass, and a watch! The movement is attributed to Piguet & Capt, active in Geneva, c 1810.

303

WATCHES

Michelle Ong of Carnet

Michelle Ong, Co-founder and Creative Head of Carnet, is a jeweler of great distinction who caters for an elite market. Her remarkable creations have been described as "wearable art", and the merit of her watches lie in the beauty of each piece. Ms Ong's designs are most often one-of-a kind. She showcases her work across the world and has a primary Carnet boutique in Hong Kong. Her work has been featured at the Museum of Natural History in London and the Burrell Collection in Scotland. Ms Ong has an eye for detail and an appreciation of natural form so designs of plants, shells, clouds, and animals are some reoccurring motifs. Her timepieces are encased in richly colored gems and diamonds, and the watch itself is often part of a bejeweled cuff or an intricate and fluid bracelet.

RIGHT: Michelle Ong refuses to follow fashion but designs her jewel watches as objects with lasting value and significance. She devotes much time to exploratory sketches and searching for the gems that will suit each client. Her work over the past 20 years confirms her reputation as an original designer of jewelry and watches.

Michelle Ong of Carnet

ABOVE: Ong concentrates on the beauty of the gems. These are used to fashion a posy of flowers with a diamond heart. The delicate hands moving across the diamond surface confirm that this gorgeous piece is actually a watch.

ABOVE: This diagram of a labyrinth appears frequently in Chinese art. Ong has hidden a watch within the traditional maze, posing a question on the meaning and complexity of time.

ABOVE: This clasp combines diamonds and emeralds in a clever design of curved lines that incorporate a timepiece. It is a sumptuous jewel, its timekeeping qualities of secondary value.

WATCHES

In revolt against mass-produced, cheap, and cheerful products, 20th century artisans began to make 'artistic watches'. The Australian artisan, Cindy Crawford, manipulated silver strands into a forest of claws twisting around a watch. Gold is shaped into a small sculptural form to hold the watch, generally made of precious stones. Or clever abstract metal shapes incorporate a watch in the design, but these are generally one-off pieces, confined to the luxury market, often finding their way into museum collections. Such creations, although small enough, are not to be carried about, or pinned to one's clothes, and are sometimes referred to as 'artisan' pieces.

And in the 21st century world of haut horologie female customers have begun to demand their very own, very grand, novelty watches. Consequently, jewelers have become an integral part of the watch making teams at Vacheron-Constantin, Piaget, Boucheron, and other high luxury brands. Boucheron made an owl, sitting on a bracelet, and the owl's face is inlaid with diamonds. Its eyes are watches – the dials are covered with cabochon, amethysts, and tourmalines. Jaeger LeCoultre fashioned their 'Rose Noir'. Its petals, shaped and furled, are laid with diamonds and pink sapphires. The watch nestles coyly in the heart of the flower.

ABOVE: This comes from the fashion house, Karen Millen. It resembles a dog collar but the mock crocodile skin strap is worn on the wrist. Where an identity tag might hang on a collar is a stainless steel padlock case. This is a watch without numerals but Swarovski crystals mark the quarter hours, and the steel hands show hours, minutes and seconds.

Novelty Watches – In Disguise

Piaget has designed a deep, diamond 'slave' or captive bracelet, the 'Limelight Paris Diamond Cuff'. It is tied by narrow thongs; in a section of these crisscross ties, lie the arms of the watch but there are no numbers. Cartier sculpted a bracelet with two panthers chasing tortoises. Lift a shell and find a watch! Over 2,750 individual gemstones have been used on this piece. Some of these luxury novelties are made to order, each jeweled timepiece unique.

Both the luxury and the popular watch market, in the 21st century, cater to a sense of novelty, and this sense mirrors an historic attitude. The earliest watches were shaped often in ways that detracted from the timepiece; they were worn as jewelry, a proud statement of wealth and status, and the watch has returned to this role as an interesting accessory. Whether a luxury product or mass-produced, the novelty watch is either a status symbol of great wealth, or an expression of an offbeat, contemporary style. Neither is designed simply as an important mechanism to tell the time and, most times, neither even resembles a watch.

RIGHT: The color mix of yellow, pink, and torquoise warns that this is a youthful, crazy decoration for the wrist but the plastic VW Beetle model is a watch in disguise. It has a digital time display on its windscreen. This wristwatch was made by Beetland, Japan, in 1986.

RIGHT: Seiko has always lived up to its reputation for radical concepts and daring use of technology. This cuff is their 'Spectrum' and it is an E-ink watch. Crystal reinforces and protects the piece, making it expensive. The time is displayed across the surface of the cuff and is subtle, possibly even confusing but who knows, this novelty from Seiko may become standard mode for wristwatches of the future.

WATCHES

A visit to
Roger W Smith - Watchmaker

The creation of a wristwatch or pocketwatch today is normally relegated to the world of the mass produced article; most watch companies produce anywhere between 2,000 to 800,000 watches a year. Not so when it comes to the world of the independent watchmaker. Making extensive use of the hand and eye with basic tools and only a modicum of pre-machining (necessary for some parts with microns of tolerance), a watch from such a workshop harks back to the Golden Age of English horology in the 18th century, and allows clients the possibility of ordering a bespoke timepiece, if they are patient at least, since creating such watches is time consuming and production is limited to a mere 10-15 pieces per year.

LEFT: A watchmaker's world is smaller than a desktop- so that means even in a small workshop, several people can work side by side without difficulty. Although talking is of course allowed, the atmosphere is almost meditative, as the watchmakers concentrate for hours on end with the demands of microscopic accuracy and coordination.

WATCHES

For a bespoke watch from the only firm in England working in this manner, the first step at the R W Smith workshop is a decision about the kind of watch functions one desires: a tourbillon or a basic hour, minute seconds watch, with or without power reserve, moonphase, large date or day of the week indicators- all being typical examples of the kinds of mechanical possibilities that one can order.

Since the dials are made up of several parts by hand, rose engine turned and hand engraved, a variety of motifs, color combinations (such as rose gold with silver) and designs can be executed. Once these decisions for a bespoke watch have been worked out, the actual making of the timepiece can begin.

ABOVE: Each dial is composed of several hand made parts, which are later soldered together. They start out life as small square plaques of gold and silver.

ABOVE: The movement's baseplate requires micron accuracy and is milled in a special machine before the watchmakers take over filling in hundreds of details.

A visit to Roger W Smith – Watchmaker

A watch will normally have anywhere from 100 to 500 and more parts, depending on its complexity, and of course each and every one of these needs to first be drawn in detail, made, finished and then later assembled. Each of these steps requires several stages to complete. The dial, hands and case of the watch that surround the movement allow room for much visual artistry. Even the creation of the hands, sculpted from solid pieces of gold or steel, takes more than 3 days of work from start to finish.

The watchcase is created from a massive block of 18-carat gold or platinum. Different colors are available from light yellow to reddish in tint: light yellow gold (2N), regular yellow gold (3N), rose gold (4N) and red gold (5N). In addition, white gold also exists; this is a gold type with large amounts of palladium, a member of the platinum family, added to the alloy.

LEFT: The case is made of three parts of solid gold or platinum: the central caseband, and the front and back bezels that will later hold the sapphire glass.

RIGHT: Here are just a few of the main components used in a R.W. Smith series 2 wristwatch. Each piece must not only be manufactured; every corner, side and angle, including the tiny gear teeth, will require hours of fine finishing before they are perfect enough to go into the watch movement.

WATCHES

The interior of the watch, the movement is however the domain of pure accuracy and engineering, although even here, blued screws, jewels in chatons, brushed gold surfaces, 'black polished' bits of mirror finished steel and even ornamental engraving belie the fact that this is not an average watch. These kinds of details are the sign of the attention, care and respect the R W Smith workshop has for the realization of a timepiece in the traditional and century's old manner.

The balance wheel, the beating heart of the movement, (the source of the ticking sound in every mechanical watch) is also made at the R W Smith workshop on the Isle of Man, a fact almost unique in the world of watchmaking today. This most critical part, together with the lever and its two jewels that consecutively lock and release the miniscule escapement wheel, determine a watch's accuracy.

TOP RIGHT: The Flying Tourbillon (left part of the upper picture) looks at first glance unassuming, but it represents a highpoint in horological mastery. It was invented in the 18th century during many experimental quests for high accuracy.

RIGHT: The R. W. Smith Series 2 Open Dial shows off the intricacy of the movement to the viewer. This type of open-worked dial side, (not to be confused with a skeletonized movement), first originated at the end of the 18th and beginning of the 19th centuries.

A visit to Roger W Smith – Watchmaker

The energy for the watch is stored in the winding barrel, which is connected to the escapement with a series of wheels and pinions. As this escaping energy is released bit by bit through the 'ticking' of the escapement, the hour, minute and seconds hands - attached to the wheels between the barrel and the escapement- will show the time. That's how a watch works. Simple isn't it?

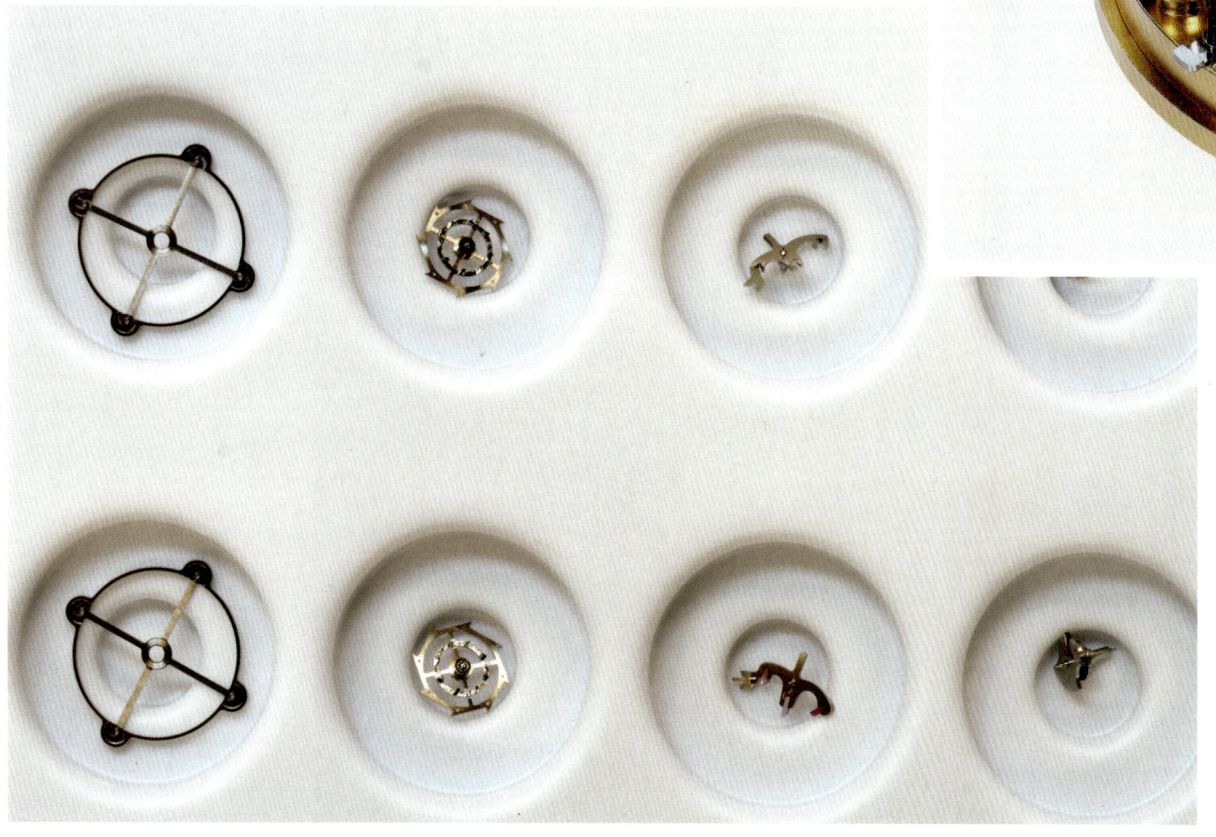

Above: Another view of the Flying Tourbillon mechanism. This system places the balance wheel within a 'cage' that turns 360 degrees continuously, thus counteracting the effects of gravity on the balance. Gravity normally has a strong influence on a balance wheel in every position of daily use.

Left: The balance wheel and the other parts of the escapement are amongst the smallest parts of the wristwatch, yet they have the lion's share in determining the accuracy of the movement.
In the second circle from the left you can see the main escapement wheel of the famed Daniels co-axial escapement. This invention of Dr. George Daniels CBE, MBE, is the first of its kind that can function with or without oil, since it eliminates the usual sources of friction normally found in wristwatch escapements.

313

WATCHES

Since the energy of the winding barrel must be sent through all these bits and pieces, you can imagine that they must be smooth and finely finished so as not to create unnecessary friction, which would affect timekeeping. This means that the watchmaker must spend a lot of time polishing and finishing many parts so that they will be as frictionless as possible.

LEFT AND ABOVE: One of the last finishing stages is burnishing using metal rubbing against metal. The final luster that is achieved is not only decorative; the surface molecules of the metal actually change during this process, becoming harder and partially protected against possible corrosive influences.

A visit to Roger W Smith – Watchmaker

Like any machine, a watch needs to be oiled, however only the tiniest amounts are used. A thimbleful of oil is enough to oil about 200 watches! Nonetheless, the oil is very special and quite expensive to produce; several types, each with a special quality, are used in a wristwatch.

RIGHT AND ABOVE: The amounts of oil used in a watch are minimal; you would need a loupe in order to see the tiny droplets that are used. The oil stays in place mainly due to surface tension of the oil film, aided by the jewels that additionally help trap the oil, keeping it where it is most needed.

WATCHES

Last but not least, the watch must be placed in a timing machine and regulated over a period of weeks. Every watch will keep time differently when the dial is facing up, facing down and all positions in between. It is the final task of the watchmaker to equal out these differences so that the watch will keep good time in all the usual positions of everyday life. This is in itself is an art of its own.

When all these stage are complete the timepiece is placed in its wooden box, made with equal care and attention as was given to the watch itself, and is ready to be shipped to its new owner.

BELOW: Gravity affects the balance wheel's to and fro movements constantly. This is why a watch will keep time slightly differently whether it is laying in positions with its dial down, dial up, crown up, 12 o' clock up or 6 o'clock up. The watchmaker aims to create good timekeeping that takes account of these so-called 'positional errors' and such things as typical walking/sitting positions in timing the movement for daily life.

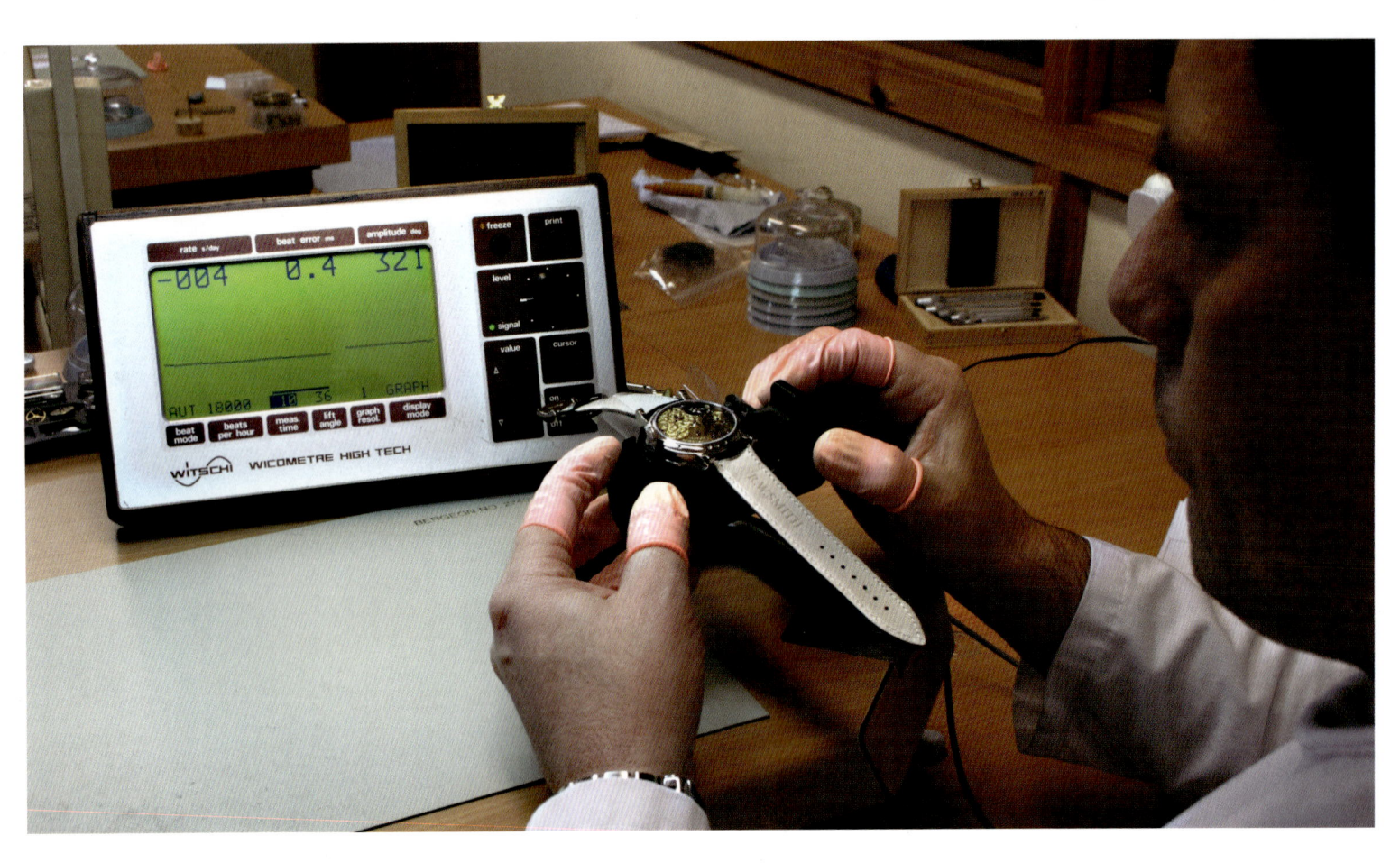

A visit to Roger W Smith – Watchmaker

LEFT: In keeping with traditional methods and philosophy, the presentation boxes for R.W. Smith watches are made by Linley of London, and created from English hardwoods, proof of the care the watchmaker gives each watch from the beginning to the end of the creative process.

WATCHES

Glossary

Automatic watch This has a mechanism to wind automatically. First introduced in the 18th century, it functions through the oscillation of a moving weight, and was refined in the 20th century by John Harwood.

Balance spring A spiral spring used with a circular balance, and helps overcome gravity. This improved the accuracy of timekeeping from an error of 20 minutes a day to less than a minute. Robert Hooke and Christiaan Huygens are both claimed as inventors.

Caliber refers to the different watch movements, and they may be marked or numbered to identify the model of the watch.

Chronograph A watch that measures short intervals on demand,

Chronometer A high precision watch able to measure time – hours, minutes, seconds or calendar, phases of the moon and such like.

Complication watch gives more information than the hours, minutes and seconds. For instance, may also have a date calendar.

Crown A small attachment on watch to wind and set the time. A few turns start an automatic watch, but a manually wound watch has to be regularly wound by the crown.

Curvette The inner back cover of the case, often having holes to show the winding and hand setting squares.

Escapement Part linking the oscillator (balance) to the power source (spring or weight) and which controls the rate of movement. There are many different arrangements of the escapement.

Fly-back hand An additional hand allowing two events to be timed without affecting each other's time, or the regular timekeeping..

Hour-jump function This has a hand on the dial for minutes but in a separate section, the hours jump to the next hour.

Oscillator The balance that controls the timepiece. (In a clock the balance is called the pendulum)

Pallet Small piece, usually shaped from a ruby, that conducts an impulse to the oscillator.

Parachute The first watch shock absorber, invented by Breguet.

Perpetual calendar This shows different lengths of months, including leap years. Shows days of the week and phases of the moon.

Power reserve indicator warns how much time before rewinding is required.

(Liquid) Quartz see page 186–7.

Skeleton dial Sections or all of dial removed to show the movements.

Tourbillon mechanism invented by Breguet to counteract effect of gravity; see page 182–3.

Train The wheels and pinions that transmit motion from the mainspring to the escapement.

Credits

We would like to thank the following people and organizations for their help in supplying pictures:

Getty Images, London, England.
Vacheron Constantin, Geneva, Switzerland.
Breitling, Grenchen, Switzerland.
Patek Philippe, Plan-les-Ouates, Switzerland.
Girard-Perrigaux, La Chaux-de-Fonds, Switzerland.
TAGHeuer, La Chaux-de-Fonds, Switzerland, and London, England.
Seiko UK Ltd., Maidenhead, Berkshire, England.
Citizen Watch Company, Wokingham, Berkshire, England.
Alberta Ferretti, London, England.
Longines, Saint-Imier, Switzerland.
Ball Watch Company, Neuchatel, Switzerland.
Fortis/Harwood Watch Company, Grenchen, Switzerland.
Oris Watches, Hölstein, Switzerland.
Bamford Watch Department, London, England.
Accurist Watches Ltd., West Hampstead, London, England
Jaeger-LeCoultre, London, England.
Audemars Piguet, Le Brassus, Switzerland.
Van Cleef & Arpels via Joan Rolls, New Bond Street, London.
Omega, Bienne, Switzerland.
The Swatch Group, Southampton, England.
Ulysee-Nardin, Le Locle, Switzerland.
Paul Schliesser (www.pixelp.com)
Michelle Ong of Carnet, Hong Kong, China.
Derek Dier, Vintage Watch Specialist (www.WatchesToBuy.com)
Page 133: Christie's Images Ltd 2010.
Page 73: Bundesarchiv, Germany.
Pieces of Time (info@antique-watch.com)

We would also like to thank the following people and organizations for allowing us to take photographs of their collections:

Beyer Uhrenmuseum, Zurich, Switzerland.
Tessa Paul collection, London, England.
Page 246
Winnie the Witch, copyright Valerie Thomas and Korky Paul, published by Oxford University Press, Oxford, England.
Copyright Winnie the Witch illustration Korky Paul.

Special Photography
Mirco De Cet, who would like to extend special thanks to:
Eva, Matthias and all the staff at the Deutsches Uhrenmuseum, Furtwangen, Germany, for supplying so many watches from their wonderful collection, and for their patience, information, help and hospitality.
Roger and Caroline Smith from R W Smith Ltd, Ramsey, Isle of Man, British Isles, for allowing us to carry out photography at their premises and for the assistance they and their staff gave.

Index

accuracy 11, 29, 32, 45
Accurist 226, 282–3
　Char 282
　Old England 282
ancient world 14
artistic references 86, 87, 206, 208, 209, 251–2
astronauts 164, 168, 194–5, 204
atomic timekeeping 166
Audemars Piguet 40, 222, 230–1
　Offshore 230
　Royal Oak 188, 230, 268
aviators 48, 76, 80, 106, 110, 136

Bailey, Banks and Biddle 59
balance spring 21
Ball Watch Company 178–9
　Engineer Hydrocarbon Spacemaster 281
　Engineer Master II Diver GMT 178
Bamford and Sons 289
Baumgartner, Francis 63
Boer War 52
Borgel 63
Boucheron 306
bracelet watches 41, 56, 57, 112, 121, 128
Breguet 22-3, 24, 29, 40, 50, 115, 182
Breitling 76–7, 106, 196, 214, 272
　Chronomat 106
　Cosmonaut 76
　Lady J 240
　Navitimer 76

brooch watches 62
Bueche Girod 191
Bulgari 230, 279
Bulova 60, 93, 156, 164, 190
　Accutron 156, 184
　Driver's Lug Tank 118

Carnet 304–5
Cartier 41, 55, 57, 60, 109, 128, 162, 190, 191, 208–9, 230, 252, 307
　Libre 86
　Santos 48, 214
　Tank Watch 55
celebrity associations 69, 90, 115, 116, 124, 132, 134, 136, 138, 147, 148–51, 152, 154, 155, 160, 173, 188, 226, 235, 237, 256
cell phones 249, 255, 256
Chanel J12 214, 266
chatelaines 26
children's market 218, 220, 247
Chopard 128, 286
　Mille Miglia 214
chronographs 36, 58, 66, 72, 107, 115, 126, 160, 204, 212, 238, 282
chronometers 31, 34, 73, 76, 80, 102, 106, 107, 214, 264
　Citizen 166–7
　Eco-Drive 166
　Promaster Aqualand 166
Co-Axial escapement 116
complications watches 8, 24, 56, 76, 102, 158, 196, 210, 244, 264
computerized manufacturing 229
Cottier, Louis 118
counterfeit watches 233–4, 249
customized watches 289

Dali, Salvador 86
Daniels, George 116, 292
date indicators 66, 115
De Trey, Cesar 80
'detective watches' 302
dollar watch 39

earliest watches 15–43
Ebauches SA 196
Ebel 88, 238-9, 272
　Classic Hexagon Chronograph 238
　Gunners 238
　Tekton Real Madrid 272
electronic watches 139, 142, 156, 163
Elizabeth I, Queen 20
Elizabeth II, Queen 121, 134
enameling 26, 140–1, 142, 144, 291
equipages 26, 28
Eterna 115

Facio, Nicholas 29
fashion accessories 200–3, 206, 208, 218, 220, 225, 256
Ferretti, Alberta 286
first wristwatches 8, 41
fob (pocket) watches 7, 28, 32, 38, 42, 46, 52
form watches 16
Fortis 204–5
　Calculator 204
　Flieger Chronograph 204
　Harwood Automatic 204
　Planet Watch 204
Foundation Cartier 208–9

Galasso, Angelo 234
gender preferences 28, 45, 56
Genta, Gerald 188, 221
Girard-Perregaux 52, 102–3
　Cat's Eye 102
　Observatory Chronometer 102
　Tourbillon 102
　Vintage 1945 102
Greenwich Mean Time (GMT) 30–1, 34
Gruen 118
　Curvex 82
Gucci 175, 177, 237

Hamilton Watch Company 106, 139, 156
　Pulsar 176
　Sekron Doctor's Dual-Dial 108
　Ventura 147, 156
Harrison, John 31, 34
Hayek, Nicolas 199–200
Hilfiger, Tommy 237
Henlein, Peter 15
hermetic watches 88
Hetzel, Max 156
Heuer 72, 107
　Carrera 107
　Daytona 107
　Micrograph 72
　Monaco 173
　Montreal 173
Hillary, Sir Edmund 138, 188
Holbein, Hans 87
Hooke, Robert 21
Horwitt, Nathan George 114
Hugo Boss
　Metropolis 240

　Spirit 240
Huygens, Christiaan 21

Ingenieur Automatic Edition 268
Ingersoll 39, 50, 92, 113, 130, 168
　Dan Dare 130
　Mickey Mouse 92, 150
international time conference 34

Jaeger-LeCoultre 121, 123, 145, 244–5, 252, 306
　Caliber 170 244
　Futurematic 123
　Gyrotourbillon 1 182
　Hybris Mechanica a Grande Sonnerie 244
　Master Grande Tradition 244
　Reverso 82, 128, 142, 244
jewels 29, 119

keyless winding system 101
Kreisler, Jacques 112

Lip, Fred 139
logo-branded watches 221, 247
Longines 74, 80, 110–11, 218
　Chronograph 110
　Flagship Heritage 110
　Lindbergh Atlantic Voyage Watch 80
　Lindbergh Hour Angle Watch 110
lugs 118

mariners 45, 52, 102
Mary, Queen of Scots 20
medical profession 36, 62, 108
Mikuna 128
Minerva 126

319

WATCHES

Index

Montblanc 71, 126–7
    Classic Watch Collection 237
    Villeret 1885 126
montre perpetual 24
Movado 55, 89, 109
    Ermeto 89
Museum 114
musk-apple watches 16
novelty watches 89, 300-7

Omega 41, 55, 74, 90, 113, 116–17, 128, 164, 190, 206
    Constellation 194
    Constellation Marine Chronometer 214
    Sapphire Art Series 216
    Seamaster Aqua Terra 266
    Seamaster Professional 235
    Speedmaster Mark II 194
    Speedmaster Professional 164
    Titanium Polaris Seamaster 188
Ong, Michelle 304–5
Oris 162, 206, 212–13
    ProDriver Chronograph 212
over-the-cuff watches 234

Panerai Mare Nostrum 115
parachute 23, 25
Patek Philippe 40, 41, 50, 58-9, 118, 132, 144, 222, 279, 291
    Nautilus 58, 188
perpetuelle 23
photocells 166
Piaget 128, 307
Polo 190
Polo Mini 242
Piccard, Jacques 73, 154, 155

Pierre Cardin 162
    Espace 184
Polso Orologia 234
Pulsar Quartz 216
purse watches 89

quartz watches 11, 76, 152, 166, 175–7, 180, 182, 184–7, 196, 200, 206, 242, 247

R W Smith 292–3, 310–17
railway watches 38, 46
Ralph Lauren 222
    Stirrup 291
Richemont 84, 126, 134
Robin, Robert 230
Rolex 64–5, 86, 88, 113, 132, 138, 168, 289
    Deep Sea Special 154, 155
    Explorer I 138, 188
    Explorer II 138, 188
    GMT Master 136, 148, 168
    Oyster 69, 104, 132, 138
    Oyster Chronograph 104
    Oyster Perpetual Datejust 115
    Oyster Perpetual Submariner 136, 148
    Prince 64, 68
    Speed King 104
    Turn-O-Graph 136
Roskopf 100, 101, 113, 123
Rotherham and Son 50

St. Laurent, Yves 216
Seiko 152-3, 168, 175, 200, 202
    35 SQ Astron 176
    Ananta 152

Kinetic 152, 242
    Spring Drive 152
    UC2000 202
Sekonda 106, 130, 168
    Poljot 106
self-winding watches 23, 24, 66, 76
Smith, Roger W 292–3
soldiers 8, 42, 50, 51, 52, 54, 104
spiral hairspring 21
sport 69, 70–83, 88, 107, 110, 115, 160, 173, 178, 210, 212–14, 218, 237, 238, 257–61, 266–71, 272
stopwatches 36, 71, 72, 74, 107, 136
Swatch 23, 90, 110, 116, 200, 206, 216, 218–19, 247, 252
    Beat 218
    Bijoux 218
    Flik-Flak 218
    Irony 218
    Scuba 218
    Skin 218
Swiss watchmaking industry 40, 94–105, 119, 123, 130, 132, 136, 139, 156, 163, 171, 177, 180, 196, 199–200

TAG Heuer 74, 136, 160, 268
    Golf Watch 160
    Kirium 237
    Ladies' Carrera 266
    Ring Master 136
Theil 60
Tiffany 41, 57, 60, 109, 113, 190, 218, 230, 302
time, measuring 7, 13–14
Timex 168, 216
Tissot 55, 74, 90–1, 218

T-Touch 90
Tompion, Thomas 21
tourbillon 59, 182–3, 230, 244
Toutin, Jean 26
transition watches 52
Tri-Synchro Regulator 152

Ulysse Nardin 264–5, 291
    Astrolabium Galileo Galilei 264
    Planeterium Copernicus 264
    Tellerium Johannes Kepler 264

Vacheron Constantin 48, 50, 84–5, 86, 109, 124, 125, 128, 171, 252
    Kallista 84
    Les Masques 84
    Patrimony 84
Van Cleef & Arpels 134–5
    Cademas 134
    Charms Mini Watch 279
    Les Pontes des Amoureux 134
vintage watches 223, 249

watch rings 303
watchmaking process 310–17
waterproofing 63, 115, 136
Werner, Casper 15
women's market 26, 39, 60, 109, 112–13, 128, 158, 190, 214, 216, 279
world time watches 118
World War I 8, 42, 50, 51, 54, 55
World War II 97, 106
Wright Brothers 48
Wunderman, Steve 175

Zenith 196